D1391996

Mitchell Symons was born in 1957 in London and educated at Mill Hill School and the LSE where he (just) got a degree in Law. Since leaving BBC TV, where he was a researcher and then a director, he has worked as a writer, broadcaster and journalist. He was a principal writer of early editions of the board game Trivial Pursuit and has devised many television formats. Currently, he writes a weekly column for the *Sunday Express* and is working on a non-fiction book. That tricky third novel remains unfinished.

Also by Mitchell Symons

Non-fiction:
That Book
Forfeit!
The Equation Book of Sports Crosswords
The Equation Book of Movie Crosswords
The You Magazine Book of Journolists (four books; co-author with John Koski)
Movielists (co-author with John Koski)
The Sunday Magazine Book of Crosswords
The Hello! Magazine Book of Crosswords (three books)
How To Be Fat: The Chip And Fry Diet (co-author, with Penny Chorlton)
The Book of Criminal Records
The Book of Lists
The Book of Celebrity Sex Lists
The Bill Clinton Joke Book
National Lottery Big Draw 2000 (co-author, with David Thomas)

Fiction:
All In
The Lot

THIS
BOOK

THIS
BOOK

MITCHELL SYMONS

BANTAM PRESS

LONDON · TORONTO · SYDNEY · AUCKLAND · JOHANNESBURG

TRANSWORLD PUBLISHERS
61–63 Uxbridge Road, London W5 5SA
a division of The Random House Group Ltd

RANDOM HOUSE AUSTRALIA (PTY) LTD
20 Alfred Street, Milsons Point, Sydney,
New South Wales 2061, Australia

RANDOM HOUSE NEW ZEALAND LTD
18 Poland Road, Glenfield, Auckland 10, New Zealand

RANDOM HOUSE SOUTH AFRICA (PTY) LTD
Endulini, 5a Jubilee Road, Parktown 2193, South Africa

Published 2004 by Bantam Press
a division of Transworld Publishers

A catalogue record for this book is available from the British Library.
ISBN 0593 053486

Printed by Mackays of Chatham plc, Chatham, Kent

10 9 8 7 6 5 4

Papers used by Transworld Publishers are natural, recyclable products made
from wood grown in sustainable forests. The manufacturing processes
conform to the environmental regulations of the country of origin.

To Penny, Jack and Charlie
– as ever and always

'A smattering of everything
and a knowledge of nothing'
CHARLES DICKENS

'It is possible to store the mind with a million
facts and still be entirely uneducated'
ALEC BOURNE

'If an idea's worth having once,
it's worth having twice'
SIR TOM STOPPARD

PURE TRIVIA

Trivia was a Roman goddess to whom sacrifices were offered at crossroads. Because travellers often engaged in idle gossip at crossroads, Trivia's name (referring to three roads coming together) came to be associated with the sort of information exchanged in such places.

Offered a new pen to try, 97 per cent of people will write their own name.

The pitches that Babe Ruth hit for his last-ever home run and that Joe DiMaggio hit for his first-ever home run were thrown by the same man.

Donald Duck's middle name is Fauntleroy. Quackmore Duck is the name of Donald Duck's father.

Until the 18th century, India produced almost all the world's diamonds.

During US conscription for World War Two, there were nine documented cases of men with three testicles.

82 per cent of the Beatles music was about love.

The name Wendy was made up for the book *Peter Pan*.

All the clocks in *Pulp Fiction* are stuck on 4:20.

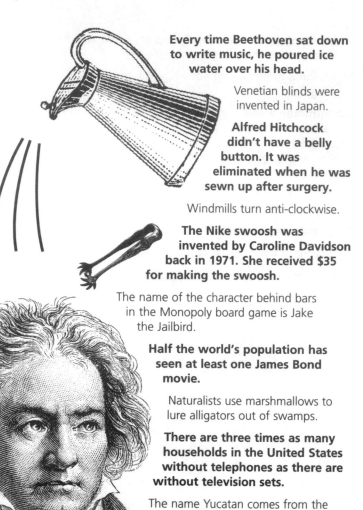

Every time Beethoven sat down to write music, he poured ice water over his head.

Venetian blinds were invented in Japan.

Alfred Hitchcock didn't have a belly button. It was eliminated when he was sewn up after surgery.

Windmills turn anti-clockwise.

The Nike swoosh was invented by Caroline Davidson back in 1971. She received $35 for making the swoosh.

The name of the character behind bars in the Monopoly board game is Jake the Jailbird.

Half the world's population has seen at least one James Bond movie.

Naturalists use marshmallows to lure alligators out of swamps.

There are three times as many households in the United States without telephones as there are without television sets.

The name Yucatan comes from the Maya for 'listen to how they speak' – which is what the Maya said when they first heard the Spanish.

M&Ms were developed so that soldiers could eat chocolate without getting their fingers sticky.

An ant lion is neither an ant nor a lion. It is the larval form of the lacewing fly.

The term 'the whole 9 yards' comes from World War Two. A .50-calibre machine-gun ammo belt measured exactly 27 feet (or 9 yards) before being loaded. If a fighter pilot fired all of it at once, the target was said to have received 'the whole 9 yards'.

The bark of the redwood tree is fireproof. Fires in redwood forests take place inside the trees.

Amethyst was once thought to prevent drunkenness.

50 per cent of Americans live within 50 miles of their birthplace.

20 per cent of all road accidents in Sweden involve an elk.

FIRSTS

The **first** time women and men used separate toilets was in 1739 at a Paris ball.

Ice-cream cones were **first** served at the 1904 World's Fair in St Louis.

Dubbed laughter was used on American television for the **first** time on 9 September 1950.

The **first** flushing toilet seen on US TV was on *Leave It To Beaver*.

Dr W.S. Halstead was the **first** to use rubber gloves during surgery in 1890.

The **first** sport to have a world championship was billiards in 1873.

Benjamin Franklin was the **first** person to suggest daylight saving.

Whoooooopi!

The **first** in-flight movie was shown on a Lufthansa flight on 6 April 1925.

The **first** couple to be shown in bed together on US prime time TV were Fred and Wilma Flintstone.

Austria was the **first** country to use postcards.

The **first** country to abolish capital punishment was Austria in 1787.

John Lennon's **first** girlfriend was named Thelma Pickles.

Whoopi Goldberg acquired her **first** name because she had a problem with flatulence.

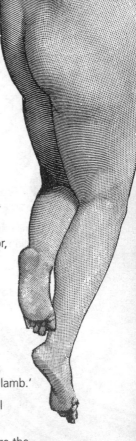

The **first** product to have a bar code was Wrigley's gum.

Britain's **first** escalator was installed in Harrods in 1878.

The **first** plastic ever invented was celluloid in 1868. It's still used today to make billiard balls.

The **first** mosque in the US was built in 1893.

Sugar was **first** added to chewing gum in 1869 – by a dentist.

The **first** telegraph message tapped by its inventor, Samuel Morse, was: 'What hath God wrought?'

Iceland was the **first** country to legalize abortion in 1935.

The **first** words spoken on the telephone by its inventor, Alexander Graham Bell, were: 'Watson, come here, I need you.'

The **first** words spoken on the phonograph by its inventor, Thomas Edison, were: 'Mary had a little lamb.'

Captain Cook was the **first** man to set foot on all continents (except Antarctica).

In 1776, Croatia was the **first** country to recognize the United States.

Beethoven's Fifth was the **first** symphony to include trombones.

90 per cent of all new restaurants fail in the **first** year. Of the ones that survive, 90 per cent fail in the second year.

THE FIRST LINES OF CLASSIC NOVELS

'It was a bright, cold day in April, and the clocks were striking thirteen.' (*1984* by George Orwell)

'Hale knew, before he had been in Brighton three hours, that they meant to murder him.' (*Brighton Rock* by Graham Greene)

'As Gregor Samsa woke one morning from uneasy dreams he found himself transformed in his bed into a gigantic insect.' (*Metamorphosis* by Franz Kafka)

'Last night I dreamt I went to Manderley again.' (*Rebecca* by Daphne du Maurier)

'Happy families are all alike, but an unhappy family is unhappy in its own way.' (*Anna Karenina* by Leo Tolstoy)

'Many years later, as he faced the firing squad, Colonel Aureliano Buendía was to remember that distant afternoon when his father took him to discover ice.' (*One Hundred Years of Solitude* by Gabriel García Márquez)

'There were 117 psychoanalysts on the Pan Am flight to Vienna and I'd been treated by at least six of them.' (*Fear of Flying* by Erica Jong)

'What's it going to be then, eh?' (*A Clockwork Orange* by Anthony Burgess)

'Stately, plump Buck Mulligan came from the stairhead, bearing a bowl of lather on which a mirror and a razor lay crossed.' (*Ulysses* by James Joyce)

'I'm going to get that bloody bastard if I die in the attempt.' (*King Rat* by James Clavell)

'On top of everything, the cancer wing was number 13.' (*Cancer Ward* by Alexander Solzhenitsyn)

'If you really want to hear about it, the first thing you'll probably want to know is where I was born, and what my lousy childhood was like and how my parents were occupied and all before they had me, and all that David Copperfield kind of crap, but I don't feel like going into it, if you want to know the truth.' (*Catcher In The Rye* by J.D. Salinger)

THE FIRST SINGLES THEY BOUGHT

Sue Perkins: 'My Camera Never Lies' (Bucks Fizz)

Brian May: 'Rock Island Line' (Lonnie Donegan)

Amanda Holden: 'I'm In The Mood For Dancing' (The Nolans)

Moby: 'Live And Let Die' (Wings)

Mick Hucknall: 'God Save The Queen' (The Sex Pistols)

Nicki Chapman: 'Killer Queen' (Queen)

Jordan: 'I Should Be So Lucky' (Kylie Minogue)

Jemma Redgrave: 'I'm The Leader of The Gang (I Am!)' (Gary Glitter)

Samantha Mumba: 'Sisters Are Doin' It For Themselves' (The Eurythmics and Aretha Franklin)

Sir Paul McCartney: 'Be-Bop-A-Lula' (Gene Vincent)

Beverley Callard: 'I'm A Believer' (The Monkees)

Dale Winton: 'I Only Want To Be With You' (Dusty Springfield)

Carol Vorderman: 'Sugar Baby Love' (The Rubettes)

Sophie Anderton: 'I Should Be So Lucky' (Kylie Minogue)

Pete Waterman: 'The Deadwood Stage' (Doris Day)

Paul Young: 'Fire And Water' (Free)

Zoë Ball: 'Merry Xmas Everybody' (Slade)

Arabella Weir: 'Daydream Believer' (The Monkees)

Steve Penk: 'Skweeze Me, Pleeze Me' (Slade)

Nicky Campbell: 'Alone Again (Naturally)' (Gilbert O'Sullivan)

Amanda Redman: 'MacArthur Park' (Richard Harris)

Paul O'Grady: 'Sugar Time' (Nancy Sinatra)

David 'Kid' Jensen: '(I Can't Get No) Satisfaction' (The Rolling Stones)

Frances Barber: 'Last Train To Clarksville' (The Monkees)

Kaye Adams: 'Ernie (The Fastest Milkman In The West)' (Benny Hill)

Jayne Middlemiss: 'Don't Stand So Close To Me' (The Police)

Philippa Forrester: 'Save Your Kisses For Me' (The Brotherhood of Man)

Griff Rhys Jones: 'I Want To Hold Your Hand' (The Beatles)

Roger Black: 'Knowing Me, Knowing You' (Abba)

Martine McCutcheon: 'Mickey' (Toni Basil)

Cilla Black: 'Why Do Fools Fall In Love' (Frankie Lymon And The Teenagers)

Mark Lamarr: 'Jake The Peg' (Rolf Harris)

Ardal O'Hanlon: 'Money, Money, Money' (Abba)

Rory McGrath: 'Don't Throw Your Love Away' (The Searchers)

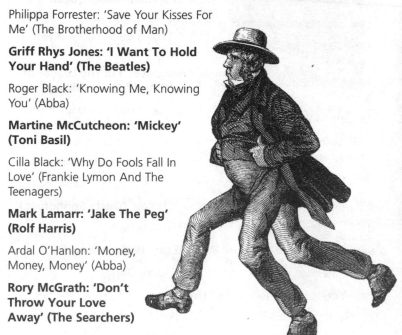

BEGINNINGS

Leonardo da Vinci invented an alarm clock that woke the sleeper by rubbing his feet.

Kiwis lay the largest eggs (relative to body size) of any bird.

Human babies born in May are on average 200 grams heavier than babies born in other months.

The word 'sex' was coined in 1382.

From fertilization to birth, a baby's weight increases 5,000 million times.

Clark Gable was listed on his birth certificate as a girl.

One female mouse can give birth to 100 babies in a year.

When Harold Robbins was a child he used to run errands for Lucky Luciano.

Mel Gibson broke the school record for the most strappings in a week – 27.

Martine McCutcheon was shortlisted for the Pears Baby.

Bela Lugosi, the great screen Dracula, was actually born in Transylvania.

Roy Walker was in the Vienna Boys' Choir.

Numbering houses in London streets began only in 1764.

When a polar bear cub is born, it can't see or hear for the first month.

The first novel written on a typewriter was *The Adventures of Tom Sawyer*.

The ancient Greeks believed that boys developed in the right-hand side of the womb and girls in the left.

Paper was invented early in the 2nd century by a Chinese eunuch.

Bruce Oldfield didn't see an inside loo until the age of 12.

Carnegie Hall in New York City opened in 1891 with Tchaikovsky as guest conductor.

Pamela Anderson was Canada's Centennial Baby, having been the first baby born on the centennial anniversary of Canada's independence.

The drinking straw was invented in 1886.

Daryl Hannah was so shy as a child that at one point she was diagnosed as borderline autistic.

Carbonated soda water was invented in 1767 by Joseph Priestley, the discoverer of oxygen.

Screwdrivers were first used to help knights put on armour.

As a child Sheryl Crow used to pretend she was Stevie Wonder by playing the piano with the lights off.

The smoke detector was invented in 1969.

The wristwatch was invented in 1904 by Louis Cartier.

Dido, Emily Watson and Oliver Letwin were banned from watching TV as children.

Sylvester Stallone was kicked out of 14 schools in 11 years.

Jodie Foster was mauled by a lion when she was a child.

A newborn kangaroo is small enough to fit in a teaspoon.

Were foster children

Vidal Sassoon, George Cole, Kathy Burke, Sylvester Stallone, Gary Glitter, Jane Lapotaire, Kriss Akabusi, Eartha Kitt, Neil Morrissey, Marilyn Monroe, Barbara Stanwyck, Shirley Anne Field (sent to a baby home and then to an orphanage), Seal (until his Nigerian mother reclaimed him), Rosie Perez, Paul Barber, Samantha Morton, Kerry McFadden

Were barnardo's boys

John Fashanu, Justin Fashanu, Leslie Thomas, Bruce Oldfield, Chris Armstrong

Born with a club foot

**Dudley Moore, Josef Goebbels, Dr David Starkey,
Mother Teresa, Emperor Claudius, Eric Richard, Lord Byron,
Callan Pinckney**

Born in India

Spike Milligan, Joanna Lumley, William
Makepeace Thackeray, Angela Thorne,
Sir Cliff Richard, Sir Basil Spence, Nigel
Dempster, Lord Beveridge, Julie
Christie, Kenneth Kendall, Engelbert
Humperdinck, George Orwell, Lord
Colin Cowdrey, Tiny Rowland,
Kim Philby, Lindsay Anderson,
John Aspinall, Margaret
Lockwood, Googie Withers,
Isla Blair, Vivien Leigh, Anna
Carteret, Pete Best

Born in Canada

**Saul Bellow, David 'Kid' Jensen, William Shatner,
k.d. lang, Joni Mitchell, Bryan Adams, Rick Moranis,
Leonard Cohen, Greg Rusedski, Margot Kidder, Mary Pickford,
Genevieve Bujold, Michael J. Fox, Donald Sutherland, Leslie
Nielsen, Lou Jacobi, Mike Myers, Shania Twain, Jason Priestley,
Michael Ondaatje, James Randi, Robbie Robertson, Lionel Blair,
Natasha Henstridge, Alanis Morissette, Jim Carrey, Norman
Jewison, Raymond Massey, Martin Short, Linda Thorson, Oscar
Peterson, Christopher Plummer, Lynda Bellingham, Celine Dion,
Norma Shearer, John Candy, David Cronenberg, Wayne
Gretzky, Neil Young**

BORN IN WALES

Ian Hislop, Heather Small, Carol Vorderman, Christian Bale, Ryan Giggs, The Edge, Dawn French, Jonathan Pryce, Paul Whitehouse, H, John Prescott, Anneka Rice, Neil Aspinall, Sir Stanley Baker, Michael Owen, Dame Shirley Bassey, Jessica Garlick, Keith Allen, Paula Yates, Julian Cope, John Humphrys, Gabby Logan, Doris Hare, Jeff Banks, Peter Greenaway, Ioan Gruffudd, Catherine Zeta-Jones, Jeremy Bowen, Tommy Cooper, Terry Jones, Ivor Novello, Michael Heseltine, Martyn Lewis, Helen Lederer, Timothy Dalton, Hywel Bennett, Ray Milland, David Broome, Leslie Thomas, T.E. Lawrence, Noel Sullivan, Patrick Mower, Roald Dahl, Me-One, Charlotte Church, Roger Rees, Griff Rhys Jones, Victor Spinetti, Christopher Timothy

BORN IN SCOTLAND

Sir Sean Connery, Alan Cumming, Sheena Easton, Carol Smillie, Tony Blair, Robbie Coltrane, David McCallum, Annie Lennox, Maxwell Caulfield, Hannah Gordon, Lulu, Ewan McGregor, Midge Ure, Donovan, Rory Bremner, Sharleen Spiteri, Stanley Baxter, Siobhan Redmond, Jimmy Somerville, Stephen Hendry, Fish, Andrew Marr, Matthew MacFadyen, Sylvester McCoy, John Sessions, Graeme Garden, John Hannah, Shirley Manson, Mark Knopfler, Ian Anderson, Barbara Dickson, Kaye Adams, Billy Connolly, Kenneth Cranham, Sir Jackie Stewart, Phyllida Law, Charles Kennedy, Jenni Falconer, Kirsty Gallacher, Ian McCaskill, Gail Porter, Tom Conti, Jack Bruce, Ronnie Corbett, Rhona Cameron, Sir Ludovic Kennedy, Jeff Stewart, Gordon Ramsay, Eddie Large, Ian Richardson, David Byrne, Sir Malcolm Rifkind, Marti Pellow, Irvine Welsh, Sally Magnusson, Lindsay Duncan, Robert Carlyle, Darius Danesh, John Gordon Sinclair, Jim Kerr, Annette Crosbie, Dame Muriel Spark, Nicky Campbell, Lorraine Kelly

BORN IN GERMANY

Ken Adam, John McEnroe, Andre Previn, Marsha Fitzalan, Charles Wheeler, Jackson Browne, Peter Alliss, Dominic Monaghan, Bruce Willis, Lucien Freud, Ruth Prawer Jhabvala, Henry Kissinger, Paul Ackford, Andrew Sachs, Gyles Brandreth, Jeri Ryan, Martin Lawrence, Pam Ferris, Peter Gilmore

BORN IN AFRICA

Nicola Pagett (Egypt)

Thomas Dolby (Egypt)

Fiona Fullerton (Nigeria)

Claudia Cardinale (Tunisia)

Derek Pringle (Kenya)

Glynis Barber (South Africa)

Stephanie Beacham (Morocco)

Patrick Allen (Nyasaland)

Moira Lister (South Africa)

Phil Edmonds (Zambia)

Debbie Thrower (Kenya)

Born elsewhere

Terry Butcher (Singapore)

Katie Boyle (Italy)

Chris De Burgh (Argentina)

Pamela Armstrong (Borneo)

Ted Dexter (Italy)

Fiona Bruce (Singapore)

Lisa Butcher (Singapore)

Minnie Driver (Barbados)

Louis Theroux (Singapore)

Dom Joly (Lebanon)

Eddie Izzard (Aden – now Yemen)

Robert Bathurst (Gold Coast – now Ghana)

Jenny Seagrove (Malaysia)

Dulcie Gray (Malaysia)

Born part-irish

Muhammad Ali, Joan Baez, Dolly Parton, Anthony Quinn, Emilio Estevez, Robert Mitchum, Valerie Harper, Don Ameche, Lucille Ball, Marlon Brando, James Clavell, Alex Haley, Kiri Te Kanawa, Robert De Niro, Freddie Prinze Jr, Lindsay Lohan

GYPSY BLOOD

Pat Phoenix, Elvis Presley, Eric Clapton, Vita Sackville-West, Django Reinhardt, Eric Cantona, David Essex, Bob Hoskins, Charlie Chaplin, Ava Gardner, Pablo Picasso, Nadja Auermann, Miguel de Cervantes, Yul Brynner

NATIVE AMERICAN BLOOD

Burt Reynolds (one-quarter Cherokee)

Johnny Depp (part Cherokee)

Waylon Jennings (part Cherokee and part Comanche)

Cher (part Cherokee)

Mike McShane

Tiger Woods

Johnny Cash (one-quarter Cherokee)

Lena Horne (one-eighth Blackfoot)

Jimi Hendrix (part Cherokee)

James Garner (part Cherokee)

Roy Rogers (part Choctaw)

Kim Basinger (part Cherokee)

Dolly Parton (one-eighth Cherokee)

Dennis Weaver (part Osage)

Eartha Kitt (half Cherokee)

Farrah Fawcett (one-eighth Choctaw)

Sandy Duncan (part Cherokee)

Chuck Norris (half Cherokee)

John Phillips (half Cherokee)

Sally Field (part Cherokee)

Redd Foxx (one-quarter Seminole)

Joe Mantana (part Sioux)

Johnny Ray (part Blackfoot)

Oral Roberts (part Cherokee)

Will Rogers (part Cherokee)

Tommy Tune (part Shawnee)

Tori Amos (part Cherokee)

Jerry Hall (part Cherokee – her mother's father's grandmother was a Cherokee)

Val Kilmer (part Cherokee)

Jessica Biel (part Choctaw)

Hilary Swank

Sir Winston Churchill (one-sixteenth Iroquois)

Carmen Electra (part Cherokee)

Lou Diamond Phillips (one-eighth Cherokee)

Shannon Elizabeth (part Cherokee)

NB Benjamin Bratt's mother, a Peruvian Indian, is an activist for Native Americans

THE HUMAN CONDITION

If your body's natural defences failed, the bacteria in your gut would consume you within 48 hours, eating you from the inside out.

Only 4 per cent of babies are born on their due date.

People who smoke have 10 times as many wrinkles as people who don't smoke.

People who suffer from gum disease are twice as likely to have a stroke or heart attack.

We use 43 muscles to frown.

We use 17 muscles to smile.

The fastest-moving muscle in the human body is the one that opens and closes the eyelid.

Women smile more than men do

14 million people were killed in World War One; 20 million died in the flu epidemic that followed it.

Right-handed people tend to scratch with their left hand, and vice-versa.

It takes the typical person 7 minutes to fall asleep.

Every year, there are more births in India than there are people in Australia.

Someone who eats little is said to eat like a bird, even though many birds eat twice their weight in a day.

Men have on average 10 per cent more red blood cells than women do.

One square inch of human skin contains 625 sweat glands.

The Islands of Langerhans are a group of cells located in the pancreas.

Most people have lost 50 per cent of their taste buds by the time they reach 60.

15 million blood cells are produced and destroyed in the human body every second.

The human head is a quarter of our total length at birth, but an eighth of our total length by the time we reach adulthood.

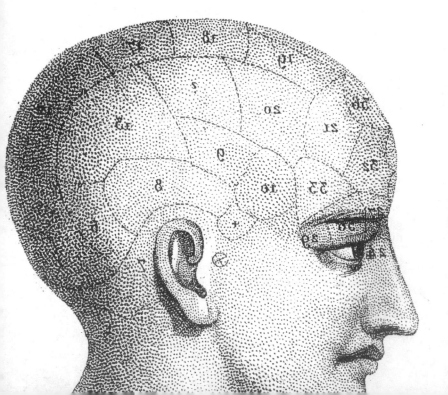

The hydrochloric acid in the human stomach is strong enough to dissolve a nail.

The foot is the most common part of the body bitten by insects.

There are over 100 million light-sensitive cells in the retina.

The opposite of 'cross-eyed' is 'wall-eyed'.

We use 54 muscles every time we step forward.

The surface area of a human lung is equivalent to a tennis court.

Between the ages of 20 and 70, the typical person spends about 600 hours having sex.

Our hearing is less sharp after eating too much.

The hardest bone in the human body is the jawbone.

The largest cell in the human body is the ovum; the smallest is the sperm.

The most sensitive cluster of nerves is at the base of the spine.

By lying on your back and raising your legs slowly you can't sink in quicksand.

The longest-recorded tapeworm found in the human body was 33 metres in length.

Vegetarians live longer and have more stamina than meat-eaters, but they have a higher chance of getting blood disorders.

An eyelash lives about 5 months.

There are approximately 100 million acts of sexual intercourse each day.

In an average lifetime a person will walk the equivalent of three times around the world.

Men get hiccoughs more often than women do.

Every year 100 people choke to death on ballpoint pens.

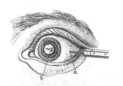

The colour red has been found to promote the hunger reflex in humans. This is why so many fast-food establishments use the colour in their logos and décor.

A human eyeball weighs an ounce.

Only 30 per cent of humans can flare their nostrils.

The average adult has about 18 square feet of skin.

A human being loses around 40 to 100 strands of hair a day.

A person will die from total lack of sleep more quickly than they will from starvation. Death will occur after about 10 days without sleep; starvation takes a few weeks longer.

If you go blind in one eye, you lose about a fifth of your vision, but all your sense of depth.

The human body contains enough iron to make a 3-inch nail.

Women have more genes than men, and because of this are better protected from things like colour blindness and haemophilia.

It takes about 200,000 frowns to make a permanent wrinkle.

The average nipple size is 0.27 inches for women and 0.22 for men.

The risk of a heart attack is higher on a Monday than on any other day of the week.

Intelligent people have more zinc and copper in their hair.

90 degrees below zero your breath will freeze in mid-air and fall to the ground.

Women are twice as likely as men to have panic attacks.

Schizophrenics hardly ever yawn.

The best way for a man to know whether he will go bald is to look at his mother's father.

An average pair of feet sweats a pint of perspiration a day.

There are twice as many left-handed men as there are left-handed women.

It takes about 150 days for a fingernail to grow from cuticle to fingertip.

Vision requires more brain power than the other four senses.

Women can detect smell better than men.

Men can read smaller print than women.

The average beard grows 5 inches a year.

The average newborn baby cries 113 minutes a day.

In one day an average person will take about 18,000 steps.

Women's hair is about half the diameter of men's

Women have a higher incidence of tooth decay than men.

The cartilage in the nose never stops growing.

The average person opens the fridge 22 times a day.

The average clean-shaven man will spend five months of his life shaving and will remove 28 feet of hair.

If you live to 70, your heart will have pumped 55 million gallons of blood.

In a lifetime, you eat around 35 tons of food.

The average reader can read 275 words per minute.

The vocabulary of the average person consists of 5,000 to 6,000 words.

In the adult human body, there are 46 miles of nerves.

When you stub your toe, your brain registers pain in 1/50th of a second.

The size of your foot is approximately the size of your forearm.

You burn 3.5 calories each time you laugh.

Women blink twice as often as men.

The kidneys use more energy than the heart (kidneys use 12 per cent of available oxygen; the heart uses 7 per cent).

The most common disease in the world is tooth decay.

You inhale about 700,000 of your own skin flakes each day.

83 per cent of people hit by lightning are men.

Human thighbones are as strong as concrete.

The thumbnail grows the slowest; the middle nail the fastest.

When you sneeze, your heart stops.

The average lifespan of a taste bud is 10 days.

According to medical experts, babies dream in the womb.

One out of every 200 women is endowed with an extra nipple.

Men are four times more likely than women to sleep naked.

The average person's eyes will be closed about 30 minutes a day because of blinking.

You'd have to walk 34 miles to melt away one pound of fat.

Women can hear better than men

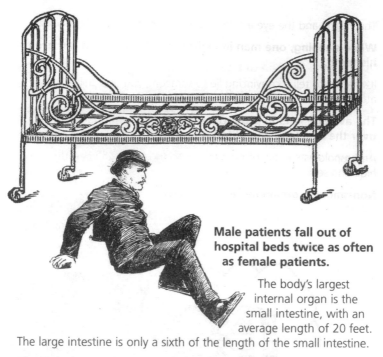

Male patients fall out of hospital beds twice as often as female patients.

The body's largest internal organ is the small intestine, with an average length of 20 feet. The large intestine is only a sixth of the length of the small intestine.

The right lung takes in more air than the left (because the left lung is smaller to make room for the heart).

Women have a wider peripheral vision than men.

The average person grows up to 6 feet of nose hair in a lifetime.

It takes 25 muscles to swallow.

More people are allergic to cow's milk than any other food.

Teenagers are 50 per cent more susceptible to colds than people over 50.

The mouth produces 2 pints of saliva a day.

The vagina and the eye are self-cleaning organs.

While sleeping, one man in eight snores, and one in ten grinds his teeth.

It's harder to tell a convincing lie to someone you find sexually attractive.

The average person produces about 12,000 gallons of urine over the course of their lifetime.

Anthropologists know of no human society whose children don't play hide and seek.

Non-smokers dream more than smokers.

AIRLINE ACRONYMS

Aer Lingus
Arousing Erotic Randy Ladies In Nice Green Uniform Suits

Aeroflot
Aircraft Everywhere Run On Fuel Left Over by Tanks

Air India
An Interesting Ride, I'll Not Do It Again

Alitalia
Always Late In Transit, Always Late In Arrival

American
A Miracle Each Rider Is Currently Alive Now
Airline Meals Eaten Regularly Induce Cramps And Nausea

BWIA
But Will I Arrive?

Delta
Departures Extra-Late, Tardy Arrivals
Doesn't Even Leave The Airport

El Al
Every Landing Always Late
Everyone's Luggage Always Lost

Emirates
English Managed, Indian Run, A
Thousand Ex-pats Suffering

Finnair
Flies Ideally? Nah, Not Airborne In Reality

Garuda
Go And Relax Until Delay Announcement

Gulf Air
Get Used to Late Flights – Aircraft In Repair

KLM
Kamikaze Loving Maniacs

Liat
Luggage Is Always Tardy

Lot
Lots Of Trouble

Lufthansa
Let Us Fondle The Hostess And Not Say Anything

Olympic
Onassis Likes Your Money Paid In Cash

Qantas
Quick And Nasty Transportation, Australian Style
Quite A Neat Trick, Arriving Safely
Quits Air-travel, Next Time Approaches Ship

Ryanair
Running Your Ailing National Airline Into Receivership

Sabena
Such A Bad Experience – Never Again

SAS
Sex Always Supplied
Same As Sabena

Swissair
Sexy Women In Swissair Service Are
Incredibly Rare

United
Usually Not Inclined To Eliminate
Disasters

Virgin
Very Interesting Ride: Going
Into Nowhere

ANIMALS ETC.

An elephant's trunk can hold 2 gallons of water.

An adult lion's roar is so loud, it can be heard up to 5 miles away.

The word rodent comes from the Latin word 'rodere', meaning to gnaw.

A mole can dig over 250 feet of tunnel in a single night.

A cow's only sweat glands are in its nose.

When a horned toad is angry, it squirts blood from its eyes.

The average gorilla has a penis that is 2 inches long.

Bats have sex in the air.

Chameleons can move their eyes independently: one eye can look forward at the same time as the other looks back.

The pocket gopher, a burrowing rodent, can run backwards as fast as it can run forwards.

A chamois goat can balance on a point of rock the size of a £1 coin.

Frogs don't drink water – they absorb it through their skin.

A giraffe's erect penis is 4 feet long.

Bulls and crocodiles are colour-blind.

The ragdoll is the largest breed of domesticated cat in the world.

The sloth moves so slowly that green algae can grow undisturbed on its fur.

Male boars excite females by breathing on their faces.

The poison arrow frog has enough poison to kill 2,200 people.

Emus can't walk backwards.

Pigs can cover a mile in 7.5 minutes when running at top speed.

Iguanas can and do commit suicide.

The giraffe has the highest blood pressure of any animal.

A crocodile's tongue is attached to the roof of its mouth.

Crocodiles swallow stones to help them dive deeper.

Gorillas sleep for up to 14 hours a day.

Giraffes can't cough.

The last of a cat's senses to develop is its sight.

The ancient Egyptians trained baboons to wait at their tables.

A woodchuck breathes only 10 times during hibernation.

Sloths spend 75 per cent of their lives asleep.

Camels are born without humps.

Despite the hump, a camel's spine is straight.

Elephants sleep for about 2 hours per day.

A crocodile can open and close its jaw but cannot move it side to side.

Armadillos can be house-trained.

Elephants are not afraid of mice.

Mice will nurse babies that are not their own.

The orangutan's warning signal to would-be aggressors is a loud belch.

During mating, the male Californian sea-otter grips the nose of the female with his teeth.

Pumas can leap a distance of about 60 feet.

Crocodiles carry their young in their mouths.

A sloth can move twice as fast in water as it can on land.

A hippopotamus is born under water.

Kangaroos can't walk backwards.

Crocodiles cannot stick out their tongues.

A crocodile can run at speeds of 11 mph.

A sow always has an even number of teats or nipples, usually 12.

Hog is a generic name for all swine – so a pig is a hog but a hog is not necessarily a pig.

The distance between an alligator's eyes, in inches, is equivalent to its length in feet.

Horses, rabbits and rats can't vomit.

A rat's performance in a maze can be improved by playing Mozart to it.

African heart-nosed bats have such a keen sense of hearing that they can hear the footsteps of a beetle on sand 6 feet away.

The pupils in goat's and sheep's eyes are rectangular.

A female ferret can die if she goes into heat and can't find a mate.

A hedgehog's heart beats 190 times a minute but drops to 20 beats per minute during hibernation.

Lions cannot roar until they reach the age of two.

Male goats will pee on each other in order to attract mates.

All the pet hamsters in the world are descended from one female wild golden hamster found with a litter of 12 young in Syria in 1930.

The Argentinian horned toad can consume an entire mouse in one swallow.

Cows can hear lower and higher frequencies than we can.

A dog can't hear the lowest key on a piano.

Elephants walk on tiptoe – the back of the foot is made up of fat and no bone.

Human birth-control pills work on gorillas.

It takes a sloth up to 6 days to digest the food it eats.

A rhinoceros's horn is made of compacted hair.

A dog can suffer from tonsillitis, but not appendicitis. It doesn't have an appendix.

An elephant has about 100 gallons of blood.

The average dairy cow produces 4 times its weight in manure each year.

A cat's jaws can't move sideways.

A chimpanzee can learn to recognize itself in a mirror, but a monkey can't.

Nose prints are the most reliable way to identify dogs.

The normal temperature of a cat is 101.5 degrees Fahrenheit.

A polecat is not a cat. It is a nocturnal European weasel.

All cats step with both left legs, then both right legs, when they walk or run. The only other animals to do this are the giraffe and the camel.

Every known dog except the chow has a pink tongue – the chow's tongue is jet black.

Every year in the US, more people are killed by deer than by any other animal.

Sex between snakes lasts from 6 to 12 hours.

The tenrac, a Madagascan insectivore, has 22 to 24 nipples.

The two-toed sloth is the only other animal (apart from humans) that mates face to face.

A mouse has more bones than a man: mouse 225, man 206.

Greyhounds can reach their top speed of 45 miles per hour in just three strides.

Cows and horses sleep standing up.

A giraffe can clean its ears with its 50cm (20-inch) tongue.

An elephant trunk has 40,000 muscles but no bone.

A giraffe has the same number of bones in its neck as a human.

Snakes hear through their jaws.

The South American giant anteater eats more than 30,000 ants a day.

The red kangaroo of Australia can leap 27 feet in one bound.

Camel milk does not curdle.

Beaver teeth are so sharp that Native Americans once used them as knife blades.

The stomach of a hippopotamus is 10 feet long.

A grasshopper needs a minimum air temperature of 62 degrees Fahrenheit before it's able to hop.

An elephant can eat a quarter of a ton of grass in one day.

Being near-sighted, sometimes a moose will approach a car, thinking it is another moose.

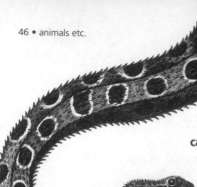

A python is capable of devouring a pig whole.

A rat can last longer without water than a camel can.

Rabbits have been known to reach a speed of 47 mph.

An iguana can stay under water for 28 minutes.

Brand-new baby giraffes are 6 feet tall and weigh almost 200 pounds.

Moose intercourse typically lasts about five seconds.

Giraffes rarely sleep more than 20 minutes a day.

A cat has 32 muscles in each ear.

Kangaroo means 'I don't understand' in Aborigine.

A polar bear's skin is black. Its fur is not white, but clear.

Polar bear liver contains so much vitamin A that it could be fatal to a human.

Minks have sex that lasts about 8 hours.

Cats can't taste sweet food.

Gorillas can't swim.

A rat can fall from a five-storey building without injury.

Greyhounds have the best eyesight of any dog.

When a giraffe is born, it has to fall around 6 feet to the ground.

The greater dwarf lemur in Madagascar always gives birth to triplets.

A giraffe's heart is 2 feet long.

Sheep are mentioned 45 times and goats 88 times in the Bible.

The placement of a donkey's eyes in its head enables it to see all four feet at one time.

Camels have three eyelids to protect themselves from blowing sand.

Frogs and toads never eat with their eyes open because they have to push food down into their stomach with the back of their eyeballs.

Hamsters blink one eye at a time.

A chameleon's tongue is twice the length of its body.

Brazil, Argentina, Australia and New Zealand all have more cattle than people.

Australia, Uruguay, Syria and Bolivia all have more sheep than people.

Somalia has more goats than people.

Denmark has twice as many pigs as people.

Alaska has almost twice as many caribou as people.

Paris is said to have more dogs than people.

Giraffes have no vocal cords.

A full-grown bear can run as fast as a horse.

The cheetah is the only cat that can't retract its claws.

A rodent's teeth never stop growing.

Beavers can hold their breath for 45 minutes.

Porcupines can float in water.

Deer sleep for only 5 minutes a day.

The skin of a hippopotamus is nearly bulletproof.

BIRDS ETC.

Lyre birds can imitate any sound they hear, from a car alarm to an electric chainsaw.

The owl can't move its eyes but it's the only creature able to turn its head in a complete circle.

Apart from chocolate and avocados, which are highly toxic to the parrot, pet parrots can eat most of the food we eat.

Kiwis are the only birds that hunt by smell.

Bluebirds can't see the colour blue.

Condors can fly 10 miles without flapping their wings.

A male emperor penguin spends 60 days or more protecting his mate's eggs, which he keeps on his feet, covered with a feathered flap. During this time he doesn't eat and loses about 25 pounds. When the chicks hatch, he feeds them a liquid from his throat. When the female penguin returns to care for the young, the male goes to sea to eat and rest.

A pigeon can't lay an egg

The smallest bird in the world is the bee hummingbird: it's 2.24 inches long and weighs less than a tiny coin.

The pouch under a pelican's bill holds up to 25 pounds of fish and water.

Geese often mate for life, and can pine to death at the loss of their mate.

The kiwi is the only bird with nostrils at the end of its bill.

Turkeys often look up at the sky during a rainstorm, and have been known to drown as a result.

Penguins are the only bird that can leap into the air like a porpoise.

The shell constitutes 12 per cent of an egg's weight.

Only the male nightingale sings.

The emu gets its name from the Portuguese word for ostrich.

An eagle can kill a young deer and fly away with it.

A pigeon can't lay an egg unless she sees another pigeon. If another pigeon isn't available, her own reflection in a mirror will do.

unless she sees another pigeon

There is a type of parrot in New Zealand that likes to eat the rubber strips that line car windows.

The fastest bird in the world is the peregrine falcon, which can fly faster than 200mph.

When the air force was conducting test runs and breaking the sound barrier, fields of turkeys dropped dead.

The bones of a pigeon weigh less than its feathers.

Ostriches stick their heads in the sand to look for water.

When the first duck-billed platypus arrived at the British Museum, the curators thought it was a fake and tried to pull its beak off.

A vulture will never attack a human or animal that is moving.

The albatross can sleep in flight.

Unlike humans, canaries can regenerate their brain cells.

It takes about 40 minutes to hard-boil an ostrich egg.

75 per cent of wild birds die before they reach 6 months old.

A woodpecker can peck 20 times a second.

Fish etc.

Nine out of every ten living things live in the ocean.

A male catfish keeps the eggs of his young in his mouth until they are ready to hatch.

Sharks will continue to attack, even when disembowelled.

A shark is the only fish that can blink with both eyes.

In order to mate, a male deep-sea anglerfish will bite a female and never let go – eventually merging his body into hers and spending the rest of his life inside her.

The red mullet only turns red after death.

Many male fish blow bubbles when they want to mate.

Whales increase their weight 30,000,000,000 times in their first 2 years.

A large whale needs more than 2 tons of food a day.

The closest relative to the manatee is the elephant.

A dolphin's hearing is so acute that it can pick up an underwater sound from 15 miles away.

When young, black sea basses are mostly female, but at the age of five many become male.

Whales can't swim backwards.

To change its line of sight, a whale must move its entire body.

The walking catfish can live on land.

A baby oyster is called a spat.

If a lobster loses an eye it can grow a new one.

If a mackerel stops swimming, it dies.

A red sponge can be broken into a thousand pieces and still reconstitute itself.

The heart of a blue whale is the size of a small car.

The flounder, a flat fish, has both eyes on one side of its body.

One species of shark is so competitive that the babies fight each other within the womb, until only one is left to be born alive.

Bluefin tuna can swim at 50 miles per hour.

Sharks are immune to all known diseases.

A shark can grow a new set of teeth in a week.

Squids sometimes commit suicide by eating their own tentacles.

Oysters can change from one gender to the other and back again.

The female starfish produces 2 million eggs a year. 99 per cent of them are eaten by other fish.

The European freshwater mussel lives for at least 90 years.

5 piranha fish could chew a horse and rider up in 7 minutes.

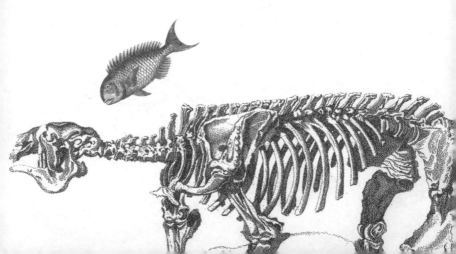

Sharks will eat anything except something in the vicinity of where they give birth. This is the only way nature protects them from accidentally eating their own babies.

To keep from being separated while sleeping, sea otters tie themselves together with kelp.

The shrimp's heart is in its head.

An octopus has 3 hearts.

A humpback whale's penis can be longer than 10 feet.

A whale can swim for 3 months without eating.

A whale's penis is called a dork.

85 per cent of all life on Earth is plankton.

Turtles can live for more than 100 years.

At 188 decibels, the whistle of the blue whale is the loudest sound produced by any animal.

All clams start out as males; some decide to become females at some point in their lives.

INSECTS ETC.

There are more insects in one square mile of rural land than there are human beings on Earth.

A queen bee lays about 1,500 eggs a day.

The only food cockroaches won't eat is cucumber.

Flies take off backwards.

A moth has no stomach.

The size of a mosquito penis is 1/100th of an inch.

Some ribbon worms will eat bits of themselves if they can't find any food.

The average bee yields only one-twelfth of a teaspoon of honey in its life.

Bees flap their wings 11,400 times a minute.

A female mosquito can produce 150,000,000 young in one year.

Mosquitoes are attracted to people who have recently eaten bananas.

Mosquitoes like the scent of oestrogen, so women get bitten by mosquitoes more than men do.

After eating, a housefly regurgitates its food and then eats it again.

A butterfly warms its body up to 81 degrees Fahrenheit before flying.

A typical bed houses over 6 billion dust mites.

A leech has 32 brains.

A greenfly born on Sunday can be a grandparent by Wednesday.

Insects shiver when they're cold.

The cicada spends 17 years of its life sleeping. In the 2 weeks it's awake, it mates and then dies.

Earthworms have 5 hearts.

The silkworm has 11 brains. But it uses only 5 of them.

Leeches can drink up to 5 times their weight in blood.

There are over 1,800 known species of flea.

The longest earthworm ever found was 22 feet long.

Mosquitoes are attracted to the colour blue twice as much as to any other colour.

A snail can crawl across a razor blade without getting injured because it excretes a protective slime.

 Cockroaches can survive underwater for 15 minutes.

Australian termites have been known to build mounds 20 feet high and at least 100 feet wide.

Slugs have 4 noses.

If a cockroach breaks a leg it can grow another one.

A spider's web is a natural clotting agent; applied to a cut it quickly stops the flow of blood.

The aphid's reproductive cycle is so fast that females are born pregnant.

The world's termites outweigh the world's humans 10 to 1.

Stag beetles have stronger mandibles than humans.

More people are killed each year by bees than snakes.

Adult earwigs can float in water for up to 24 hours.

The black widow spider can devour as many as 20 'mates' in a single day.

Bees are born fully grown.

In relation to its size, the ordinary house spider is 8 times faster than an Olympic sprinter.

The creature with the largest brain in relation to its body is the ant.

Ants can't chew their food so they move their jaws sideways to extract the juices from it.

Mexican jumping beans jump because of a moth larva inside the bean.

A snail has about 25,000 teeth.

The average garden snail has a top speed of 0.03 mph.

The sensors on the feet of a red admiral butterfly are 200 times more sensitive to sugar than the human tongue.

The female praying mantis devours her partner while they're mating.

A snail's reproductive organs are in its head.

Termites do more damage in the US every year than all the fires, storms and earthquakes combined.

A mosquito has 47 teeth.

A dragonfly's penis has a shovel on the end that scoops out a rival male's semen.

Slugs can fertilize their own eggs.

Ants don't sleep.

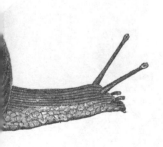

ONLYS

The bloodhound is the **only** animal whose evidence is admissible in an American court.

Monday is the **only** day of the week that has an anagram: dynamo.

Libra (the scales) is the **only** inanimate symbol in the zodiac.

The **only** countries in the world with one syllable in their names are Chad, France, Greece and Spain.

The **only** rock that floats in water is pumice.

There wasn't a single pony in the Pony Express, **only** horses.

Malayalam, spoken in Kerala, southern India, is the **only** language with a palindromic name.

A person from the country of Nauru is called a Nauruan; this is the **only** palindromic nationality.

In Germany, there's a flea that lives and breeds **only** in beer mats.

Almonds and pistachios are the **only** nuts mentioned in the Bible.

'Subbookkeeper' is the **only** word found in an English dictionary with four pairs of double letters in a row.

St John's Wood is the **only** London Underground station that doesn't contain any letters from the word 'mackerel'.

Only male turkeys (Toms) gobble; females make a clicking noise.

Rudyard Kipling wrote **only** in black ink.

'Forty' is the **only** number that has its letters in alphabetical order.

Your tongue is the **only** muscle in your body that is attached at **only** one end.

'One' is the **only** number with its letters in reverse alphabetical order.

The **only** Dutch word to contain eight consecutive consonants is 'angstschreeuw'.

Only female mosquitoes bite, and only female mosquitoes buzz.

The **only** two people in the Baseball Hall of Fame who had nothing to do with baseball are Abbott and Costello.

No president of the United States was an **only** child.

If there were an ocean big enough, Saturn would be the **only** planet that could float because its density is lighter than that of water (it is mostly gas).

Goethe could write **only** if he had an apple rotting in the drawer of his desk.

The **only** bone not broken so far in a ski accident is one located in the inner ear.

The **only** person ever to decline a Pulitzer Prize for Fiction was Sinclair Lewis.

Hummingbirds are the **only** birds able to fly backwards.

Christopher Lee was the **only** member of the cast (and crew) of the *Lord of the Rings* movies to have met J.R.R. Tolkien.

New Zealand is the **only** country that contains every type of climate in the world.

Pierre, the capital of South Dakota, is the **only** US state capital name that shares no letters with the name of its state.

Earth is the **only** planet not named after a God.

Black lemurs are the **only** primates, other than humans, that might have blue eyes.

The Dutch town of Abcoude is the **only** town or city in the world whose name begins with ABC.

Maine is the **only** US state with just one syllable. Maine is also the only US state that borders only one other state.

Theodore Roosevelt was the **only** US president to deliver an inaugural address without using the word 'I'. (Abraham Lincoln, Franklin D. Roosevelt and Dwight D. Eisenhower tied for second place, using 'I' only once in their inaugural addresses.)

Only two US states have names beginning with double consonants: Florida and Rhode Island (if you don't count Wyoming).

Only two countries have borders on three oceans – the US and Canada.

The Boston University Bridge (on Commonwealth Avenue, Boston, Massachusetts) is the **only** place in the world where a boat can sail under a train going under a car driving under an aeroplane.

Europe is the **only** continent without a desert.

The letter W is the **only** letter in the alphabet that has three – rather than one – syllables.

Sir Alec Douglas-Home is the **only** prime minister to have made it into *Wisden*, having played for Middlesex and, in 1926, toured Argentina with the MCC.

Samuel Beckett is the **only** Nobel prizewinner to have made it into *Wisden* – having played in a first-class fixture for Dublin University against Northamptonshire (scoring 18 and 12) in 1926.

Nauru is the **only** country in the world with no official capital.

Snails mate **only** once in a lifetime, but it can take up to 12 hours.

Lake Nicaragua boasts the **only** freshwater sharks in the world.

The **only** wild camels in the world are in Australia.

The polar bear is the **only** mammal with hair on the soles of its feet.

The **only** chancellor to have previously worked for the Inland Revenue is James Callaghan.

Pecans are the **only** food that astronauts can take untreated into space.

A Dalmatian is the **only** dog that can get gout.

Devon is the **only** county in Great Britain to have two coasts.

A bowling pin has to tilt **only** 7.5 degrees to fall down.

General Robert E. Lee is the **only** person ever to have graduated from the West Point military academy without a single demerit.

Only two female mammals possess hymens: humans and horses.

Only two male mammals possess prostates: humans and dogs.

Bruce Forsyth, Brenda Fricker, Kerry Packer and Steven Spielberg have **only** one kidney each. (NB Mel Gibson has a horseshoe kidney – two kidneys fused into one.)

Early Greek and Roman physicians believed the **only** way to grow a good crop of basil was to curse while scattering the seeds.

Things said by W.C. Fields

'Start every day off with a smile and get it over with.'

'I never vote for anyone; I always vote against.'

'Say anything that you like about me except that I drink water.'

'After two days in hospital, I took a turn for the nurse.'

'I certainly don't drink all the time. I have to sleep, you know.'

'Anybody who hates children and dogs can't be all bad.'

'I exercise extreme self-control: I never drink anything stronger than gin before breakfast.'

'Women are like elephants to me; they're nice to look at but I wouldn't want to own one.'

'Horse sense is the thing a horse has which keeps it from betting on people.'

'A thing worth having is a thing worth cheating for.'

'I've been on a diet for two weeks and all I've lost is two weeks.'

'The funniest thing a comedian can do is not do it.'

'Once, during Prohibition, I was forced to live for days on nothing but food and water.'

'A rich man is nothing but a poor man with money.'

'Never give a sucker an even break.'

'I'm just looking for loopholes.' (When caught reading the Bible on his deathbed.)

'On the whole, I'd rather be in Philadelphia.' (His epitaph.)

Only in Britain

Only in Britain ... can a pizza get to your house faster than an ambulance.

Only in Britain ... do chemists make ill people walk all the way to the back of the store to get their prescriptions while healthy people can buy chocolate bars at the front.

Only in Britain ... are more than 200 people a year admitted to A&E after opening bottles of beer with their teeth.

Only in Britain ... do people order double cheeseburgers, large fries and a Diet Coke.

Only in Britain ... do banks leave both doors open and chain the pens to the counters.

Only in Britain ... do we leave cars worth thousands of pounds on the drive and put our rubbish in the garage.

Only in Britain ... do we use answering machines to screen calls and then have call waiting so we won't miss a call from someone we didn't want to talk to in the first place.

Only in Britain ... do we buy hot dogs in cans of ten and buns in packs of eight.

Only in Britain ... do three people die each year testing a 9v battery on their tongue to see if it works.

Only in Britain ... were 142 men injured in a single year because they didn't remove all the pins from new shirts.

Only in Britain ... are 58 people injured every year by using sharp knives instead of screwdrivers.

Only in Britain ... can 18 people in a single year suffer serious burns trying on a new jumper with a lit cigarette in their mouth.

Only in Britain ... have 31 people died since 1996 because they watered their Christmas tree while the fairy lights were plugged in.

PURE TRIVIA

Amber was once thought to be solidified sunshine or the petrified tears of gods.

1,929,770,126,028,800 different colour combinations are possible on a Rubik's Cube.

Cleopatra used pomegranate seeds for lipstick.

The decibel was named after Alexander Graham Bell.

'Honcho' comes from the Japanese word meaning 'squad leader'.

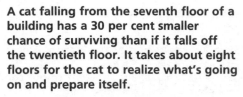

A cat falling from the seventh floor of a building has a 30 per cent smaller chance of surviving than if it falls off the twentieth floor. It takes about eight floors for the cat to realize what's going on and prepare itself.

English soldiers of the Hundred Years' War were known to the French as 'Les Goddamns' because of their propensity to swear.

Hydrangeas produce pink and white flowers in alkaline soil and blue ones in acidic soil.

Rabbits love licorice.

Malaria was originally believed to be caused by the vapours rising from swamps (the name comes from 'bad air').

Portland, Oregon was named in a coin-toss in 1844. Heads Portland, tails Boston.

50 per cent of all marshmallows consumed in the US have been toasted.

One superstition to get rid of warts is to rub them with a peeled apple and then feed the apple to a pig.

The 'live long and prosper' sign by *Star Trek*'s Mr Spock is the sign that Jewish priests (Cohenim) used while saying certain prayers.

St Cassian was a schoolmaster whose pupils stabbed him to death with their pens.

Mel Blanc, the voice of Bugs Bunny, was allergic to carrots.

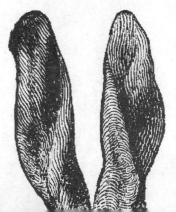

According to the ancient Chinese, swinging your arms cures headache pain.

Syphilis was known as the French disease in Italy and the English disease in France.

Pliny believed that the souls of the dead resided in beans.

Coffee drinkers have sex more frequently and enjoy it more than non-coffee drinkers.

Ham radio operators got the term 'ham' coined from the expression 'ham-fisted operators', a term used to describe early radio users who sent Morse code (i.e. pounded their fists).

Traditionally, a groom must carry a bride over the threshold to protect her from being possessed by the evil spirits that hang around in doorways.

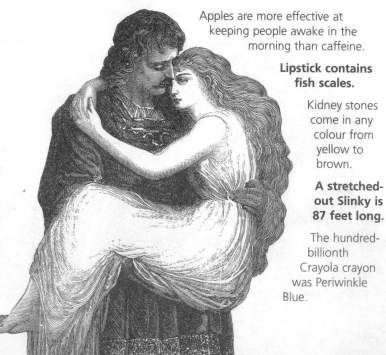

Apples are more effective at keeping people awake in the morning than caffeine.

Lipstick contains fish scales.

Kidney stones come in any colour from yellow to brown.

A stretched-out Slinky is 87 feet long.

The hundred-billionth Crayola crayon was Periwinkle Blue.

A can of Spam is opened every 4 seconds.

Pinocchio was made of pine.

More people are killed annually by donkeys than in aeroplane crashes.

Maine is the toothpick capital of the world.

New Jersey has a spoon museum with over 5,400 spoons.

There was once a town in West Virginia called '6'.

The colder the room you sleep in, the more likely you are to have a bad dream.

The Gulf Stream would carry a message in a bottle at an average of 4 miles per hour.

The monkey wrench was invented by Charles Moncke.

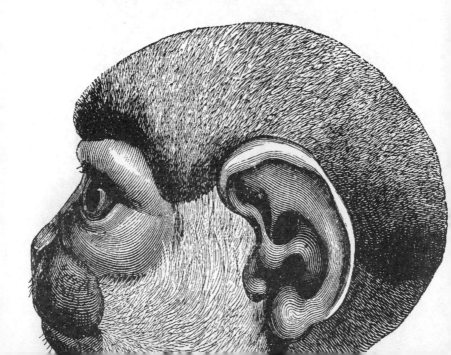

Before fame

Noel Gallagher used to be a roadie for the Inspiral Carpets (and Liam got the name Oasis from an Inspiral Carpets poster).

Shirley Williams screen-tested for the lead role in *National Velvet*.

Catherine Zeta-Jones broke into showbusiness as a teenage Shirley Bassey impersonator. Her father drove her around the working men's clubs to perform.

Geena Davis has an elbow that bends the wrong way (and when she was young, she'd do things like stand in a lift and the doors would close and she'd pretend that her arm had got caught).

Fidel Castro was voted Cuba's best schoolboy athlete (in 1944).

Simon Le Bon has taken part in the Whitbread Round-The-World yacht race.

Peter Snow auditioned to be James Bond (in the late 1960s) but was too tall.

Axl Rose used to earn $8 an hour for smoking cigarettes (for a science experiment at UCLA).

Michael Crichton handed in a paper written by George Orwell to see if his college professor had a down on him. He scored a B minus.

Billie Piper made her TV debut impersonating Posh Spice.

Emma Bunton played one of the bridesmaids catapulted onto a giant wedding cake in a Halifax Building Society TV commercial. Tina Barrett appeared in the same commercial.

Matt Damon used to break dance for money in Harvard Square.

Michelle Pfeiffer used to be a clerk at Von's grocery store in California where she learned to tie cherry stems in knots with her tongue.

Oprah Winfrey once approached Aretha Franklin as she got out of a limo and convinced the singer that she was abandoned. Aretha gave her $100, which she used to stay in a hotel.

FORMER ALTAR BOYS

Pierce Brosnan, Stephen Tompkinson, Phil Donahue, Jimmy Wray, Sir Michael Gambon, Frankie Fraser, Nigel Pivaro, Neil Jordan, Martin Scorsese, Louis Farrakhan, Bob Guccione, Paul McGann, Patric Walker, Tony Monopoly, Ron Todd, Bernhard Langer, Oliver North, Frank Bough, Danny La Rue, Engelbert Humperdinck, Eamonn Andrews, Charles Kennedy, Philip Treacy, Bernard Manning

DROPPED OUT OF COLLEGE

Ben Affleck (two colleges), Beau Bridges, Vin Diesel, Bill Murray, Dennis Quaid, Steven Spielberg, Stephen Stills, Eric Stoltz, Paula Abdul, Courteney Cox, Rosie O'Donnell, Marisa Tomei

SPENT PART OF THEIR CHILDHOOD IN A BROTHEL

James Brown

Louis Armstrong

Chico Marx (played piano in one)

Harpo Marx (also played piano but only knew two songs which he played over and over again at different speeds)

Edith Piaf (her grandmother was the cook. She also lived in one as an adult during the German occupation because it was one of the few buildings in Paris that was heated)

Richard Pryor (his grandmother was the owner)

NB Henri de Toulouse-Lautrec lived in a brothel as an adult

TEENAGE RUNAWAYS

Courtney Love, Oprah Winfrey, Bob Dylan, Daniel Day-Lewis, Billy Connolly, Errol Flynn, Roy Walker, Pierce Brosnan, Hazel O'Connor, Cary Grant, Ella Fitzgerald, Clare Higgins

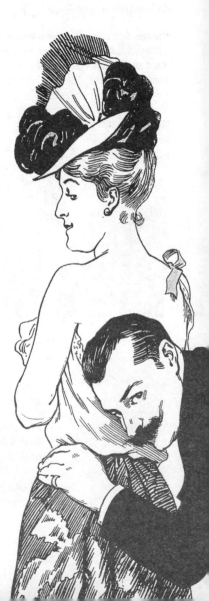

ATTENDED ART SCHOOL

Robbie Coltrane, Charles Dance, Trevor Eve, Ralph Fiennes, Bob Holness, Jonathan Pryce, Alexei Sayle, Bryan Ferry, David Byrne, John Lennon, Sofia Coppola, Fran Healey, Muriel Gray, Vic Reeves, Jim Broadbent

RHODES SCHOLARS

Bill Clinton, Bryan Gould, Bill Bradley, Kris Kristofferson, Bob Hawke, Terrence Malick, Naomi Wolf, David Kirk, Dom Mintoff, Edward de Bono, Carl Albert, J. William Fulbright, Robert Penn Warren, Dean Rusk, General Wesley Clark

ATTENDED THE SORBONNE

Alan Alda, Jean-Luc Godard, Sam Waterston, Jacqueline Kennedy Onassis, Rose Tremain, Verity Lambert, Spencer Batiste, Michael Bogdanov, Dale Campbell-Savours, Lord Killanin, Prue Leith, Magnus Linklater, Sir Julian Critchley, Christian Lacroix, Clare Balding, Liza Minnelli

FORMER CHEERLEADERS

Reese Witherspoon, Meryl Streep, Paula Abdul, Madonna, Sally Field, Raquel Welch, Carly Simon, Jerry Lewis, Angela Bassett, Sandra Bullock, Renée Zellweger (star cheerleader), Cameron Diaz, Charisma Carpenter (for the San Diego Chargers), Steve Martin, Alicia Silverstone, Calista Flockhart, Jack Lemmon, Sela Ward, Teri Hatcher (for the San Franciso 49ers)

NB Uma Thurman abandoned her dreams of becoming a cheerleader at the age of ten after a bad experience at summer camp. 'The players were kind of embarrassed. We certainly didn't turn them on.'

FORMER (BOY) SCOUTS

Rolf Harris, Bill Clinton, David Bellamy, Sir Bobby Robson, Mark Spitz, Russell Grant, Georgie Fame, Richard Gere, Trevor Brooking, Sir Derek Jacobi, Frank Bough, Neil Armstrong, President Jacques Chirac, Sir David Attenborough, Leslie Thomas, Lord Brian Rix, Michael Parkinson, Lord Jeffrey Archer, Jason Donovan, Roger Rees, Brian Clough, Sir Stirling Moss, Tony Benn, Sir Norman Wisdom, Danny La Rue, James Stewart, Lord Richard Attenborough, Sir Richard Branson, Edward Woodward, Keith Richards, Michael Barrymore, George Michael, Lord Melvyn Bragg, Ken Dodd, John Major, Sir Paul McCartney, Jim Davidson, Ronnie Corbett, Sir Cliff Richard, Chris Tarrant

FORMER (GIRL) GUIDES

Janet Street-Porter, Mo Mowlam, Angela Rippon, Dame Anita Roddick, Helen Sharman, Björk, Michelle Gayle, Linda Robson, Sally Magnusson, Clare Short, Penny Junor, Emma Forbes, Emma Thompson, Diana Quick, Baroness Thatcher, Ann Widdecombe, Belinda Lang, Mariah Carey, Princess Margaret, Teresa Gorman, Venus Williams, Alice Beer, Glenda Jackson, The Princess Royal, Pauline Quirke, Susan Tully, Mandy Rice-Davies, Carol Vorderman, Anneka Rice, Delia Smith, Kim Wilde, Carol Smillie, Cherie Blair, The Queen, Cat Deeley, Lorraine Kelly, Sarah Kennedy, Davina McCall, Gail Porter, Kate Hoey, Claire Rayner, Jenni Murray, Sandi Toksvig, Lysette Anthony, Natasha Richardson, Hillary Clinton, Belinda Carlisle, Lesley Garrett, Kate Moss

HOMECOMING QUEENS

Rosie O'Donnell, Sela Ward, Caprice, Meryl Streep, Sissy Spacek, Meg Ryan, Lynne Cheney, Barbara Bush (Dubya's daughter), Kay Hartenstein, Tori Amos, Elizabeth Dole, Nicole Brown (O.J. Simpson's ex-wife), Sharon Tate

ACHIEVEMENTS BEFORE THE AGE OF 10

At the age of 3, Elizabeth Taylor danced in front of King George V.

At the age of 3, the 19th-century English philosopher John Stuart Mill was able to read Greek.

At the age of 4, Lulu sang in public for the first time.

At the age of 5, Natalie Wood appeared in her first film.

At the age of 5, Tori Amos won a scholarship to study piano in a Baltimore conservatory (but was kicked out by the age of 11).

At the age of 6, Shirley Temple was awarded an honorary Oscar 'in grateful recognition of her outstanding contribution to screen entertainment during the year 1934'.

At the age of 7, Fred Astaire was performing in vaudeville.

At the age of 8, Jamie Oliver was cooking in his father's pub.

At the age of 9, Ruth Lawrence passed A-level maths.

At the age of 9, Macaulay Culkin was cast as the lead character in *Home Alone*, the movie that made him famous.

WASHED DISHES FOR A LIVING

Ronald Reagan, Jacques Chirac, Burt Reynolds, Roseanne, Little Richard, Eddie 'The Eagle' Edwards, Sir Roger Moore, Steve Collins, Chrissie Hynde, Uma Thurman, Warren Beatty, Dustin Hoffman, Carlos Santana, Robert Duvall

TRAINED AS COMMERCIAL ARTISTS

Lynsey De Paul, David Bowie, Bob Hoskins, Roy Hudd, Sir Dirk Bogarde, Gene Hackman, Ian Hunter, Len Deighton, Pete Townshend, Leo Sayer

TOOK PART IN UNIVERSITY CHALLENGE AS COMPETITORS

David Mellor (Christ's College, Cambridge)

Clive James (Pembroke College, Cambridge)

Sebastian Faulks (Emmanuel College, Cambridge)

Miriam Margolyes (Magdalene College, Cambridge)

Alastair Little (Downing College, Cambridge)

John Simpson (Magdalene College, Cambridge)

Stephen Fry (Queens' College, Cambridge)

Andrew Morton (Sussex)

Malcolm Rifkind (Edinburgh)

WORKED AS USHERS/USHERETTES

Sylvester Stallone, Barbra Streisand, Marianne Jean-Baptiste, Charlene Tilton, George Michael, Elizabeth Garvie, George Segal, Nadia Sawalha, Jayne Irving, Kirk Douglas, Heather Graham, Al Pacino

Worked as models

Joaquin Phoenix, Sharon Stone, Jessica Biel, Penelope Cruz, Bijou Phillips, Denise Richards, Chloe Sevigny, Mena Suvari, Christopher Walken, Emily Watson (for Laura Ashley, aged 4), Carol Smillie, Paul Marazzi, Rachel Stevens, Sophie Ellis-Bextor, Ralf Little, Willem Dafoe, Ashton Kurcher, Brooke Shields, Jacqueline Bisset, Sylvia Kristel, President Gerald Ford, Ali MacGraw, Charlotte Rampling, George Lazenby, Ellen Burstyn, Richard Jobson, Burt Reynolds, Jessica Lange, Dyan Cannon, Courteney Cox, Ted Danson, Susan Dey, Farrah Fawcett, Tom Selleck, Cybill Shepherd, Antonio Banderas, Cameron Diaz, Nick Nolte, Lindsay Lohan

Started out as extras

Dustin Hoffman, Marilyn Monroe, Ronald Reagan, Clint Eastwood, Donald Sutherland, John Wayne, Robert De Niro, Bill Cosby, Clark Gable, Robert Duvall, Gary Cooper, Marlene Dietrich, Paulette Goddard, Stewart Granger, Jean Harlow, Sophia Loren, David Niven, Rudolph Valentino, Cate Blanchett (when she was 18, in a boxing movie filmed in Egypt where she was holidaying. She appeared in a crowd scene cheering for an American boxer who was losing to an Egyptian; she hated it so much she walked off the set), Gary Sinise (in *General Hospital*), Phil Collins (in *A Hard Day's Night*), Ben Affleck & Matt Damon (in *Field of Dreams*).

SERVED IN KOREA

Neil Armstrong, Sir Michael Caine, Frank Gorshin (as an entertainer), James Garner, Ty Hardin, Screamin' Jay Hawkins, Lee Hazlewood, Ed McMahon, Chaim Potok (as an army chaplain), Jamie Farr (Corporal Klinger in the TV series M*A*S*H – the only member of the cast to have served in Korea), Faron Young, P.J. Kavanagh, Berry Gordy Jr, Charlie Rich, Link Wray, John Mayall, Leonard Nimoy, John Wells, Robert Duvall

SERVED IN VIETNAM

Oliver Stone, Al Gore, Steve Kanaly (awarded the Purple Heart for the injuries he suffered there), Charles Lindbergh (as a brigadier-general), Oliver North, Colin Powell (two tours; awarded the Purple Heart), Dennis Franz (11 months in an elite airborne division), Brian Dennehy (was in the Marines for over five years and served eight months in Vietnam before returning home with shrapnel wounds and concussion), General Wesley Clark (was shot; awarded Silver Star for bravery), James Avery, Troy Evans

Stephen King failed the medical on four counts: flat feet, limited vision, high blood pressure and a punctured eardrum.

Roger Ebert went to the draft for the Vietnam War but was rejected for being overweight. He was 26 years old and weighed 206 pounds.

Micky Dolenz was drafted to serve in the US Army in 1967 despite medical grounds for deferment – trouble with Perthese disease in childhood had left him with one leg shorter than the other. Dolenz was eventually excused from military service for being underweight. Davy Jones was also drafted, but was excused as his family's sole source of support.

CONSCIENTIOUS OBJECTORS

Bill Clinton, Paul Eddington, Sir Michael Redgrave, Carl Wilson, Muhammad Ali, Lord Soper, Dom Mintoff, Donald Swann, Richard Dreyfuss, Harold Pinter

MICKEY MOUSE CLUB 'MOUSEKETEERS' ON US TV

Justin Timberlake, Christina Aguilera, Britney Spears, J.C. Chasez, Keri Russell

STUDIED TO BE ARCHITECTS

Art Garfunkel, Rifat Ozbek, Janet Street-Porter, Queen Noor of Jordan, Justine Frischmann, Carla Bruni, Alan Plater, Lord Snowdon, Chris Lowe, Roger Waters

LIVED ON A KIBBUTZ

Sacha Baron Cohen, Sigourney Weaver, Dame Anita Roddick

BUTLINS REDCOATS

Ted Rogers, Des O'Connor, Roy Hudd, Michael Barrymore, Russell Grant, Darren Day, Jimmy Tarbuck, Ken Dodd, William G. Stewart, Dave Allen, Sir Cliff Richard, Johnny Ball

QUALIFIED (MEDICAL) DOCTORS

Graeme Garden, Che Guevara, David Owen, Harry Hill, Rob Buckman, W. Somerset Maugham, Lady Isobel Barnett, J.P.R. Williams, Graham Chapman, Sir Jonathan Miller, Anton Chekhov

WORKED IN THE CIRCUS

Pierce Brosnan (fire-eater in his teens)

Roberto Benigni (clown)

Christopher Walken (assistant lion tamer)

Harry Houdini (escapologist)

Burt Lancaster (acrobat)

Bob Hoskins (fire-eater)

Rupert Graves (clown)

Jack Higgins (odd jobs)

**W.C. Fields
(elephant attendant)**

Jeremy Beadle (ringmaster)*

Charlie Dimmock (trapeze artist)*

Cantinflas (prizefighter)

**Graham Cripsey (rode the wall
of death)**

Trevor Baylis (underwater
stunt in the Berlin Circus)

*After finding fame

LEFT-HANDED

Sarah Jessica Parker, Jean-Paul Gaultier, Angelina Jolie, Drew Barrymore, Charlie Dimmock, Eminem, Bruce Willis, Demi Moore, Rik Mayall, Goldie Hawn, Sir Bobby Charlton, Shirley MacLaine, Sir Henry Cooper, Phil Mickelson, Steve Ovett, Michael Crawford, Diane Keaton, Robert De Niro, Emma Thompson, Nicholas Lyndhurst, William Roache, Matthew Broderick, Paul Nicholas, Cheryl Baker, Ringo Starr, George Michael, Tom Cruise, Julia Sawalha, Syd Little, Loyd Grossman, Richard Dreyfuss, Robert Redford, Bob Geldof, Mark Spitz, Jennifer Saunders, Jean Shrimpton, Tony Robinson, Ruud Gullit, Phil Collins, Oprah Winfrey, Magnus Magnusson, Julian Clary, Julia Roberts, Michael Parkinson, Ross Kemp, Ryan O'Neal, Prince William, Bill Clinton, Uri Geller, George Bush, Sir Paul McCartney, Esther Rantzen, Terence Stamp, Seal

UNFORTUNATELY NAMED PRODUCTS AND CAMPAIGNS

Sharwoods launched its Bundh sauces – without realizing that, in Punjabi, the word 'bundh' is perilously close to a word meaning 'arse'.

Parker Pens' slogan, 'Avoid embarrassment – use Quink', when translated into Spanish came out as: 'Avoid pregnancy – use Quink'.

Plessey and **GEC** had a joint company in France called GPT. When this is pronounced in French, it comes out as Jay-Pay-Tay, which sounds like 'J'ai pété', meaning 'I have farted'.

Mitsubishi launched its Pajero 4WD without realizing that 'pajero' is Spanish for 'wanker'.

The computer company **Wang** ran an Australian TV commercial that contained the slogan, 'Wang cares'. It ran for just the one day.

KFC's 'finger-lickin' good' slogan was translated into China as 'eat your fingers off'.

Ford's car, the Pinto, couldn't be sold in Brazil because the word 'pinto' is slang for a small penis.

Electrolux was obliged to abandon its slogan 'Nothing sucks like Electrolux'.

The lager **Coors** had a slogan 'turn it loose' which, when translated into Spanish, became 'suffer from diarrhoea'.

Pepsi-Cola had a slogan 'Come alive with the Pepsi generation' which, when translated into Chinese, became 'Pepsi brings your ancestors back from the grave'.

Similarly, the name **Coca-Cola** was, at first, Ke-kou-ke-la in Chinese until the company discovered that the phrase means 'bite the wax tadpole' or 'female horse stuffed with wax', depending on the dialect.

The **Rolls-Royce** Silver Mist range had to be renamed for the German market because 'mist' means 'dung' in German.

Puffs tissues didn't sell well in Germany because 'puff' in German means 'brothel'.

The German hardware store chain **Götzen** opened a mall in Turkey but had to change the name as 'göt' means 'bum' in Turkish.

The Italian mineral water **Traficante** means 'drug dealer' in Spanish.

Honda launched its new car the Fitta in Scandinavia – only to find that 'fitta' was a slang word for vagina in Swedish, Norwegian and Danish.

Ford's Comet was called the Ford Caliente in Mexico, but although 'caliente' literally means hot (as in temperature), it's also used colloquially as 'horny'. Ford had a similar problem in Latin American countries with their Fiera, which means 'ugly old woman' there.

When **Mazda** launched the Laputa they didn't take into account the fact that 'puta' is the Spanish word for prostitute. The ads claiming that 'Laputa is designed to deliver maximum utility in a minimum space while providing a smooth, comfortable ride' took on a new meaning.

A **Nike** TV commercial for hiking shoes was shot in Kenya using Samburu tribesmen, one of whom was caught mouthing – in native Maa – 'I don't want these. Give me big shoes.'

Nissan launched the Moco before discovering that 'moco' is the Spanish for 'mucus'.

Frank Perdue's Chicken was advertised in Mexico with the slogan, 'It takes a tough man to make a tender chicken.' When translated into Spanish, this became: 'It takes a hard man to make a chicken aroused.'

The American slogan for **Salem** cigarettes, 'Salem – Feeling Free', was translated into Japanese as: 'When smoking Salem, you feel so refreshed that your mind seems to be free and empty.'

Hunt-Wesson introduced its Big John products in French Canada as Gros Jos before discovering that this is a slang expression for 'big breasts'.

Samarin, a Swedish remedy for upset stomachs, ran an ad that was a series of three pictures. The first was of a man looking sick, the second was of him drinking a glass of Samarin and the third was of him smiling. The company ran the ad in Arabic newspapers – where people read from right to left.

Toyota launched its MR2 model without realizing that, in France, it would be pronounced 'em-er-deux', which sounds very similar to 'merde', meaning 'shit'.

Bacardi brought out a fruit drink which they named 'Pavian' to suggest French chic, but, alas, 'pavian' means 'baboon' in German.

When **Gerber** first started selling baby food in Africa, they used their standard packaging with the cute baby on the label. Unfortunately, they were obliged to change it when they discovered that, in Africa, the standard practice is to put pictures of the contents on foods.

Jolly Green Giant translated into Arabic means 'Intimidating Green Ogre'.

When **Braniff** boasted about its seats in Spanish, what should have read 'Fly in leather' became 'Fly naked'.

SLOGANS SEEN OUTSIDE CHURCHES

No God – No Peace. Know God – Know Peace

Free Trip to heaven. Details Inside!

Try our Sundays. They're better than Baskin-Robbins

Have trouble sleeping? We have sermons – come and hear one!

God so loved the world that He did not send a committee

When down in the mouth, remember Jonah. He came out all right

Sign broken. Message inside this Sunday

How will you spend eternity – Smoking or Non-smoking?

Dusty Bibles lead to Dirty Lives

Come work for the Lord. The work is hard, the hours are long and the pay is low. But the retirement benefits are out of this world

It is unlikely there will be a reduction in the wages of sin

Do not wait for the hearse to take you to church

If you're headed in the wrong direction, God allows U-turns

Forbidden fruit creates many jams

In the dark? Follow the Son

If you can't sleep, don't count sheep. Talk to the Shepherd

GEOGRAPHY

Tasmania has the cleanest air in the inhabited world.

The furthest point from any ocean would be in China.

There are no public toilets in Peru.

The Red Sea is not red.

China uses 45 billion chopsticks per year.

The Pacific Ocean covers 28 per cent of the Earth's surface.

The poorest country in the world is Mozambique. (Switzerland is the richest.)

At the nearest point, Russia and America are less than 4 km apart.

Alaska is the most northern, western and eastern state; it also has the highest latitude, the most eastern longitude and the most western longitude, and could hold the 21 smallest states.

Birmingham has 22 more miles of canal than Venice.

The coastline of Alaska is longer than the entire coastline of the rest of the US (excluding Hawaii).

 If an Amish man has a beard, he's married.

The people of Iceland read more books per capita than any other people in the world.

La Paz in Bolivia is so high above sea level there is barely enough oxygen in the air to support a fire.

Antarctic means 'opposite the Arctic'.

Fewer than 1 per cent of the Caribbean Islands are inhabited.

The volume of water in the Amazon river is greater than the next eight largest rivers in the world combined.

There is no point in England more than 75 miles from the sea.

Seoul, the South Korean capital, means 'the capital' in the Korean language.

Despite having a land mass over 27 times smaller, Norway's total coastline is longer than the US's.

Coca-Cola is Africa's largest private-sector employer.

Parsley is the most widely used herb in the world.

The Coca-Cola company is the largest consumer of sugar in the world.

In Albania nodding the head means 'no' and shaking the head means 'yes'.

The Coca-Cola company is the largest consumer of vanilla in the world.

Everything weighs 1 per cent less at the equator.

The East Alligator River in Australia's Northern Territory harbours crocodiles, not alligators.

Mongolia is the largest landlocked country.

More redheads are born in Scotland than in any other part of the world.

Eskimos use refrigerators to keep their food from freezing.

Two-thirds of the world's aubergines are grown in New Jersey.

28 per cent of Africa is wilderness; 38 per cent of North America is wilderness.

The University of Alaska covers four time zones.

Approximately 20 per cent of Americans have passports.

Canada has more lakes than the rest of the world combined.

One third of all the fresh water on Earth is in Canada.

10 per cent of the salt mined in the world each year is used to de-ice the roads in America.

Own/owned islands

Marlon Brando (Tetiaroa)

Sir Richard Branson (Necker)

Carla Lane (St Tedwell's East)

Charles Haughey (Inis Mhicileain)

Lord Peter Palumbo (Ascrib)

Björn Borg (Kattilo)

Malcolm Forbes (Lacaula)

Nick Faldo (Bartrath)

Björk (Ellidaey – given to her by the Icelandic government)

History

The first-known contraceptive was crocodile dung, used by Egyptians in 2000BC.

Armoured knights raised their visors to identify themselves when they rode past their king. This custom has become the modern military salute.

Nobody knows where Mozart is buried.

In the latter part of the 18th century, Prussian surgeons treated stutterers by snipping off portions of their tongues.

From 1807 till 1821, the capital of Portugal was moved to Rio de Janeiro, Brazil (at the time a colony of Portugal), while Portugal was fighting France in the Napoleonic Wars.

Abdul Kassem Ismael, the Grand Vizier of Persia in the 10th century, carried his library with him wherever he went. The 117,000 volumes were carried in alphabetical order by 400 camels.

Ethelred the Unready, King of England in the 10th century, spent his wedding night in bed with his wife and his mother-in-law.

The lance ceased to be an official battle weapon in the British Army in 1927.

The Toltecs, 7th-century native Mexicans, went into battle with wooden swords so as not to kill their enemies.

China banned the pigtail in 1911 as it was seen as a symbol of feudalism.

During World War One, the future Pope John XXIII was a sergeant in the Italian army.

Emperor Caligula once decided to go to war against the Roman god of the sea, Poseidon, and ordered his soldiers to throw their spears into the water.

Between the two world wars, France was controlled by 40 different governments.

In 1939 the American Nazi Party had 200,000 members.

Richard II died in 1400. A hole was left in the side of his tomb so people could touch his royal head, but 376 years later someone stole his jawbone.

Albert Einstein was once offered the presidency of Israel. He declined, saying he had no head for problems.

Instant coffee has been around since the 18th century.

The Incas and the Aztecs were able to function without the wheel.

In about 1597, William Shakespeare gave *The Merry Wives of Windsor* to Queen Elizabeth I for Christmas because she wanted to see a play that featured Falstaff in love.

The people of East Anglia used to mummify cats and place them in the walls of their homes to ward off evil spirits.

The River Nile has frozen over only twice – once in the ninth century, and again in the eleventh century.

In ancient Egypt, if a patient died during an operation, the surgeon's hands were cut off.

In ancient China, doctors only got paid if the patient stayed in good health. If the patient's health deteriorated, sometimes the doctor had to pay him.

In medieval times, Welsh mercenary bowmen wore one shoe at a time.

Alfred Nobel invented dynamite; his father Emmanuel invented plywood.

Roman emperor Caligula made his horse a senator.

In ancient Egypt, when a cat died, it was mandatory for its owner to shave off his eyebrows to show his grief.

In Sweden in the Middle Ages, a mayor was once elected by a louse. The candidates rested their beards on a table and the louse was placed in the middle. The louse's chosen host became mayor.

The ancient Celts believed that rivers were the urine of goddesses. Many European rivers (Seine, Severn, Danube, etc.) were named after these urinating Celtic deities.

Legend has it that after he was beheaded, St Denis, the patron saint of Paris, carried his head around and walked for some distance.

During World War Two, the American automobile industry produced just 139 cars.

The imperial throne of Japan has been occupied by the same family for the last thirteen hundred years.

During the Crusades, the difficulty of transporting bodies off the battlefield for burial was resolved by taking a huge cauldron on to the battlefield, boiling down the bodies and taking away the bones.

Adolf Hitler's mother considered having an abortion but was talked out of it by her doctor.

Cleopatra wrote a book on cosmetics. One of the ingredients was burnt mice.

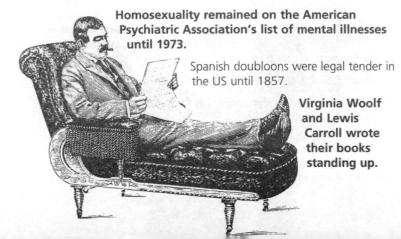

Homosexuality remained on the American Psychiatric Association's list of mental illnesses until 1973.

Spanish doubloons were legal tender in the US until 1857.

Virginia Woolf and Lewis Carroll wrote their books standing up.

The Pentagon has twice as many toilets as necessary because in the 1940s, when it was built, Virginia still had segregation laws requiring separate facilities for blacks and whites.

All 18 of Queen Anne's children (including 13 miscarriages) died before she did.

Mexico once had three presidents in one day.

Between 1839 and 1855, Nicaragua had 396 different rulers.

The Wright brothers' first flight was shorter than the wingspan of a 747.

Lady Macbeth had a son called Lulach the Fatuous.

Sultan Murad IV inherited 240 wives when he assumed the throne of Turkey in 1744. He put each wife into a sack and tossed them one by one into the Bosphorus.

During World War Two, it was against the law in Germany to name a horse Adolf.

Napoleon constructed his battle plans in a sandbox.

Ancient Egyptians slept on pillows of stone.

Richard the Lionheart spent just four months of his life in England

The Egyptians thought it was good luck to enter a house left foot first.

Mark Twain was born on a day in 1835 when Haley's Comet came into view. When he died in 1910, Haley's Comet came into view again.

Leonardo da Vinci could write with one hand and draw with the other at the same time.

Louis XIV took just three baths in his lifetime (and he had to be coerced into taking those).

George I, King of England from 1714 to 1727, was German and couldn't speak a word of English.

In ancient Greece, tossing an apple to a girl was a traditional proposal of marriage. Catching it meant she accepted.

In the 1500s, one out of 25 coffins was found to have scratch marks on the inside.

GOLD

There is 200 times more gold in the world's oceans than has ever been mined.

All the gold ever mined would be as big as a 3-bedroom house; all the gold that's still to be mined (on land) would only be big enough to make the garage.

Gold is the only metal that doesn't rust – even if it's buried in the ground for thousands of years.

India is the world's largest consumer of gold.

There are just 6 grams of gold in an Olympic Gold medal.

NB In the original story of Cinderella, her slippers were made of gold, not glass. And her stepsisters were beautiful on the outside – their ugliness lay within.

WOULD HAVE TURNED 100 IN 2005

Sir Michael Tippett, British composer

Tex Ritter, American actor

Christian Dior, French fashion designer

Bill O'Reilly, Australian cricketer

Jule Styne, American composer

Anthony Powell, British writer

Leslie Ames, British cricketer

Lord Longford, British politician

Dalton Trumbo, American film writer

Gilbert Roland, Mexican actor

Mantovani, Italian musician

Tommy Dorsey, American musician

Emlyn Williams, British actor and playwright

C.P. Snow, British writer

Joel McCrea, American actor

Max Schmeling, German boxer

Greta Garbo, Swedish actress

Howard Hughes, American industrialist

Michael Powell, British film director

Anna May Wong, American actress

Sterling Holloway, American actor

Jean Vigo, French film director

Helen Wills Moody, American tennis player

Arthur Koestler, British philosopher and writer

Clara Bow, American actress

Albert Speer, German architect and war criminal

Jack Teagarden, American musician

Dore Schary, American film producer

Leo Genn, American actor

Dag Hammarskjöld, Swedish diplomat

Thelma Todd, American actress

Dolores Del Rio, American actress

Hastings Banda, Malawi politician

James Robertson Justice, British actor

Lillian Hellman, American writer

Jean-Paul Sartre, French writer

Thelma Ritter, American actress

J. William Fulbright, American politician

Joseph Cotten, American actor

Henry Fonda, American actor

Robert Donat, British actor

Maria Von Trapp, Austrian singing nun

Harold Arlen, American composer

Franchot Tone, American actor

Geoffrey Grigson, British poet

Myrna Loy, American actress

Robert Newton, British actor

Turn 90 in 2005

Saul Bellow, Canadian writer

Herman Wouk, American writer

John Profumo, British politician

Augusto Pinochet, Chilean politician

Sargent Shriver, American politician

Arthur Miller, American playwright

John Freeman, British politician and ambassador

Eli Wallach, American actor

Harry Morgan, American actor

Sir Norman Wisdom, British actor

Would have turned 90 in 2005

Dennis Price, British actor

Don Budge, American tennis player

Lorne Green, Canadian actor

Dick Emery, British comedian

Victor Mature, American actor

Sir Stanley Matthews, British footballer

Curt Jürgens, German actor

Frank Sinatra, American singer

Michael Denison, British actor

Edith Piaf, French singer

Edmond O'Brien, American actor

Billie Holiday, American singer

Muddy Waters, American musician

Arthur Lowe, British actor

Ring Lardner Jr, American writer

Yul Brynner, American actor

Ingrid Bergman, Swedish actress

Memphis Slim, American musician

Abba Eban, Israeli politician

Phyllis Calvert, British actress

Mark Goodson, American TV programme-maker

Nathaniel Benchley, American writer

Anthony Quinn, American actor

Alice Faye, American actress

Orson Welles, American actor and director

Denis Thatcher, British politician's husband

Moshe Dayan, Israeli politician

Jay Livingston, American composer

Dorothy Squires, British singer

Zero Mostel, American actor

Ann Sheridan, American actress

Turn 80 in 2005

Harry Carpenter, British TV boxing commentator

Herbert Kretzmer, British writer and lyricist

B.B. King, American musician

Elmore Leonard, American writer

Tony Hart, British TV presenter

Angela Lansbury, British actress

Art Buchwald, American writer

Bernard Hepton, British actor

Johnny Carson, American TV presenter

Paul Raymond, British theatrical impresario

Charlie Drake, British actor and comedian

Cliff Robertson, American actor

Oscar Peterson, Canadian musician

Brian Aldiss, British writer

William Styron, American writer

Pierre Salinger, American press spokesman for JFK

Richard Baker, British broadcaster

Maureen Stapleton, American actress

Miriam Karlin, British actress

Tony Curtis, American actor

Barbara Bush, American First Lady

Peter Brook, British film and theatre director.

George Cole, British actor

Yoga Berra, American sports commentator

Alec McCowen, British actor

Doris Hart, American tennis player

Jacques Delors, French politician

Farley Granger, American actor

Mikis Theodorakis, Greek composer

Alan Whicker, British broadcaster

William F. Buckley Jr, American writer

Tony Benn, British politician

George MacDonald Fraser, British writer

William Lucas, British actor

Abel Muzorewa, Zimbabwean politician

John De Lorean, American car designer

Everton Weekes, West Indian cricketer

Jonathan Winters, American comedian and actor

June Whitfield, British actress and comedienne

Julie Harris, American actress

Dick Van Dyke, American actor

Dory Previn, American singer/songwriter

Robert Hardy, British actor

Charles Haughey, Irish politician

Gore Vidal, American writer

Baroness Margaret Thatcher, British politician

Hal Holbrook, American actor

Paul Newman, American actor

Robert Altman, American film director

George Kennedy, American actor

Nina Bawden, British writer

Elaine Stritch, American actress

WOULD HAVE TURNED 80 IN 2005

Richard Burton, British actor

Rock Hudson, American actor

Peter Sellers, British actor and comedian

Ross McWhirter, British writer and broadcaster

Norris McWhirter, British writer and broadcaster

Donald O'Connor, American actor and dancer

Stratford Johns, British actor

Malcolm X, American activist

Mai Zetterling, Swedish actress

John Stonehouse, British politician

Bill Haley, American singer

Robert F. Kennedy, American politician

Alun Owen, British playwright

Ernie Wise, British comedian

Rod Steiger, American actor

Sam Peckinpah, American film director

Richard Vernon, British actor

Lee Van Cleef, American actor

Gerald Durrell, British naturalist

Sammy Davis Jr, American entertainer

Harry Guardino, American actor

Hildegard Neff, German actress

Mel Torme, American singer

Lenny Bruce, American comedian

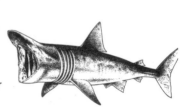

Harry H. Corbett, British actor

Jack Lemmon, American actor

Kim Stanley, American actress

Pol Pot, Cambodian dictator

John Ehrlichman, American presidential aide

Yukio Mishima, Japanese writer

TURN 70 IN 2005

Michael Jayston, British actor

Sir Mark Tully, British broadcaster

Thomas Keneally, Australian writer

Johnny Briggs, British actor

Michael Winner, British film director

Gary Player, South African golfer

Albert Roux, French chef

Duke of Kent, British royal

Don McCullin, British photographer

Sam Moore, American singer

Barry McGuire, American singer

Don Howe, British footballer

Luciano Pavarotti, Italian singer

Michael Heath, British cartoonist

Ted Edgar, British showjumper

Johnny Mathis, American singer

Sir Roy Strong, British arts administrator

Julian Pettifer, British broadcaster

John Saxon, American actor

Geraldine Ferraro, American politician

Michael Holroyd, British writer

Dalai Lama, Tibetan spiritual leader

John Inman, British actor

Roy Barraclough, British actor

Jack Kemp, American politician

Ken Kercheval, American actor

William G. Stewart, British TV producer and presenter

Donald Sutherland, Canadian actor

Diahann Carroll, American actress

Lee Meriwether, American actress

Sir Norman Foster, British architect

Françoise Sagan, French writer

Eddie Floyd, American singer

David Nobbs, British writer

Judd Hirsch, American actor

Sheila Steafel, British actress

Brian Clough, British footballer and manager

Lester Piggott, British jockey

Alain Delon, French actor

Bibi Andersson, Swedish actress

Lord George Carey, British Archbishop

Sir Magdi Yacoub, British surgeon

M. Emmet Walsh, American actor

Lord Peter Palumbo, British architect

Jim Dale, British actor

Vernon Jordan, American political aide

Susan Brownmiller, American writer

Robert Conrad, American actor

Topol, Israeli actor

John Spencer, British snooker player

Jimmy Armfield, British footballer

Henry Gibson, American actor

Jerry Lee Lewis, American singer/songwriter

Dame Julie Andrews, British actress

Jeremy Kemp, British actor

Bamber Gascoigne, British broadcaster and writer

Jimmy Swaggart, American evangelist

David Lodge, British writer

Julian Mitchell, British playwright

Jack Charlton, British footballer

Ted Dexter, British cricketer

Trevor Griffiths, British writer

Erich von Däniken, Swiss writer

Rohan Kanhai, West Indian cricketer

Woody Allen, American writer, actor and director

Barbara Leigh-Hunt, British actress

Phil Donahue, American talk show host

Geoff Lewis, British racehorse trainer

Alan Plater, British playwright

Bobby Vinton, American singer

Barry Cryer, British writer and comedian

Michael Parkinson, British TV presenter and journalist

Herb Alpert, American musician

Ronnie Hawkins, American musician

Lou Rawls, American singer

Sally Jessy Raphael, American TV presenter

Loretta Lynn, American singer

Charles Grodin, American actor

Floyd Patterson, American boxer

Would have turned 70 in 2005

Elvis Presley, American singer

Rod Hull, British ventriloquist

John Phillips, American singer/songwriter

Eldridge Cleaver, American activist

King Hussein of Jordan

Michael Williams, British actor

Ted Rogers, British comedian and TV presenter

Sonny Bono, American singer and politician

Alex Harvey, British singer

Ken Kesey, American writer

Johnny 'Guitar' Watson, American musician

Gene Vincent, American singer

Dennis Potter, British playwright

Lee Remick, American actress

Esther Phillips, American singer

Dudley Moore, British actor and comedian

Ruby Murray, British singer

Bryan Pringle, British actor

Doug McClure, American actor

John Cazale, American actor

Turn 60 in 2005

John Balding, British horseracing trainer

Ralph Stubbs, British horseracing trainer

Goldie Hawn, American actress

Henry Winkler, American actor

Anni-Frid Lyngstad, Swedish singer

Neil Young, Canadian singer/songwriter

Jeremy Hanley, British politician

John McVie, British musician

Bette Midler, American singer and actress

Doug Walters, Australian cricketer

Paul Nicholas, British actor

Roger Glover, British musician

Deborah Harry, American singer

Ken Buchanan, British boxer

Bill Kenwright, British theatrical impresario

Al Stewart, British singer/songwriter

Van Morrison, British singer/songwriter

Itzhak Perlman, Israeli musician

Margaret Ewing, British politician

Eddy Merckx, Belgian cyclist

Peter Storey, British footballer

Jose Feliciano, American musician

Franz Beckenbauer, German footballer

Maria Aitken, British actress

Jessye Norman, American singer

Kate Adie, British TV news journalist

Bryan Ferry, British singer

Don McLean, American singer/songwriter

Burt Ward, American actor

Michael Ancram, British politician

John Motson, British football commentator

Virginia Wade, British tennis player

Rod Argent, British musician

Pat Jennings, British footballer

Nicola Pagett, British actress

Ken Livingstone, British politician

Aung San Suu Kyi, Burmese democracy campaigner

Betty Stove, Dutch tennis player

Colin Blunstone, British singer/songwriter

Carly Simon, American singer/songwriter

Jasper Carrott, British comedian

Micky Dolenz, American singer

Katharine Houghton, American actress

Brenda Fricker, British actress

Mia Farrow, American actress

Maud Adams, American actress

Michael Stoute, British horseracing trainer

Kevin Godley, British musician

John Lithgow, American actor

Jeannie C. Riley, American singer

David Jessel, British TV presenter

Wayne Fontana, British singer

Gerd Müller, German footballer

Martin Shaw, British actor

Nick Raynsford, British politician

Marthe Keller, Swiss actress

Tom Selleck, American actor

Rod Stewart, British singer

Maggie Bell, British singer

Patrick Malahide, British actor

Eric Clapton, British musician

Pete Postlethwaite, British actor

Linda Hunt, American actress

Gerry Cottle, British circus proprietor

John Patten, British politician

John Lowe, British darts player

Helen Mirren, British actress

Ken Norton, American boxer

Steve Martin, American actor and comedian

Tony Scannell, Irish actor

Lemmy, British singer

Christopher Cazenove, British actor

Ian Gillan, British musician

Martyn Lewis, British TV newsreader

Ritchie Blackmore, British musician

Michael Brandon, American actor

Björn Ulvaeus, Swedish musician

Bob Seger, American singer/songwriter

Bianca Jagger, Nicaraguan model

Alan Ball, British footballer

Nicky Henson, British actor

David Pleat, British football manager

Princess Michael of Kent, British royal

Jacky Ickx, Belgian racing driver

Stephen Stills, American rock musician

Sir Rocco Forte, British hotelier

Eric Stewart, British musician

Christopher Martin-Jenkins, British journalist

Pete Townshend, British musician

Steven Norris, British politician

Priscilla Presley, American actress

Dave Lee Travis, British DJ

John Fogerty, American musician

Martin Pipe, British racehorse trainer

Brian Barnes, British golfer

Hale Irwin, American golfer

Bill Paterson, British actor

Derek Underwood, British cricketer

Gordon Waller, British singer

Davy Jones, British singer

Roy 'Chubby' Brown, British comedian

Douglas Hogg, British politician

Gerald Davies, British rugby union player/writer

Patch Adams, American doctor

Daniel Topolski, British oarsman and coach

WOULD HAVE TURNED 60 IN 2005

Bob Marley, Jamaican musician

Noel Redding, British musician

Bob Peck, British actor

Donny Hathaway, American singer

Bob 'The Bear' Hite, American singer

Divine, American actor

Jacqueline du Pre, British musician

Turn 50 in 2005

Steve Jones, British guitarist

Jose Rivero, Spanish golfer

Carlene Carter, American singer

Abdul Qadir, Pakistani cricketer

Janet Ellis, British TV presenter

Lord Colin Moynihan, British politician

Phil Oakey, British singer/songwriter

John Rutherford, British rugby union player

Yo-Yo Ma, French-born musician

Steve Ovett, British athlete

Bill Gates, American businessman

Jeff Stewart, British actor

Sally Magnusson, British TV presenter

Glynis Barber, South African actress

Sam Bottoms, American actor

Tanya Roberts, American actress

Eric Faulkner, British musician

Paul Bradley, British actor

Ben De Lisi, British fashion designer

Sandra Bernhard, American actress

Dean Sullivan, British actor

Griffin Dunne, American actor

Tony Allcock, British bowls player

Tony Knowles, British snooker player

Alan Hansen, British footballer and pundit

Julie Hagerty, American actress

Jonathan Lunn, British dancer and choreographer

Catherine Panton-Lewis, British golfer

Paul O'Grady, British comedian

Oliver Sherwood, British racehorse trainer

Judy Davis, Australian actress

Gary Sinise, American actor

Derek Longmuir, British musician

Bruce Willis, American actor

Reba McEntire, American singer/songwriter

Timothy Laurence, Princess Anne's husband

Jeff Daniels, American actor

Alain Prost, French racing driver

Garry Christian, British singer

Kelsey Grammer, American actor

Helen Atkinson Wood, British actress

Howard Jones, British musician

Jay Osmond, American singer

Michael Troughton, British actor

Michel Platini, French footballer

Tina Charles, British singer

Kirsty Wark, British TV presenter

Virginia Elliot (formerly Leng), British equestrian

John Grisham, American writer

Carol Harrison, British actress

Olga Korbut, Russian gymnast

Hazel O'Connor, British actress and singer

Bill Paxton, American actor

Debra Winger, American actress

Chow Yun-Fat, Hong Kongese actor

Dale Winton, British TV presenter

Rosanne Cash, American singer

Dominic Grieve, British politician

Connie Sellecca, American actress

Vivien Creegor, British TV newsreader

Iman, Somalian model

Allan Border, Australian cricketer

Desmond Douglas, British table-tennis player

Curtis Strange, American golfer

Maggie Philbin, British TV presenter

Vic Marks, British cricketer

Mick Jones, British musician

Isabelle Adjani, French actress

Shirley Cheriton, British actress

Billy Idol, British singer

Steve Coppell, British footballer

Jimmy Smits, American actor

Willem Dafoe, American actor

Billy Bob Thornton, American actor

John Whitaker, British showjumper

Gordon Brand, British golfer

John Reid, Irish jockey

Bruce Foxton, British musician

Billy Blanks, American fitness expert and actor

Ed Moses, American athlete

Gillian Taylforth, British actress

Lesley Garrett, British singer

Mike Smith, British TV presenter

Janice Long, British DJ

Pete Shelley, British musician

Donna Hartley, British athlete

Les McKeown, British singer

Andy Gray, British footballer and commentator

Ian Botham, British cricketer

Arsenio Hall, American TV presenter

Maria Shriver, American broadcaster

Belinda Lang, British actress

Karen Dotrice, British actress

Ray Liotta, American actor

Donatella Versace, Italian designer

Greg Norman, Australian golfer

Steve Earle, American musician

Jay McInerney, American writer

Rowan Atkinson, British actor

Kevin Costner, American actor

Sir Simon Rattle, British orchestral conductor

Whoopi Goldberg, American actress

Eddie Van Halen, American musician

Trudie Styler, British producer

Dana Carvey, American actor

Gary Grimes, American actor

Turn 40 in 2005

Martin Lawrence, American actor

Rob Wainwright, British rugby union player

Steve Bull, British footballer

Ardal O'Hanlon, Irish actor

Tiggy Legge-Bourke, British socialite

Emmanuelle Béart, French actress

Robert Downey Jr, American actor

Sean Wilson, British actor

Alice Beer, British TV presenter

Susannah Harker, British actress

Julia Ormond, American actress

Guy Forget, French tennis player

Beth Gibbons, British musician

Paul Prichard, British cricketer

Iain Dowie, British footballer

Joely Richardson, British actress

Nathan Moore, American musician

Sarah Jessica Parker, American actress

Jesper Parnevik, Danish golfer

Michael Watson, British boxer

Laurence Llewelyn-Bowen, British designer and TV presenter

Colin Calderwood, British footballer

Victoria Sellers, British-born actress

Sophie Rhys-Jones, Countess of Wessex

Diane Lane, American actress

Robbie Earle, British footballer

Alan Cumming, British actor and comedian

Sherilyn Fenn, American actress

Princess Stephanie of Monaco

Chris Rock, American actor and comedian

Zinzan Brooke, New Zealander rugby union player

John Leslie, British TV presenter

Helena Sukova, Czech tennis player

Veronica Webb, American model

Kristin Davis, American actress

Julia Carling, British TV presenter

Lembit Opik, British politician

Linda Evangelista, Canadian model

Elizabeth Hurley, British actress

Brooke Shields, American actress

Norman Whiteside, British footballer

Ben Volpeliere-Pierrot, British singer

Aravinda De Silva, Sri Lankan cricketer

Ruben Sierra, American baseball player

Matt Biondi, American swimmer

Evan Harris, British politician

Denis Irwin, Irish footballer

Annabella Lwin, Burmese singer

Famke Janssen, Dutch actress

Robert Jones, British rugby union player

Björk, Icelandic singer

Will Carling, British rugby union player

Sean Hughes, British comedian

Des Walker, British footballer

Ben Stiller, American actor and director

Illeana Douglas, American actress

Garry Schofield, British rugby league player

Jeremy Guscott, British rugby union player

Tony Cottee, British footballer

Trent Reznor, American singer and musician

Emma Forbes, British TV presenter

Hazel Irvine, British TV presenter

Pat Cash, Australian tennis player

Steve & Mark Waugh, Australian cricketers

Jill Greenacre, British actress

Angus Fraser, British cricketer

J.K. Rowling, British writer

Sam Mendes, British theatre and film director

Kevin Dillon, American actor

Kyra Sedgwick, American actress

Slash, American musician

Gunnar Halle, Norwegian footballer

Marlee Matlin, American actress

Shania Twain, Canadian singer/songwriter

Craig McLachlan, Australian actor

Lennox Lewis, British boxer

Derek Redmond, British athlete

Charlie Sheen, American actor

Zak Starkey, British musician

Andrea Jaeger, American tennis player

Damien Hirst, British artist

Colin Alldridge, British actor

Simon O'Brien, British actor

Paul Jarvis, British cricketer

Gary Pallister, British footballer

Moby, American musician

Steve Coogan, British actor

Cathy Tyson, British actress

Sonique, British singer

Luke Perry, American actor

Goldie, British actor and rapper

Dougray Scott, British actor

Turn 30 in 2005

David Beckham, British footballer

Enrique Iglesias, Spanish singer

John Higgins, Irish snooker player

Jonah Lomu, New Zealander rugby union player

Lauryn Hill, American singer

Mel B, British singer

Andy Farrell, British rugby league player

Angelina Jolie, American actress

Ralf Schumacher, German motor racing driver

Tobey Maguire, American actor

Ronnie O'Sullivan, British snooker player

Milla Jovovich, Ukrainian actress

Tiger Woods, American golfer

Balthazar Getty, American actor

Jamie Oliver, British chef

Paul Marazzi (aka Funk a1), British singer

Lee Latchford-Evans, British singer

Mary Pierce, French tennis player

James Major, British son of ex-PM John

Nicky Butt, British footballer

Sara Gilbert, American actress

Rick McMurray, British singer

Lil' Kim, American rapper

Charlize Theron, South African actress

Eric Miller, Irish rugby union player

Lee Brennan, British singer

Kate Winslet, British actress

Sean Lennon, American singer

Jacqueline Pirie, British actress

Michael Duberry, British footballer

Shaznay Lewis, British singer

Jacques Kallis, South African cricketer

Faye Tozer, British singer

Ant McPartlin (of Ant & Dec), British entertainer

Declan Donnelly (of Ant & Dec), British entertainer

Natalie Imbruglia, Australian singer
Keith Gillespie, British footballer
Gary Neville, British footballer
Brian Littrell, American singer
Drew Barrymore, American actress
Niki Taylor, American model
Kelle Bryan, British musician
Magdalena Maleeva, Bulgarian tennis player
John Hartson, British footballer
Robbie Fowler, British footballer
Chris Martin, Canadian actor
Melanie Blatt, British singer
Hannah Waterman, British actress

Turn 25 in 2005

Sergio Garcia, Spanish golfer
Jenson Button, British motor racing driver
Nick Carter, American singer
Christina Ricci, American actress
Chelsea Clinton, American daughter of Bill
Lady Rose Windsor, British royal
Bijou Phillips, American actress and singer
Bryan McFadden, Irish singer
Daniel MacPherson, Australian actor

Kian Egan, Irish singer

Mark Feehily, Irish singer

Steven Gerrard, British footballer

Venus Williams, American tennis player

Robbie Keane, Irish footballer

Jessica Simpson, American singer

Gisele Bundchen, Brazilian model

Michelle Williams, American singer

Noel Sullivan, British singer

Dominique Swain, American actress

Macaulay Culkin, American actor

Kerry McFadden, British singer

Michelle Williams, American actress

Martina Hingis, Swiss tennis player

Isaac Hanson, American singer

Adele Silva, British actress

**Christina Aguilera,
American singer**

Monica, American singer

**Simon (Baz) Bright,
British TV presenter**

BORN ON THE SAME DAY

Barry Goldwater & Dana Andrews (1.1.1909)

J.D. Salinger & Sheila Mercier (1.1.1919)

John Paul Jones & Victoria Principal (3.1.1946)

Julia Ormond & Guy Forget & Beth Gibbons (4.1.1965)

Robert Duvall & Alfred Brendel (5.1.1931)

Umberto Eco & Raisa Gorbachev (5.1.1932)

Capucine & E.L. Doctorow (6.1.1931)

Robin Ellis & Professor Stephen Hawking (8.1.1942)

Freddie Starr & Jimmy Page (9.1.1944)

Anthony Andrews & Brendan Foster (12.1.1948)

Suggs & Julia Louis-Dreyfus (13.1.1961)

Mark Bosnich & Nicole Eggert (13.1.1972)

LL Cool J & Ruel Fox (14.1.1968)

David Pleat & Princess Michael of Kent (15.1.1945)

Konstantin Stanislavsky & David Lloyd George (17.1.1863)

Nevil Shute & Al Capone (17.1.1899)

Moira Shearer & Sir Clyde Walcott (17.1.1926)

David Bellamy & John Boorman (18.1.1933)

Julian Barnes & Dolly Parton (19.1.1946)

Benny Hill & Telly Savalas (21.1.1924)

Placido Domingo & Richie Havens (21.1.1941)

Sam Cooke & Claire Rayner (22.1.1931)

John Hurt & Gillian Shepherd (22.1.1940)

Randolph Scott & Sergei Eisenstein (23.1.1898)

Neil Diamond & Aaron Neville (24.1.1941)

Robbie Earle & Alan Cumming (27.1.1965)

Nick Price & Frank Skinner (28.1.1957)

Vanessa Redgrave & Boris Spassky (30.1.1937)

Christian Bale & Jemima Khan (30.1.1974)

Sherilyn Fenn & Princess Stephanie & Brandon Lee (1.2.1965)

Lisa Marie Presley & Rupert Moon (1.2.1968)

Melanie & Farrah Fawcett (2.2.1947)

Michael Dickinson & Morgan Fairchild (3.2.1950)

Charles Lindbergh & Sir Hartley Shawcross (4.2.1902)

Red Buttons & Andreas Papandreou (5.2.1919)

Douglas Hogg & Roy 'Chubby' Brown (5.2.1945)

Sven Goran Eriksson & Christopher Guest & Barbara Hershey (5.2.1948)

Patrick Macnee & Denis Norden (6.2.1922)

Rip Torn & Mamie Van Doren & Fred Trueman (6.2.1931)

Pete Postlethwaite & Gerald Davies (7.2.1945)

Garth Brooks & Eddie Izzard (7.2.1962)

Carmen Miranda & Dean Rusk (9.2.1909)

Sandy Lyle & Cyrille Regis (9.2.1958)

Jimmy Durante & Bill Tilden (10.2.1893)

Mary Quant & John Surtees (11.2.1934)

Simon MacCorkindale & Michael McDonald (12.2.1952)

Edwina, Countess Mountbatten & Arthur Pentelow (14.2.1924)

Sir Alan Parker & Carl Bernstein (14.2.1944)

Gerald Harper & Graham Hill (15.2.1929)

Melissa Manchester & Jane Seymour (15.2.1951)

Patricia Routledge & Nicholas Ridley (17.2.1929)

Jeremy Edwards & Denise Richards (17.2.1971)

Johnny Hart & Ned Sherrin (18.2.1931)

Roberto Baggio & Colin Jackson (18.2.1967)

Jimmy Greaves & Judy Cornwell (20.2.1940)

Brenda Blethyn & Sandy Duncan (20.2.1946)

Eddie Hemmings & Ivana Trump (20.2.1949)

Anthony Head & Patricia Hearst (20.2.1954)

Kurt Cobain & Andrew Shue (20.2.1967)

Alan Rickman & Tyne Daly (21.2.1946)

Jonathan Demme & Tom Okker (22.2.1944)

Michael Chang & Jo Guest (22.2.1972)

Anton Mosimann & Shakira Caine (23.2.1947)

Denis Law & Pete Duel (24.2.1940)

Dame Elizabeth Taylor & Lord Young of Graffham (27.2.1932)

Mario Andretti & Joe South (28.2.1940)

Mike D'Abo & Roger Daltrey (1.3.1944)

Catherine Bach & Ron Howard (1.3.1954)

John Irving & Lou Reed (2.3.1942)

Rory Gallagher & Dame Naomi James & J.P.R. Williams (2.3.1949)

James Doohan & Ronald Searle (3.3.1920)

Kenny Dalglish & Chris Rea (4.3.1951)

Alan Greenspan & Andrzej Wajda (6.3.1926)

Kiki Dee & Rob Reiner (6.3.1947)

David Wilkie & Cheryl Baker (8.3.1954)

Trish Van Devere & Bobby Fischer (9.3.1943)

Garth Crooks & Sharon Stone (10.3.1958)

Virginia Bottomley & James Taylor (12.3.1948)

John B. Sebastian & Patti Boyd (17.3.1944)

Lee Dixon & Rob Lowe (17.3.1964)

Kenny Lynch & Ron Atkinson (18.3.1939)

Spike Lee & Theresa Russell (20.3.1957)

Matthew Broderick & Rosie O'Donnell (21.3.1962)

Wilfrid Brambell & Karl Malden (22.3.1912)

Stephen Sondheim & Pat Robertson (22.3.1930)

William Shatner & Leslie Thomas (22.3.1931)

George Benson & Keith Relf (22.3.1943)

Clyde Barrow & Tommy Trinder (24.3.1909)

Archie Gemmill & Sir Alan Sugar (24.3.1947)

Aretha Franklin & Richard O'Brien (25.3.1942)

Jung Chang & Stephen Dorrell (25.3.1952)

Maria Ewing & Terry Yorath (27.3.1950)

Gary Stevens & Quentin Tarantino (27.3.1963)

Richard Eyre & Richard Stilgoe (28.3.1943)

Matthew Corbett & Dianne Wiest (28.3.1948)

Shirley Jones & Richard Chamberlain (31.3.1934)

Al Gore & Rhea Perlman (31.3.1948)

Marsha Mason & Wayne Newton (3.4.1942)

Cherie Lunghi & Gary Moore (4.4.1952)

Hugo Weaving & Jonathan Agnew (4.4.1960)

Natasha Lyonne & Heath Ledger (4.4.1979)

Bette Davis & Herbert Von Karajan (5.4.1908)

Max Clifford & Roger Cook (6.4.1943)

Andrew Sachs & Cliff Morgan (7.4.1930)

Tony Banks & James Herbert (8.4.1943)

Alec Stewart & Julian Lennon (8.4.1963)

Gerry Fitt & Hugh Hefner (9.4.1926)

Jack Smethurst & Carl Perkins (9.4.1932)

Iain Duncan-Smith & Dennis Quaid (9.4.1954)

Adrian Henri & Omar Sharif (10.4.1932)

Gloria Hunniford & Ricky Valance (10.4.1940)

Nicholas Ball & Bob Harris (11.4.1946)

David Cassidy & Maeve Haran (12.4.1950)

Seamus Heaney & Paul Sorvino (13.4.1939)

Bishop Abel Muzorewa & Rod Steiger (14.4.1925)

Julian Lloyd Webber & Anthea Redfern (14.4.1951)

Sir John Harvey-Jones & Henry Mancini (16.4.1924)

Clare Francis & Henry Kelly (17.4.1946)

Melissa Joan Hart & Sean Maguire (18.4.1976)

Harold Lloyd & Joán Miró (20.4.1893)

Lord Beeching & Norman Parkinson (21.4.1913)

Hugh Lloyd & Aaron Spelling (22.4.1923)

Peter Frampton & Jancis Robinson (22.4.1950)

Lloyd Honeyghan & Gary Rhodes (22.4.1960)

Fiona Bruce & Hank Azaria (25.4.1964)

Darcey Bussell & Mica Paris (27.4.1969)

Dickie Davies & Willie Nelson (30.4.1933)

Richard E. Grant & Peter Howitt (5.5.1957)

Tony Blair & Graeme Souness (6.5.1953)

Sir David Attenborough & Don Rickles (8.5.1926)

Peter Benchley & Ricky Nelson (8.5.1940)

Katharine Hepburn & Leslie Charteris (12.5.1907)

Tony Hancock & Jackie Milburn (12.5.1924)

Susan Hampshire & Dr Miriam Stoppard (12.5.1937)

Ian Dury & Billy Swan (12.5.1942)

Alan Ball & Nicky Henson (12.5.1945)

Bob Carolgees & Steve Winwood (12.5.1948)

Gabriel Byrne & Jenni Murray (12.5.1950)

Joe Brown & Ritchie Valens (13.5.1941)

Selina Scott & James Whale (13.5.1951)

George Lucas & Francesca Annis (14.5.1944)

Sue Carpenter & Sugar Ray Leonard (17.5.1956)

Joe Cocker & Keith Fletcher (20.5.1944)

Bob Dylan & Harold Melvin (24.5.1941)

Matt Busby & Aldo Gucci (26.5.1909)

Hubert Humphrey & Vincent Price (27.5.1911)

Duncan Goodhew & Siouxie Sioux (27.5.1957)

Lynda Bellingham & John Bonham (31.5.1948)

Gemma Craven & Tom Robinson (1.6.1950)

Anita Harris & Curtis Mayfield (3.6.1942)

Chris Finnegan & Michelle Phillips (4.6.1944)

Mike Gatting & Javed Miandad (6.6.1957)

Tom Jones & Ronald Pickup (7.6.1940)

Tara Lipinski & Leelee Sobieski (10.6.1982)

Carmine Coppola & Jacques Cousteau (11.6.1910)

Brigid Brophy & Anne Frank (12.6.1929)

Johnny Hallyday & Xaviera Hollander (15.6.1943)

Sir Paul McCartney & Roger Ebert (18.6.1942)

Phil Middlemiss & Rory Underwood (19.6.1963)

Chet Atkins & Audie Murphy (20.6.1924)

Kate Hoey & Sir Malcolm Rifkind & Lord Maurice Saatchi (21.6.1946)

King Edward VIII, Duke of Windsor & Alfred Kinsey (23.6.1894)

Jean Anouilh & Ted Tinling (23.6.1910)

Bob Fosse & Kenneth McKellar (23.6.1927)

Adam Faith & Lord Alexander Irvine & Wilma Rudolph (23.6.1940)

Frances McDormand & Robert Norster (23.6.1957)

Brian Johnston & Mary Wesley (24.6.1912)

Jeff Beck & Arthur Brown & Julian Holloway (24.6.1944)

Betty Stove & Colin Blunstone (24.6.1945)

Tommy Cannon & Alan Coren & Shirley Ann Field (27.6.1938)

David Duckham & Gilda Radner (28.6.1946)

Jamie Farr & Jean Marsh & Sydney Pollack (1.7.1934)

Sir Alec Douglas-Home & King Olav V of Norway (2.7.1903)

Gina Lollobrigida & Neil Simon (4.7.1927)

Alan Freeman & Janet Leigh (6.7.1927)

Vladimir Ashkenazy & Ned Beatty & Gene Chandler (6.7.1937)

Jet Harris & Dame Mary Peters (6.7.1939)

Bill Oddie & Michael Howard (7.7.1941)

Louis Jordan & Nelson Rockefeller (8.7.1908)

Jim Kerr & Ben De Haan (9.7.1959)

Courtney Love & Gianluca Vialli (9.7.1964)

John Motson & Virginia Wade (10.7.1945)

Sir Alastair Burnet & Kathy Staff (12.7.1928)

Sir Alec Rose & Sir Garfield Todd (13.7.1908)

Harrison Ford & Roger McGuinn (13.7.1942)

Ken Kercheval & William G. Stewart (15.7.1935)

Linda Ronstadt & The Sultan of Brunei (15.7.1946)

Lolita Davidovich & Forest Whitaker (15.7.1961)

Desmond Dekker & Sir George Young (16.7.1941)

Margaret Court & Frank Field (16.7.1942)

Donald Sutherland & Diahann Carroll (17.7.1935)

Phoebe Snow & David Hasselhoff (17.7.1952)

Brian Auger & Dion Dimucci (18.7.1939)

Norman Jewison & Bill Pertwee & Karel Reisz (21.7.1926)

Albert Brooks & Don Henley (22.7.1947)

Coral Browne & Michael Foot (23.7.1913)

Chris Smith & Lynda Carter (24.7.1951)

Peter Bottomley & Frances de la Tour (30.7.1944)

Geraldine Chaplin & Jonathan Dimbleby & Sherry Lansing (31.7.1944)

Dean Cain & Marina Ogilvy (31.7.1966)

James Baldwin & Carroll O'Connor (2.8.1924)

Julia Foster & Rose Tremain (2.8.1943)

Josh Gifford & Martha Stewart (3.8.1941)

Mary Decker Slaney & Ian Broudie (4.8.1958)

Joan Hickson & John Huston (5.8.1906)

Alan Howard & Carla Lane (5.8.1937)

Garrison Keillor & B.J. Thomas (7.8.1942)

Brian Conley & Walter Swinburn (7.8.1961)

Rory Calhoun & Esther Williams (8.8.1922)

Reginald Bosanquet & Tam Dalyell (9.8.1932)

Lawrence Dallaglio & Angie Harmon (10.8.1972)

Adrian Lester & Jason Leonard (14.8.1968)

Tony Robinson & Jimmy Webb (15.8.1946)

Robert Culp & Tony Trabert (16.8.1930)

Nelson Piquet & Guillermo Vilas (17.8.1952)

Claire Richards & Thierry Henry (17.8.1977)

Johnny Nash & Jill St John (19.8.1940)

Kevin Dillon & Kyra Sedgwick (19.8.1965)

Jason Starkey & Lucy Briers (19.8.1967)

Alan Parry & Robert Plant (20.8.1948)

Dame Janet Baker & Barry Norman (21.8.1933)

Geoff Capes & Shelley Long & Rick Springfield (23.8.1949)

Leonard Bernstein & Richard Greene (25.8.1918)

Martin Amis & John Savage & Gene Simmons (25.8.1949)

Blair Underwood & Joanne Whalley (25.8.1964)

Howard Clark & Steve Wright (26.8.1954)

Gerhard Berger & Siobhan Redmond & Jeanette Winterson
(27.8.1959)

Ben Gazzara & Windsor Davies (28.8.1930)

Timothy Bottoms & Dana (30.8.1951)

Van Morrison & Itzhak Perlman (31.8.1945)

Freddie Mercury & Buddy Miles & Loudon Wainwright III
(5.9.1946)

Malcolm Bradbury & Sir Paul Getty (7.9.1932)

Cynthia Lennon & David Hamilton (10.9.1939)

Herbert Lom & Ferdinand Marcos & Jessica Mitford (11.9.1917)

Carol Barnes & Jacqueline Bisset & Pete Cetera (13.9.1944)

Paul Allott & Ray Wilkins (14.9.1956)

Charles Haughey & B.B. King (16.9.1925)

Linda Lusardi & Derek Pringle (18.9.1958)

Brian Epstein & Austin Mitchell (19.9.1934)

Keith Harris & Stephen King (21.9.1947)

Charles Clarke & Bill Murray (21.9.1950)

Scott Baio & Liam Fox & Catherine Oxenberg (22.9.1961)

Tony Gubba & Julio Iglesias (23.9.1943)

Jack Dee & Ally McCoist (24.9.1962)

Bishen Bedi & Felicity Kendal (25.9.1946)

Mary Beth Hurt & Olivia Newton-John (26.9.1948)

Denís Lawson & Meat Loaf (27.9.1947)

Peter Egan & Majid Khan & Helen Shapiro (28.9.1946)

Madeline Kahn & Ian McShane (29.9.1942)

Angie Dickinson & Teresa Gorman (30.9.1931)

Jimmy Carter & William Rehnquist (1.10.1924)

Tom Bosley & Sandy Gall (1.10.1927)

Laurence Harvey & George Peppard (1.10.1928)

Duncan Edwards & Stella Stevens (1.10.1936)

Trevor Brooking & Donna Karan (2.10.1948)

Zeinab Badawi & Fred Couples & Greg Proops (3.10.1959)

Sir Terence Conran & Basil D'Oliveira (4.10.1931)

Sarah Lancashire & Yvonne Murray (4.10.1964)

Robin Bailey & Robert Kee & Donald Pleasence (5.10.1919)

Camille Saint-Saëns & Alastair Sim (9.10.1900)

Don Howe & Sam Moore & Luciano Pavarotti (12.10.1935)

Lenny Bruce & Baroness Margaret Thatcher (13.10.1925)

Paul Simon & John Snow (13.10.1941)

Sir Cliff Richard & Christopher Timothy (14.10.1940)

Vicki Hodge & Sir Cameron Mackintosh (17.10.1946)

Margot Kidder & George Wendt (17.10.1948)

Chuck Berry & Klaus Kinski (18.10.1926)

Mark King & Viggo Mortensen (20.10.1958)

Geoff Boycott & Manfred Mann (21.10.1940)

Sir Derek Jacobi & Christopher Lloyd (22.10.1938)

Nick Hancock & Steve Hodge (25.10.1962)

Jenny McCarthy & Toni Collette (1.11.1972)

John Barry & Mike Dukakis & Albert Reynolds (3.11.1933)

Sean (P Diddy) Combs & Matthew McConaughey (4.11.1969)

Kazuo Ishiguro & Rickie Lee Jones (8.11.1954)

Ronald Harwood & Carl Sagan (9.11.1934)

Andy Kershaw & Tony Slattery (9.11.1959)

Jonathan Winters & June Whitfield (11.11.1925)

Wallace Shawn & Julie Ege (12.11.1943)

Harold Larwood & Dick Powell (14.11.1904)

Prince Charles & Michael Dobbs (14.11.1948)

Bob Gaudio & Martin Scorsese (17.11.1942)

Bill Giles & Baroness Margaret Jay & Brenda Vaccaro (18.11.1939)

Elizabeth Perkins & Kim Wilde (18.11.1960)

Gareth Chilcott & Bo Derek (20.11.1956)

Dr. John & Natalya Makarova (21.11.1940)

Andy Caddick & Alex James (21.11.1968)

Billy Connolly & Marlin Fitzwater (24.11.1942)

John Gummer & Tina Turner (26.11.1939)

John Alderton & Bruce Lee (27.11.1940)

Jacques Chirac & Diane Ladd (29.11.1932)

Sir Ridley Scott & Frank Ifield (30.11.1937)

Andy Gray & Billy Idol (30.11.1955)

Mike Denness & Richard Pryor (1.12.1940)

Jaco Pastorius & Treat Williams (1.12.1951)

Scott Hastings & Marisa Tomei & Anna Walker (4.12.1964)

Harry Chapin & Stan Boardman (7.12.1942)

John Cassavetes & Bob Hawke (9.12.1929)

Clive Anderson & Susan Dey (10.12.1952)

Rita Moreno & Bhagwan Shree Rajneesh (11.12.1931)

Paula Wilcox & Robert Lindsay (13.12.1949)

Patty Duke & Michael Ovitz & Stan Smith (14.12.1946)

Christopher Ellison & Benny Andersson (16.12.1946)

Uri Geller & Lesley Judd (20.12.1946)

Donald Regan & Kurt Waldheim (21.12.1918)

Noel Edmonds & Chris Old (22.12.1948)

Princess Alexandra & Ismail Merchant (25.12.1936)

Kenny Everett & Nigel Starmer-Smith (25.12.1944)

Lightning & Dido (25.12.1971)

Jane Lapotaire & Anna Scher (26.12.1944)

Harvey Smith & Jon Voight (29.12.1938)

Ted Danson & Cozy Powell (29.12.1947)

Sir Alex Ferguson & Sarah Miles (31.12.1941)

Pure trivia

The oldest known vegetable is the pea.

To strengthen a Damascus sword, the blade was plunged into a slave.

Catherine the Great relaxed by being tickled.

A coward was originally a boy who took care of cows.

There are 2,598,960 possible hands in a five-card poker game.

Cows can be identified by noseprints.

82 per cent of the workers on the Panama Canal suffered from malaria.

60 per cent of all US potato products originate in Idaho.

The Forth railway bridge in Scotland is a metre longer in summer than in winter as a result of thermal expansion.

In the Andes, time is often measured by how long it takes to smoke a cigarette.

Brazil got its name from the nut, not the other way around.

It would take about 2 million hydrogen atoms to cover the full stop at the end of this sentence.

Dirty snow melts quicker than clean snow.

The model ape used in the 1933 film *King Kong* was 18 inches tall.

Rodin's *The Thinker* is a portrait of the Italian poet Dante.

Johann Sebastian Bach once walked 230 miles to hear the organist at Lübeck in Germany.

After retiring from boxing, ex-World heavyweight champion Gene Tunney lectured on Shakespeare at Yale University.

The Beatles' song 'A Day In The Life' ends with a note sustained for 40 seconds.

Miss Piggy's measurements are 27–20–32.

In 1517, the *Mona Lisa* was bought by King Francis I of France to hang in a bathroom.

Salvador Dalí once arrived at an art exhibition in a limousine filled with turnips.

'Mary, Mary, Quite Contrary' was based on Mary, Queen of Scots.

There are 256 semihemidemisemiquavers in a breve.

There are two independent nations in Europe smaller than New York's Central Park: Vatican City and Monaco.

If the world's total land area were divided equally among the world's people, each person would get 8.5 acres.

Seattle, like Rome, was built on seven hills.

The Dutch town of Leeuwarden can be spelled 225 different ways.

The geographical centre of North America is in North Dakota.

The only city whose name can be spelled completely with vowels is Aiea in Hawaii.

John Wilkes Booth's brother once saved the life of Abraham Lincoln's son.

ALL THE RECIPIENTS OF THE AUSTRALIAN OF THE YEAR AWARD

2004: Steve Waugh

2003: Professor Fiona Stanley

2002: Pat Rafter

2001: Lt-General Peter Cosgrove

2000: Sir Gustav Nossal

1999: Mark Taylor

1998: Cathy Freeman

1997: Professor Peter Doherty

1996: Dr John Yu

1995: Arthur Boyd

1994: Ian Kiernan

1993: ** No award given

1992: Mandawuy Yunupingu

1991: Archbishop Peter Hollingworth

1990: Fred Hollows

1989: Allan Border

1988: Kay Cottee

1987: John Farnham

1986: Dick Smith

1985: Paul Hogan

1984: Lois O'Donoghue

1983: Robert de Castella

1982: Sir Edward Williams

1981: Sir John Crawford

1980: Manning Clark

1979: *Senator Neville Bonnor

1979: *Harry Butler

1978: *Alan Bond

1978: *Galarrwuy Yunupingu

1977: *Sir Murray Tyrall

1977: *Dame Raigh Roe

1976: Sir Edward 'Weary' Dunlop

1975: *Sir John Cornforth

1975: *Major General Alan Stretton

1974: Sir Bernard Heinze

1973: Patrick White

1972: Shane Gould

1971: Evonne Goolagong Cawley

1970: His Eminence Cardinal Sir Norman Gilroy

1969: The Rt Hon Richard Gardiner Casey Baron of Berwick, Victoria and of the City of Westminster

1968: Lionel Rose

1967: The Seekers

1966: Sir Jack Brabham

1965: Sir Robert Helpmann

1964: Dawn Fraser

1963: Sir John Eccles

1962: Alexander 'Jock' Sturrock

1961: Dame Joan Sutherland

1960: Sir MacFarlane Burnet

* In some years the Canberra Australia Day Council also recognized an Australian of the Year.

** The award dating system changed – no award made.

A GUIDE TO 'STRINE (AUSTRALIAN SLANG)

Bend the elbow (to) = have a drink (as in 'g'day, sport, fancy bending the elbow?')

Bonza or **beaut** = wonderful, great

Chook = chicken (as eaten on a 'barbie')

Crook = unwell (as in 'strewth, I'm crook')

Dead as a dead dingo's donga = in a parlous condition

Drink with the flies (to) = to drink alone (as in 'That cobber's drinking with the flies!')

Dunny = toilet

Fair dinkum = the real thing (sometimes uttered in spite of oneself, as in, 'Fair dinkum, that Pom can bat')

Fair go = Good chance (as in 'Shane's got a fair go of taking a wicket against these pommie bastards')

Godzone – God's own country (i.e. Australia)

Grog = booze ('BYOG' on an invitation means bring your own grog)

Hit your kick = open your wallet (as in 'come on, blue, hit your kick and pay for those tinnies')

Hooly dooly = I say! (as in 'Hooly dooly, have you seen the state of that dunny?')

Ripper = super

A sausage short of a barbie = not in possession of all (his) faculties

She'll be right = No problem (as in 'I'll be there at the cricket, she'll be right')

Spit the dummie (to) = lose one's cool (as in 'I think that poofter's spitting the dummie')

Spunky = good-looking (as in 'That Kylie sure is spunky')

True blue = honest or straight (said approvingly as in 'he may be an ocker but he's true blue' see also 'good as gold')

Tucker = food

Wowser = killjoy, spoilsport

WORDS

The longest one-syllable word is SCREECHED.

ALMOST is the longest word in the English language with all the letters in alphabetical order. APPEASES, ARRAIGNING, HOTSHOTS, SIGNINGS and TEAMMATE all have letters which occur twice and only twice.

The syllable -OUGH can be pronounced nine different ways – as evidenced by the following sentence: 'A rough, dough-faced, thoughtful ploughman emerged from a slough to walk through the streets of Scarborough, coughing and hiccoughing.'

The sentence 'He believed Caesar could see people seizing the seas' contains seven different spellings of the 'ee' sound.

In English, only three words have a letter that repeats six times: DEGENERESCENCE (six Es), INDIVISIBILITY (six Is) and NONANNOUNCEMENT (six Ns).

The French equivalent of 'the quick brown fox jumps over the lazy dog', a sentence containing every letter of the alphabet (useful when learning to type), is 'allez porter ce vieux whisky au juge blond qui fume un Havane', which translates as 'go and take this old whisky to the fair-haired judge smoking the Havana cigar'.

The word QUIZ was allegedly invented in 1780 by a Dublin theatre manager, who bet he could introduce a new word of no meaning into the language within 24 hours.

***Alice in Wonderland* author Lewis Carroll invented the word CHORTLE – a combination of 'chuckle' and 'snort'.**

Dr Seuss invented the word NERD for his 1950 book *If I Ran the Zoo*.

The word GIRL appears just once in the Bible.

The word QUEUEING is the only English word with five consecutive vowels.

WEDLOCK is derived from the old English words for pledge ('wed') and action ('lac').

DIXIE is derived from the French word for 10 – *dix* – and was first used by a New Orleans bank that issued French-American $10 bills. Later the word expanded to represent the whole of the southern states of the US.

The shortest English word that contains the letters A, B, C, D, E, and F is FEEDBACK.

The word FREELANCE comes from a knight whose lance was free for hire.

The word SHERIFF comes from 'shire reeve'. In feudal England, each shire had a reeve who upheld the law for that shire.

The Sanskrit word for 'war' means 'desire for more cows'.

SOS doesn't stand for 'Save Our Ship' or 'Save Our Souls' – it was chosen by a 1908 international conference on Morse Code because the letters S and O were easy to remember. S is dot dot dot, O is dash dash dash.

The word CORDUROY comes from the French 'cord du roi' or 'cloth of the king'.

AFGHANISTAN, KIRGHISTAN and TUVALU are the only countries with three consecutive letters in their names.

RESIGN has two opposed meanings depending on its pronunciation ('to quit' and 'to sign again').

The word SET has the highest number of separate definitions in the Oxford English Dictionary.

In Chinese, the words 'crisis' and 'opportunity' are the same.

UNDERGROUND and UNDERFUND are the only words in the English language that begin and end with the letters 'und'.

The Chinese ideogram for 'trouble' shows 'two women living under one roof'.

Only three words in the English language end in 'dous': TREMENDOUS, HORRENDOUS, HAZARDOUS.

The tennis player, GORAN IVANISEVIC, has the longest name of a celebrity that alternates consonants and vowels.

UNITED ARAB EMIRATES is the longest name of a country consisting of alternating vowels and consonants.

TARAMASALATA (a type of Greek salad) and GALATASARAY (name of a Turkish football club) each have an A for every other letter.

TAXI is spelled the same way in English, French, German, Swedish, Spanish, Danish, Norwegian, Dutch, Czech and Portuguese.

The word THEREIN contains thirteen words spelled with consecutive letters: the, he, her, er, here, I, there, ere, rein, re, in, therein, and herein.

SWIMS is the longest word with 180-degree rotational symmetry (if you were to view it upside-down it would still be the same word and perfectly readable).

UNPROSPEROUSNESS is the longest word in which no letter occurs only once.

www as an abbreviation for 'World Wide Web' has nine spoken syllables, whereas the term being abbreviated has only three spoken syllables.

You look different

In French, OISEAU (bird) is the shortest word containing all five vowels.

ULTRAREVOLUTIONARIES has each vowel exactly twice.

FACETIOUS and ABSTEMIOUS contain the five vowels in alphabetical order.

SUBCONTINENTAL, UNCOMPLIMENTARY and DUOLITERAL contain the five vowels in reverse alphabetical order.

The shortest sentence in the English language is 'Go!'

PLIERS is a word with no singular form. Other such words are: ALMS, CATTLE, EAVES and SCISSORS.

ACCEDED, BAGGAGE, CABBAGE, DEFACED, EFFACED and FEEDBAG are seven-letter words that can be played on a musical instrument.

The word DUDE was coined by Oscar Wilde and his friends. It is a combination of the words 'duds' and 'attitude'.

'Hijinks' is the only word in common usage with three dotted letters in a row.

EARTHLING is first found in print in 1593. Other surprisingly old words are SPACESHIP (1894), ACID RAIN (1858), ANTACID (1753), HAIRDRESSER (1771), MOLE (in connection with espionage, 1622, by Sir Francis Bacon), FUNK (a strong smell, 1623; a state of panic, 1743), MILKY WAY (ca. 1384, but earlier in Latin) and MS (used instead of Miss or Mrs, 1949).

EWE and YOU are pronounced exactly the same, yet share no letters in common.

The words BORSCHTS, LATCHSTRING and WELTSCHMERZ each have six consonants in a row.

Ewe too!

TONGUE TWISTERS

Six sharp smart sharks

The sixth sick sheik's sixth sheep's sick

If Stu chews shoes, should Stu choose the shoes he chews?

Rory the warrior and Roger the worrier were wrongly reared in a rural brewery

Black-back bat

Sheena leads, Sheila needs

Wunwun was a racehorse, Tutu was one too. Wunwun won one race, Tutu won one too.

Lesser leather never weathered wetter weather better

A box of biscuits, a batch of mixed biscuits

The local yokel yodels

Eleven benevolent elephants

Red lorry, yellow lorry, red lorry, yellow lorry

Is this your sister's sixth zither, sir?

A big black bug bit a big black bear, made the big black bear bleed blood

Scissors sizzle, thistles sizzle

We shall surely see the sun shine soon

A noisy noise annoys an oyster

Three free throws

Cheap ship trip

How much wood would a woodchuck chuck if a woodchuck could chuck wood?

Mrs Smith's Fish Sauce Shop

Black bug's blood

Fred fed Ted bread and Ted fed Fred bread

Six slick slim sick sycamore saplings

Irish wristwatch

Six slippery snails slid slowly seaward

Friendly Frank flips fine flapjacks

Selfish shellfish

Peter Piper picked a peck of pickled peppers
Did Peter Piper pick a peck of pickled peppers?
If Peter Piper picked a peck of pickled peppers,
Where's the peck of pickled peppers Peter Piper picked?

OXYMORONS

Army Intelligence, Civil Servant, Easy Payments, Working Lunch, Corporate Hospitality, Amicable Divorce, Business Trip, Friendly Fire, Metal Woods, Executive Decision, Operator Service, Guest Host, Mercy Killing, Business Ethics, Microsoft Works, Virtual Reality, Jumbo Shrimp, Committee Decision, Same Difference, Free Trade, Student Teacher, Airline Food, Floppy Disk, Civil Disobedience, Working Holiday, Crash Landing, Educated Guess, Martial Law, Paid Volunteer

A WRITING GUIDE

Steer well clear of clichés; give them a wide berth.

Do not be redundant; do not use more words to express an idea or concept than you really need to use.

All verbs has to agree with subjects.

Always avoid annoying alliteration.

Be specific, more or less.

Parenthetical remarks (however pertinent) are (almost certainly) superfluous.

Complete sentences only, please.

The passive voice is to be avoided.

Foreign words and phrases are *de trop*.

Delete commas, that are, not necessary.

One should never generalize.

Eschew ampersands & abbreviations, etc.

Analogies in writing are like pyjamas on a cat.

Never use a big word where a diminutive expression would suffice.

Eliminate quotations. As Ralph Waldo Emerson said, 'I hate quotations.'

A mixed metaphor, even one that flies like a bird, should be given its marching orders.

Who needs rhetorical questions?

Exaggeration is a million times worse than understatement.

Proofread carefully to see if you any words out.

Foreign words and phrases are de trop

THE WINNING WORD IN ALL US NATIONAL SPELLING BEES

2003: Pococurante

2002: Prospicience

2001: Succedaneum

2000: Demarche

1999: Logorrhea

1998: Chiaroscurist

1997: Euonym

1996: Vivisepulture

1995: Xanthosis

1994: Antediluvian

1993: Kamikaze

1992: Lyceum

1991: Antipyretic

1990: Fibranne

1989: Spoliator

1988: Elegiacal

1987: Staphylococci

1986: Odontalgia

1985: Milieu

1984: Luge

1983: Purim

1982: Psoriasis

1981: Sarcophagus

1980: Elucubrate

1979: Maculature

1978: Deification

1977: Cambist

1976: Narcolepsy

1975: Incisor

1974: Hydrophyte

1973: Vouchsafe

1972: Macerate

1971: Shalloon

1970: Croissant

1969: Interlocutory

1968: Abalone

1967: Chihuahua

1966: Ratoon

1965: Eczema

1964: Sycophant

1963: Equipage

1962: Esquamulose

1961: Smaragdine

1960: Troche

1959: Cacolet

1958: Syllepsis

1957: Schappe

1956: Condominium

1955: Crustaceology

1954: Transept

1953: Soubrette

1952: Vignette

1951: Insouciant

1950: Haruspex

1949: Dulcimer

1948: Psychiatry

1947: Chlorophyll

1946: Semaphore

1943–5: No spelling bee was held

1942: Sacrilegious

1941: Initials

1940: Therapy

1939: Canonical

1938: Sanitarium

1937: Promiscuous

1936: Interning

1935: Intelligible

1934: Deteriorating

1933: Propitiatory

1932: Knack

1931: Foulard

1930: Fracas

1929: Asceticism

1928: Albumen

1927: Luxuriance

1926: Abrogate

1925: Gladiolus

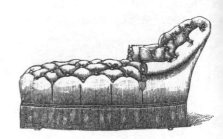

Botox treatment

Gloria Hunniford, Jennifer Ellison, Madonna, Sir Cliff Richard, Patsy Kensit, Joan Rivers, Elizabeth Hurley, Meg Mathews, Celine Dion, Kirstie Alley, Tom Cruise, Jamie Lee Curtis

Facelifts

Loni Anderson, Cher, Jane Fonda, Dolly Parton, Joan Rivers, Ivana Trump, Mary Tyler Moore, Angela Lansbury, Fay Weldon, Roseanne, Liberace, Lucille Ball, Gary Cooper, Joan Crawford, Julie Christie, Marlene Dietrich, Rita Hayworth, Kirk Douglas, Henry Fonda, Michael Jackson, Dean Martin, Jacqueline Kennedy, Mary Pickford, Elvis Presley, Debbie Reynolds, Frank Sinatra, Barbara Stanwyck, Dame Elizabeth Taylor, Lana Turner, Cherri Gilham, Bea Arthur, Phyllis Diller, Nicky Haslam, Debbie Harry, Mary Archer, Barbra Streisand, Sharon Osbourne

Had their lips done

Madonna, Lynne Perrie, Suzanne Mizzi, Cher, Loni Anderson, Pamela Anderson, Melanie Griffith, Ivana Trump, Dame Elizabeth Taylor, Leslie Ash, Sharon Osbourne

Breasts enlarged

Brigitte Nielsen, Jane Fonda, Mariel Hemingway, Melanie Griffith, Iman, Danniella Westbrook, Melinda Messenger, Paula Yates, Cher, Pamela Anderson, Demi Moore, Dannii Minogue, Gena Lee Nolin, Courtney Love (later had her implants removed), Scorpio (Nikki Diamond), Rhona Nitra, Anna Nicole Smith, Nicole Eggert (later had her breasts reduced), Alana Hamilton, Loni Anderson, Heather Locklear, Tanya Roberts, Caprice, Jilly Johnson, Bo Derek, Jessica Hahn, Emma Noble, Sharron Davies, Donna Rice, Linda Lovelace, Britt Ekland, Paula Abdul, Dyan Cannon, Geena Davis, Jerry Hall, Janet Jackson, LaToya Jackson, Mary Tyler Moore, Jennifer Tilly, Stevie Nicks (later had them reduced), Della Bovey, Meg Mathews, Mariah Carey, Mel B (removed in 2001), Christina Aguilera, Nell McAndrew, Victoria Beckham, Samantha Robson, Jordan (three ops), Toni Braxton, Carmen Electra, Natasha Hamilton

Nose jobs

Peter O'Toole, Cilla Black, Edwina Currie, Caroline Aherne, Bonnie Langford, Tom Jones, Cher, Belinda Lang, Dale Winton, Marilyn Monroe, Fanny Brice, Barbara Eden, Rhonda Fleming, Annette Funicello, Eva Gabor, Zsa Zsa Gabor, Mitzi Gaynor, Lee Grant, Juliette Greco, Joan Hackett, Carole Landis, Rita Moreno, Stefanie Powers, Jill St John, Talia Shire, Dinah Shore, Sissy Spacek, Raquel Welch, Milton Berle, Vic Damone, Joel Grey, George Hamilton, Al Jolson, Dean Martin, Lynsey De Paul, Natalie Appleton, Melanie Blatt, Shaznay Lewis, Charlie O'Neil, Lisa Kudrow, Natasha Richardson, Jodie Marsh, Roseanne

LIPOSUCTION

Michael Ball (from his stomach)

Demi Moore (from her thighs, bottom and stomach)

Joan Rivers (from her thighs)

Anna Nicole Smith (from her stomach)

Sir Michael Caine (from his stomach)

Melanie Griffith (from her stomach and thighs)

Kenny Rogers (from his stomach)

Roseanne (from her stomach)

Don Johnson (from his chin and cheeks)

Dolly Parton (from her hips and waist)

Alexander McQueen (from his stomach)

Nicole Appleton (from her thighs and hips)

Mariah Carey (from her midsection)

Linsey Dawn McKenzie (from her thighs)

Geri Halliwell (from her stomach and thighs)

Jordan (from her thighs)

Jamie Lee Curtis (from underneath her eyes)

Pierced nipples

Tim Roth, Tommy Lee, Howard Donald, Jaye Davidson, Drew Carey, Gail Porter, Davina McCall, Faye Tozer, Meg Mathews, Lene Nystrom, Billy Connolly, Sarah Cawood, Steve Tyler, Liv Tyler, Paul Cattermole, Christina Aguilera, Britney Spears, Paloma Bailey, Janet Jackson, Evan Davis

Pierced tongues

Mel B, Keith Flint, Kathy Acker, Ross Hale, Zara Phillips, Sinéad O'Connor, Janet Jackson, Ashia Hansen

Pierced navels

Oona King, Sarah Michelle Gellar, Britney Spears, Ashia Hansen, Della Bovey, Stella Tennant, Denise Van Outen, Lisa Faulkner, Rachel Stevens, Tracy Shaw, Denise Welch, Naomi Radcliffe, Jo O'Meara, Jennifer Ellison, Paloma Bailey, Danniella Westbrook, Serena Williams, Harriet Scott, Zara Phillips, Princess Charlotte of Monaco, Jessie Wallace, Madonna, Janet Jackson, Rosie Millard, Andrea Catherwood, Keira Knightley

ACTORS ON ACTING

'The art of acting is not to act. Once you show them more, what you show them is, in fact, bad acting.' (Sir Anthony Hopkins)

'I'm pragmatic. American actors tear themselves apart for a scene. British actors are lazy. We just do it.' (Sir Michael Caine)

'It's a difficult business to be in. Bernard Shaw said, "Never tangle with actresses; they keep such terrible hours" – and he should have known as he was always trying to tangle with actresses.' (Susannah York)

'When an actor marries an actress they both fight for the mirror.' (Burt Reynolds)

'My old drama coach used to say: "Don't just do something, stand there."' (Clint Eastwood)

'I didn't say actors are cattle. I said actors should be treated like cattle.' (Alfred Hitchcock)

'Being a star is an agent's dream, not an actor's.' (Robert Duvall)

'There are lots of reasons why people become actors. Some to hide themselves, and some to show themselves.' (Sir Ralph Richardson)

'An actor's a guy who, if you ain't talking about him, he ain't listening.' (Marlon Brando)

'Basically, when you whittle everything away, I'm a grown man who puts on make-up.' (Brad Pitt)

'I always say that acting isn't conducive to life.' (Cindy Crawford)

'Never mistake having a career with having a life.' (Sean Young)

'Acting is not an important job. Plumbing is.' (Spencer Tracy)

'You gotta be a nut to be in this profession.' (Rod Steiger)

'It does seem sometimes that acting is hardly the occupation of an adult.' (Sir Laurence Olivier)

'Actors are rogues and vagabonds. Or they ought to be. I can't stand it when they behave like solicitors from Penge.' (Helen Mirren)

'Nobody became an actor because he had a good childhood.' (William H. Macy)

'Don't think for a moment that I'm really like any of the characters I've played. I'm not – that's why it's called acting.' (Leonardo DiCaprio)

MNEMONICS AND AIDES-MEMOIRE

The kings and queens of England and the United Kingdom since 1066

Willie, Willie, Harry, Ste
Harry, Dick, John, Harry three
One two three Edward, Richard two
Henry, four, five, six then, who?
Edward four, five, Dick the Bad
Harry twain then Ned the lad
Mary, Bessie, James the vain
Charlie, Charlie, James again
William and Mary, Ann Gloria
Four Georges, William, then Victoria
Edward, George, then Ned the eighth
quickly goes and abdicateth
Leaving George, then Liz the second
And with Charlie next it's reckoned
That's the way our monarchs lie
Since Harold got it in the eye!

The order of planets in distance from the Sun

Mercury, Venus, Earth, Mars, Jupiter, Saturn, Uranus, Neptune, Pluto – My Very Easy Method: Just Set Up Nine Planets.

The order of colours in the rainbow

Red, Orange, Yellow, Green, Blue, Indigo, Violet
– Richard Of York Gave Battle In Vain.

The order of geological time periods

Cambrian, Ordovician, Silurian, Devonian, Carboniferous, Permian, Triassic, Jurassic, Cretaceous, Paleocene, Eocene, Oligocene, Miocene, Pliocene, Pleistocene, Recent
– Cows Often Sit Down Carefully. Perhaps Their Joints Creak? Persistent Early Oiling Might Prevent Painful Rheumatism.

The countries of Central America in geographical order
Belize, Guatemala, Honduras, Nicaragua, Costa Rica, Panama
– BeeGee's Hen! Se 'er pee?

The order of Mohs hardness scale, from 1 to 10
Talc, Gypsum, Calcite, Fluorite, Apatite, Orthoclase feldspar, Quartz, Topaz, Corundum, Diamond
– Toronto Girls Can Flirt, And Other Queer Things Can Do.

The order of sharps in music
FCGDAEB
– Father Charles Goes Down And Ends Battle.

The order of notes to which guitar strings should be tuned
EBGDAE
– Easter Bunnies Get Drunk At Easter.

The order of notes represented by the lines on the treble clef stave
EGBDF
– Every Good Boy Deserves Favour.

The order of taxonomy in biology
Kingdom, Phylum, Class, Order, Family, Genus, Species
– Kids Prefer Cheese Over Fried Green Spinach.

The four oceans
Indian, Arctic, Atlantic, Pacific
– I Am A Person.

The seven continents
Europe, Antarctica, Asia, Africa, Australia, North America, South America
– Eat AN ASpirin AFter AUgmenting Noah's Ship.

The Great Lakes
Huron, Ontario, Michigan, Erie, Superior
– HOMES.

For the Great Lakes in order of size
Superior, Huron, Michigan, Erie, Ontario
– Sam's Horse Must Eat Oats.

The Confederate States of America
South Carolina, Louisiana, Georgia, North Carolina, Alabama, Arkansas, Virginia, Mississippi, Florida, Tennessee and Texas
– Sultry Carol Languished Grumpily Near Carl, Always Aware Virginal Men Frequently Take Time.

2001: A Space Oddity
Apes, Bones, Cosmic Device … Evolution! Floating Giant Hub. Investigate Jupiter. Komputer Loopy. Man Nears Outsized Plinth. Queer Readings. Starry Turbulence. Unexpected Very Weird Xyschedelia Yielding Zen.

LUCKY CHARMS

Billy Crystal: a toothbrush he used to pretend was a microphone when he was a child. He now carries it on stage whenever he performs.

James Goldsmith: the late businessman always kept a stone frog in his pocket.

Luciano Pavarotti: a bent nail, which he always wears in his top pocket when he performs.

Damon Hill: has an Austrian lucky charm called a *Gamsbart*. It's a tassle made of goat hair and was given to Hill by his trainer Erwine Gollner.

Jo Brand: green toilet paper because: 'I did a brilliant gig once when I had a piece of green toilet paper in my pocket as I had a cold. After that I went through a phase of believing that green toilet paper was my lucky charm.'

Vic Reeves: black onyx cufflinks.

Yves Saint Laurent: a jewel, a heart made of grey diamonds with rubies. 'It's at home, in a secret place. I only take it out for collections.'

Salute Magpies

**Mel C, Robert Howley,
Sir Peter O'Sullevan, David Beckham,
Amanda Holden, Adrian Maguire**

Bite Nails

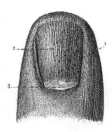

Gordon Brown, Dustin Hoffman, Phil Collins, Johnny Mathis, Liza Minnelli, Steven Spielberg, Cate Blanchett, Britney Spears (after hypnosis failed, she painted her nails with a red-hot pepper polish that burnt her tongue), Mel B (toenails), Jon Lee (toenails – 'Urgh, but I do it!'), Scott Robinson (toenails), Will Young, Elijah Wood, Gina Bellman, Emilia Fox, Melanie Sykes, Greg Proops, Jamie Theakston, Bryan Ferry, Louis Theroux

Chainsmokers

**Donatella Versace, Joaquin Phoenix,
F.W. de Klerk, Gérard Depardieu, Tom
Clancy, Robbie Williams, Rich Hall,
Emily Watson (briefly, because of her
role in *Angela's Ashes*), Kate Moss,
Michel Platini, Seamus Mallon,
Felix Dennis**

Smoke Roll-ups

Kate Winslet, Arthur Smith,
Zoë Wanamaker, Martin Amis

RECOVERING ALCOHOLICS

Mel Gibson, Barry Humphries, Sir Anthony Hopkins, Eric Clapton, Jimmy Greaves, Dick Van Dyke, Buzz Aldrin, Patrick Swayze, Mike Yarwood, Tony Adams, John Daly, Jim Davidson, Anthony Booth, Brian Barnes, Keith Chegwin, Roseanne, Dennis Quaid, Drew Barrymore, Ken Kercheval, Dame Elizabeth Taylor, Ringo Starr, Sharon Gless, Sir Elton John, Gary Oldman, Robbie Williams, Anne Robinson

HAD/HAVE AN ALCOHOLIC PARENT

Marlon Brando (both)

Jonathan Winters (father)

Suzanne Somers (father)

Lauren Hutton (mother)

Shane Richie (father)

Sir Alec Guinness (mother)

Sir Charles Chaplin (father)

Michael Barrymore (father)

Kenneth Clarke (mother)

Adam Ant (father)

Demi Moore (mother)

Richard Burton (father)

Meat Loaf (father)

Eminem (mother)

Sinéad O'Connor (mother)

Mo Mowlam (father)

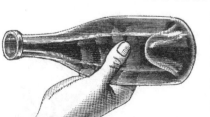

Ben Affleck (father)

Nora Ephron (both)

Halle Berry (father)

Sir Norman Wisdom (father)

Rod Steiger (mother)

Rosemary Clooney (both)

Brian Wilson (mother)

Gérard Depardieu (father)

Nell Gwyn (mother)

Andie MacDowell (mother)

Samantha Mumba (father)

Tom Cruise (father)

MONEY

American Airlines saved $40,000 in 1987 by eliminating one olive from each salad served in first class.

More Monopoly money is printed in a year than real money throughout the world.

Lee Harvey Oswald's cadaver tag sold at an auction for $6,600 in 1992.

In 1979, Judy Garland's false eyelashes were sold at auction for $125.

During World War Two, W.C. Fields kept $50,000 in Germany 'in case the little bastard wins'.

Sigmund Freud bought his first sample of cocaine for $1.27 per gram.

Woodpecker scalps, porpoise teeth and giraffe tails have all been used as money.

There are two credit cards for every person in the US.

In Monopoly, the most money you can lose in one trip round the board (going to jail only once) is £26,040. The most money you can lose in one turn is £5,070. If, on the other hand, no one ever buys anything, players could eventually break the bank.

97 per cent of paper money in the US contains traces of cocaine.

After their Civil War, the US sued Great Britain for damages caused by ships the British had built for the Confederacy. The US asked for $1 billion, but settled for $25 million.

Went bankrupt

Kevin Maxwell, Margot Kidder, Walt Disney, Alan Bond, Eddie Fisher, Grace Jones, Mark Twain, Mickey Rooney, MC Hammer, Peter Adamson, Eddie 'The Eagle' Edwards, Lionel Bart, Frank Lloyd Wright, Buster Bloodvessel, Mica Paris, Toni Braxton, John Bindon (twice), Jake Thackray, Daniel Defoe, Henry Kelly

POLONIUS'S ADVICE TO HIS SON LAERTES IN *HAMLET*

Yet here, Laertes! Aboard, aboard for shame!
The wind sits in the shoulder of your sail,
And you are stay'd for.
There ... my blessing with thee!
And these few precepts in thy memory
Look thou character. Give thy thoughts no tongue,
Nor any unproportion'd thought his act.
Be thou familiar, but by no means vulgar.
Those friends thou hast, and their adoption tried,
Grapple them to thy soul with hoops of steel;
But do not dull thy palm with entertainment
Of each new-hatch'd, unfledg'd comrade. Beware
Of entrance to a quarrel but, being in,
Bear't that th' opposed may beware of thee.
Give every man thy ear, but few thy voice;
Take each man's censure, but reserve thy judgement.
Costly thy habit as thy purse can buy,
But not express'd in fancy; rich, not gaudy;
For the apparel oft proclaims the man;
And they in France of the best rank and station
Are of a most select and generous chief in that.
Neither a borrower, nor a lender be;
For loan oft loses both itself and friend,
And borrowing dulls the edge of husbandry.
This above all: to thine own self be true,
And it must follow, as the night the day,
Thou canst not then be false to any man.
Farewell: my blessing season this
in thee!

Anagrams

ORDER IN YAWN – Winona Ryder

SO CHECK JAIL, MAN – Michael Jackson

SCREEN ANNOY – Sean Connery

BIG LEMONS – Mel Gibson

BRAIN CREEPS ON – Pierce Brosnan

RISK BIG NAME? – Kim Basinger

I LIKE 'EM YOUNG – Kylie Minogue

'CREEP,' SHE'LL MOAN – Elle Macpherson

ANIMAL WHISTLER – William Shatner

ONLY I CAN THRILL – Hillary Clinton

DEAR DEAR, RUDE PIG – Gérard Depardieu

ME MOODIER – Demi Moore

ASK TINY PEST – Patsy Kensit

LIBRARY WOMAN – Barry Manilow

CLOSE EVIL SLOT – Elvis Costello

STORY BLUNDER – Burt Reynolds

GOT SO WEIRD – Tiger Woods

A WILD OLD MENACE – Andie MacDowell

HEADING LOW – Goldie Hawn

LIKES REALITY – Kirstie Alley

LENT WORTHY GAWP – Gwyneth Paltrow

AH! POLISHED – Sophie Dahl

NO, I AM CRAZED – Cameron Diaz

TAKES CLEAN BIKE – Kate Beckinsale

GEOLOGY ENCORE – George Clooney

SLICK OR FATAL CHAT – Calista Flockhart

RAISED SOFT – Sadie Frost

MERRY GLEE MASK – Kelsey Grammer

BURY HARSHER IMP – Barry Humphries

TALKING ON SEX – Alex Kingston

I DO RAW SULK – Lisa Kudrow

SAME JOURNEY – Jane Seymour

ADORING SLAVES – Gavin Rossdale

TURNED STINKS – Kirsten Dunst

MEET JUBILANT RISK – Justin Timberlake

JEER TO LAD – Jared Leto

I'M A TRUE BOGEY – Tobey Maguire

ADJOINING FLAMES – James Gandolfini

CRASH MUCH EACH MILE – Michael Schumacher

EMPHATIC LIES – Michael Stipe

I'M MORALS NANNY – Marilyn Manson

THE CHORAL CRUTCH – Charlotte Church

WE AVOID BID – David Bowie

WOMANLY TIES – Emily Watson

NEVER NOT SICK – Kevin Costner

ODD BAT FRINGE – Bridget Fonda

SO RELAX – Axl Rose

HER SLOW CRY – Sheryl Crow

CRITICS IN CHAIR – Christina Ricci

A NAME VIRUS – Mena Suvari

OUR SNEERS – Rene Russo

HAIRS DISCERNED – Denise Richards

ANIMAL CRANK – Alan Rickman

CIAO GLANCES – Nicolas Cage

IN CLEAN CLOTHES – Chelsea Clinton

EASY RISING – Gary Sinise

HOME TWIT NAMED – Matthew Modine

AS SPEAKER JARS CHAIR – Sarah Jessica Parker

WATERY BANTER – Warren Beatty

INDOOR DANCER – Donna D'Errico

GROW ACNE GERM – Ewan McGregor

NAKED SHOUT – Kate Hudson

CANCEL THAT BET – Cate Blanchett

BENIGN NEAT TEN – Annette Bening

JAIL GENIAL ONE – Angelina Jolie

IN MOCK DENIAL – Nicole Kidman

COY VOLUNTEER – Courtney Love

I AM ONLY A LASS – Alyssa Milano

ENVY SICK APE – Kevin Spacey

CONK ALL ABSURD – Sandra Bullock

HARASSED NEAT THING – Natasha Henstridge

THIS INERT RASCAL – Christian Slater

DON'T REAR DOWN – Edward Norton

RARE MYTH WEPT – Matthew Perry

POLISHED READ – Sophie Aldred

STERN LIBEL – Ben Stiller

THEATRE RICH – Teri Hatcher

REPLENISH FAN – Ralph Fiennes

TRICK IN ARMY – Ricky Martin

I'M A TORSO – Tori Amos

LISTEN, PRAISE HER – Sharleen Spiteri

RANCID LADY CHARMER – Richard Clayderman

GLIB REPARTEE – Peter Gabriel

I AM RACY, HEAR? – Mariah Carey

MOLEST ME – ENJOY! – Tommy Lee Jones

MOLEST ME – ENJOY!

I'M STAR EVENT – Steve Martin

ONE POSH LIAR – Sophia Loren

RICH RED RAGE – Richard Gere

HE'S MAGICAL, LOUD – Michael Douglas

METAL OAF – Meat Loaf

FRIENDLY JEERS – Jerry Seinfeld

NO BRAINS ON A DATE – Antonio Banderas

WET SINK TALE – Kate Winslet

FINDS A HORROR – Harrison Ford

GRIN BY A REBEL – Gabriel Byrne

A SEVERE NUKE – Keanu Reeves

IDEAL SINEWY LAD – Daniel Day-Lewis

CAN RESEARCH ARMPIT
– Charisma Carpenter

REMARKABLE PEOPLE

Tommy Lee has a Starbucks in his house.

Marlon Brando's occupation on his passport was 'Shepherd'.

Demis Roussos was on a plane hijacked and taken to Beirut.

Julio Iglesias once had 5 gallons of water flown from Miami to LA so he could wash his hair.

Jacqueline Wilson had the magazine *Jackie* named after her.

Sir Anthony Hopkins used to be able to hypnotize people by pulling their earlobes.

David Lynch always leaves one shoelace untied.

Michael Jackson owns the rights to the South Carolina state anthem.

Jim Dale co-wrote the song 'Georgy Girl'.

Simon Le Bon has kept bees.

Christopher Trace, the first presenter of *Blue-Peter*, was Charlton Heston's body double in Ben-Hur.

Debra Winger was the voice of ET.

Robbie Williams made a cameo appearance in 1995 in *EastEnders* making a telephone call from a payphone in the Queen Vic.

Liza Tarbuck was voted Kleenex Nose of the Year by *OK!* readers.

Dusty Springfield once successfully sued Bobby Davro for an imitation he did of her.

Woody Allen won't take a shower if the drain is in the middle.

Carol Vorderman was crowned Head of the Year 2000 by the National Hairdressers' Federation.

Alan Davies bought the *Big Brother* diary room chair for £30,000.

Queen Latifah wears the key for the motorcycle on which her brother suffered a fatal crash on a chain around her neck.

John Grisham shaves just once a week – before church on Sunday.

Jewel is a champion yodeller – and has been since her childhood (even though it is 'impossible' for children to yodel because their vocal cords aren't sufficiently developed).

Anna Kournikova hasn't cut her waist-length hair since she was seven.

Robert Downey Jr once spent a night in jail with Tommy Lee.

Cate Blanchett gave her husband plaster casts of her ears as a present.

Arm wrestling is one of Helena Bonham Carter's favourite pastimes.

Kim Basinger puts sour cream and lemon juice in her bath water

Charlie Dimmock was Best Giggler 1999 – awarded by Butterkist. She had to take a bath in popcorn.

Renée Zellweger keeps a 'grateful journal', a collection of her favourite things, on her bedside table.

Cindy Crawford believes placentas should be buried under trees for good luck.

Bernard Manning did his National Service in the Military Police and one of his duties was guarding Albert Speer and Rudolf Hess in Spandau.

Sean (P Diddy) Combs wears a diamond-encrusted watch to protect against pollution from his mobile phone.

Ainsley Harriott was a Wimbledon ball boy.

Betty Boothroyd had a Belfast gay nightclub named after her.

As a teenager, Naomi Campbell used to hang around for an autograph outside Boy George's house.

Nicolas Cage was 28 before he first went abroad (to a screening in Cannes). He employs his own pizza chef and has a special pizza oven in his house.

During their marriage, Angelina Jolie and Billy Bob Thornton bought an electric chair for their dining room.

Billy Connolly topped a survey to find Britain's top fantasy cab companion (Kate Moss and Jordan were runners-up).

Gisele Bundchen owns over 200 belts.

James Woods is ambidextrous.

Missy Elliott spends four hours a day on her hair.

Diane Keaton's old college named a street after her in 2000.

Shaggy was a Royal Marine and served in the first Gulf war.

Harrison Ford has a species of spider named after him.

INVENTED OR DISCOVERED BY AMERICANS

Lightning rod (1752)

Bifocals (1760)

Cotton gin (1793)

Revolver (1835)

Telegraph (1837)

Vulcanization of rubber (1839)

Fibreglass (1839)

Ether as a human anaesthetic (1842)

Sewing machine (1846)

Safety pin (1849)

Bessemer converter (1851)

Cylinder lock (1851)

Elevator (1852)

Condensed milk (1853)

Oil well (1859)

Machine gun (1862)

Aluminium manufacture (1866)

Typewriter (1867)

Air brake (1868)

Vacuum cleaner (manual; 1869)

Barbed wire (1873)

Earmuffs (1873)

Denim jeans (1874)

Carpet sweeper (1876)

Telephone (1876)

Phonograph (1877)

Mechanical cash register (1879)

Saccharin (1879)

Light bulb (1880)

Electric fan (1882)

Fountain pen (1884)

Electric transformer (1885)

Coca-Cola (1886)

Hand-held camera (1888)

Automatic telephone exchange (1889)

Juke box (1889)

Zipper (1891)

AC electric generator (1892)

AC electric motor (1892)

Paper matchbook (1892)

Motion pictures (1893)

Escalator (1894)

Electric stove (1896)

Pepsi-Cola (1898)

Tractor (1900)

Safety razor (1901)

Gyrocompass (1905)

Electric washing machine (1906)

Vacuum cleaner (upright; 1907)

Electric toaster (1908)

Bakelite (1910)

Air conditioning (1911)

Aircraft autopilot (1912)

Moving assembly line (1913)

False eyelashes (1916)

Automatic rifle (1918)

Bulldozer (1923)

Cine camera (1923)

Frozen food (1924)

Liquid-fuelled rocket (1926)

Electric induction (1928)

Electric razor (1928)

Car radio (1929)

Scotch tape (1929)

Cyclotron (1931)

Defibrillator (1932)

FM radio (1933)

Nylon (1935)

Richter scale (1935)

Xerography (1938)

Single-rotor helicopter (1939)

Teflon (1943)

Electronic computer (1946)

Microwave oven (1947)

Transistor (1947)

Polaroid camera (1948)

Oral contraceptive (1951)

Polio vaccine (1952)

Video recorder (1952)

Measles vaccine (1953)

Nuclear submarine (1955)

Internal heart pacemaker (1957)

Superconductivity (1957)

Laser (1960)

Industrial robot (1962)

Pull-tab opener (1963)

Quasars (1963)

Electronic musical synthesizer (1965)

Quarks (1967)

Barcodes for retail use (1970)

CD (1972)

Electronic mail (1972)

Personal computer (1976)

Implantable defibrillator (1980)

Permanent artificial heart implant (1982)

PURE TRIVIA

Monaco's national orchestra is bigger than its army.

As a young and struggling artist, Pablo Picasso kept warm by burning his own paintings.

Rin Tin Tin is buried in Père-Lachaise cemetery in Paris.

Enid Blyton, writer of the Famous Five, had 59 stories published in 1959.

Pablo Picasso was abandoned by the midwife just after his birth because she thought he was stillborn. He was saved by an uncle.

Ludwig van Beethoven was once arrested for vagrancy.

The phrase 'the 3 Rs' ('reading, writing and arithmetic') was coined by Sir William Curtis, who was illiterate.

Dante died on the day he completed his masterpiece *The Divine Comedy*.

Each episode of *Dr Kildare* had three suffering patients.

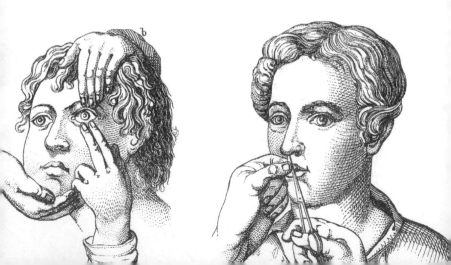

Soda water does not contain soda.

Actress Sarah Bernhardt played the part of Juliet (13 years old) when she was 70.

EMI stands for 'Electrical and Musical Instruments'.

1 kg of lemons contains more sugar than 1 kg of strawberries.

About 70 per cent of all living organisms in the world are bacteria.

The yo-yo originated in the Philippines, where it was used as a weapon in hunting.

The board game Monopoly was originally rejected by Parker Brothers who claimed it had 52 fundamental errors.

The screwdriver was invented before the screw.

The screwdriver cocktail was invented by oilmen, who used the tool to stir the drink.

At the height of his addiction, the poet Samuel Taylor Coleridge drank about 2 litres of laudanum (tincture of opium) each week.

The metre was originally defined as one 10-millionth of the distance from the equator to the pole.

A fully loaded supertanker travelling at normal speed takes at least 20 minutes to stop.

North American Indians ate watercress to dissolve stones in the bladder.

In Russia, suppositories cut from fresh potatoes were used for relief from haemorrhoids.

Opium was used widely as a painkiller during the American Civil War. More than a hundred thousand soldiers became addicts.

The girls of the Tiwi tribe in the South Pacific are married at birth.

Ralph and Carolyn Cummins had 5 children between 1952 and 1966, all of whom were born on 20 February.

The Zambian authorities don't allow tourists to take pictures of Pygmies.

Alexander Graham Bell, inventor of the telephone, never phoned his wife or mother as both were deaf.

The warrior tribes of Ethiopia used to hang the testicles of those they killed in battle on the ends of their spears.

Eau de Cologne was originally marketed as a way of protecting yourself against the plague.

The Crystal Palace at the Great Exhibition of 1851 contained 92,900 square metres of glass.

South American gauchos put raw steak under their saddles before starting a day's riding to tenderize the meat.

There are 240 white dots in a Pacman arcade game.

Blackbird, chief of the Omaha Indians, was buried sitting on his favourite horse.

A group of geese on the ground is a gaggle; a group of geese in the air is a skein.

After Custer's last stand, Sioux leader Chief Sitting Bull became an entertainer and toured the country with Buffalo Bill's Wild West Show.

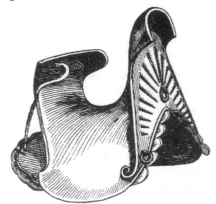

Aeschylus, the founder of Classical Greek tragedy, is said to have died when an eagle passing overhead dropped a tortoise on his head.

Aztec emperor Montezuma had a nephew, Cuitlahac, whose name meant 'plenty of excrement'.

Bananas contain about 75 per cent water.

Chewing gum while peeling onions will keep you from crying.

Chewing gum has rubber as an ingredient.

Coca-Cola was originally green.

Cuckoo clocks come from the Black Forest in Germany – not Switzerland.

An inch of snow falling evenly on one acre of ground is equivalent to about 2,715 gallons of water.

During the Middle Ages, people used spider webs to try to cure warts.

In 1967, the American Association of Typographers made a new punctuation mark that was a combination of the question mark and an exclamation point, and called it an interrobang. It was rarely used and hasn't been seen since.

Genghis Khan's cavalry rode female horses so soldiers could drink their milk.

Given sufficient amounts of chocolate, pigs can master video game skills.

BRIGHTON BUSES NAMED AFTER THEM

Norman Cook, Desmond Lynam, Sir Norman Wisdom, Lord Richard Attenborough, Dora Bryan, Chris Eubank, Adam Faith, Sally Gunnell, Derek Jameson, Annie Nightingale, Leo Sayer, Dusty Springfield, Lord Laurence Olivier, Max Miller, Dame Flora Robson, Sir Winston Churchill, Rudyard Kipling, Dame Anna Neagle

PHOTOGRAPHIC MEMORIES

Truman Capote, Carole Caplin, Sid Owen, Hu Jintao, Peter Buck, Neil Hamilton, Simon Wiesenthal, Robert Mitchum, Shaun Woodward, Anne Kirkbride

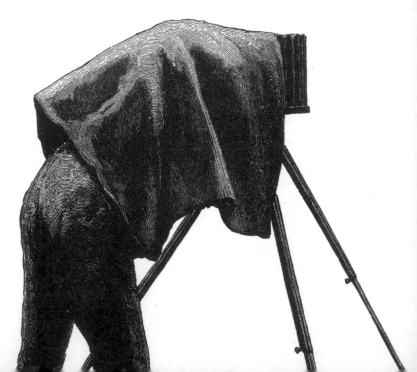

Switched on Regent Street Lights

Daniel Bedingfield (2003)

Will Young (2002)

Russell Watson (2001)

Billie Piper (2000)

David Ginola (1999)

All Saints (1998)

Frankie Dettori (1997)

John Major (1996)

Leslie Joseph, Rolf Harris, Britt Ekland and Lionel Blair (1995)

Jonathan Pryce and members of the cast of Oliver! (1994)

Sylvester Stallone (1993)

Sir Anthony Hopkins (1992)

Students from Camberwell College (1991)

Paul Gascoigne (1990)

Kylie Minogue (1989)

Dame Edna Everage (1988)

Prince Edward (1987)

The Duchess of York (1986)

Joan Collins (1985)

Prince Michael of Kent (1984)

Princess Alexandra (1983)

Prince Andrew (1982)

Diana, Princess of Wales (1981)

David Essex (1980)

Princess Michael of Kent (1979)

Prince Charles (1978)

HOTEL SUITES NAMED AFTER THEM

Sir Arthur C. Clarke (at the Hotel Club Oceanic, Sri Lanka)

Luciano Pavarotti (Pangkor Laut Island Resort, Malaysia)

Dame Barbara Cartland (Heritage Hotel at Helmsdale in Sutherland)

James Michener (Oriental Hotel in Thailand)

Dave Brubeck (The Hotel Viking, Newport, Rhode Island)

Samuel Clemens (aka Mark Twain: The Painted Lady Hotel, Elmira, New York)

Jenny Lind (Willard Intercontinental, Washington)

Sir Roger Moore (Grand Lido Sans Souci Resort, Ocho Rios, Jamaica)

Dame Agatha Christie (The Old Cataract Hotel, Aswan, Egypt)

Marlene Dietrich (The Hotel Lancaster, Paris)

Princess Michael of Kent (St George Lycabettus Hotel, Athens)

James Galway (Tara Hotel, London)

Michael Jordan (Atlantis Hotel, Bahamas)

Mata Hari (American Hotel, Amsterdam)

John Lennon (Queen Elizabeth Hotel, Montreal)

Liam Neeson (Fitzpatrick Hotel, Chicago)

Marilyn Monroe (The Legend Hotel, Kuala Lumpur)

Graham Greene (The Sofitel Metropole, Hanoi)

CELEBRITIES AND THE NUMBERS OF PAIRS OF TRAINERS THEY OWN

Goldie (1,600)

Mel C (over 200)

Justin Timberlake (450 – including every model of Air Jordans ever made)

Johnny Vegas (30)

Craig David (200)

Damon Dash (3,000)

NB Sean (P Diddy) Combs throws his away after wearing them for just one day

SPONSORED/ADOPTED AN ANIMAL AT LONDON ZOO

Paul Young (fruit bat)

George Cole (American alligator)

Letitia Dean (chimpanzee)

Fiona Fullerton (Asian elephant)

Andy Crane (crowned crane)

Robert Kilroy-Silk (black-and-white-ruffed lemur)

Cerys Matthews (Margery, a 21-year-old white-faced saki monkey)

Kym Marsh (hippo)

'SAW' GHOSTS

The Queen When they were children, the Queen and her sister, Princess Margaret, believed they saw the ghost of Queen Elizabeth I at Windsor Castle.

Daniel Day-Lewis thought he had seen the ghost of his father (the late Poet Laureate Cecil Day-Lewis) when he was acting in *Hamlet* in 1989. When the actor playing the ghost of Hamlet's father said, 'I am thy father's spirit,' Daniel Day-Lewis went off stage and wouldn't come back – convinced that he'd 'seen' his father.

Jim Davidson once lived with a girlfriend in the Old Kent Road in a flat that was said to be haunted by the ghost of a woman who'd been murdered there many years before. Jim was properly sceptical but was bothered when he couldn't find a rational explanation for all the strange noises that went on throughout the night. Eventually, after 'seeing' crucifixes moving around the room, Jim and his girlfriend moved out.

Sting awoke to 'find' a 'figure' dressed in Victorian clothes in his room. He thought it was his wife until he saw her in bed next to him. She also saw the apparition and they held each other tight, staring at it until it faded away, never to return.

Patti Boulaye In 1992, the singer was about to take on the lead role in the show *Carmen Jones* at the Old Vic, and was watching it from a private box when she felt a draught as though someone had opened the door to the box. When she turned round, no one was there. She mentioned it to someone who told her it was the ghost of the late manager of the theatre, Lilian Baylis.

Bob Hoskins Before finding fame, he was working as a porter in Covent Garden and was in a cellar when he 'saw' a nun. She held her hands out to him and spoke but he didn't understand what she said. Later he was told that Covent Garden had formerly been Convent Garden and had been owned by the Benedictines. The legend was that anyone who saw a nun's ghost would have a lucky life.

Cilla Black would be in bed at home when the ghost of a teenage girl would visit her regularly. The girl, who wore a Victorian nightdress, had a mournful expression on her face. It later turned out that the land on which Cilla's house was built had been farmland worked in the 19th century by a gardener who died, leaving a young daughter, who herself died at the age of 13.

June Brown saw something worse than a ghost, she saw a ghostly tunnel. She was walking with a friend along an abandoned single-track railway line when she saw a tunnel, which they started to walk down. Realizing that the tunnel had no end and feeling a little spooked, they turned and ran back. The next day, they went back to where they had entered the tunnel and found it had mysteriously vanished.

Miriam Karlin believes she is 'haunted' by her father's ghost whenever she has to make a speech in public. Her father was a barrister and she is convinced that he 'feeds' her her lines and makes her much more articulate than she would otherwise be.

Prince Charles Some years ago he and his valet Ken Stronach were going into the library at Sandringham when they felt inexplicably cold and became convinced that someone was standing behind them. When they looked round, no one was there. They ran out.

Paul Gascoigne believes he was attacked by a ghost while he was staying in a converted barn in Italy. The ghost, a man, was holding two foxes. It held him down until 'it sort of relaxed the pressure and I shoved my way up and out of the room and called everyone up. It happened and it wasn't a dream because I wasn't sleeping well enough to dream.'

Will Carling At Sedbergh School when he was 14, he saw a 'very dark figure wearing a cloak' standing at the other end of a long corridor. 'We stood there, facing each other, for about thirty seconds, and I can say, quite honestly, that I was pretty scared. Eventually, I couldn't face it any more and I just turned and ran downstairs.'

Noah Wyle's California ranch – bought from Bo Derek – was apparently haunted by the late John Derek. He said that John's ghost kept making 'strange noises' when he and his fiancée tried to sleep in the master bedroom, so they moved to a guest bedroom and had the main suite remodelled.

Will Young claims that he saw a ghost while staying in a converted monastery in the south of France.

Britney Spears says a ghost used to tweak her nipple ring and hide her belongings as she got ready to go out in the mornings.

Amanda Holden became so aware of a ghostly presence at London's Shaftesbury Theatre (where she was playing the title role in *Thoroughly Modern Millie*) that she required someone to walk round the theatre with her.

NB Ghosts appear in four of Shakespeare's plays: *Julius Caesar*, *Richard III*, *Hamlet* and *Macbeth*.

Made it to 100 years old

George Burns, Hal Roach, Rose Kennedy, Irving Berlin, Sir Thomas Sopwith, Emanuel Shinwell, Dorothy Dickson, Dame Freya Stark, Athene Seyler, Eubie Blake, Geoffrey Dearmer, The Queen Mother, Adolph Zukor, Bob Hope, Grandma Moses, Mother Jones, Princess Alice, Duchess of Gloucester, George Abbott, Estelle Winwood, Leni Riefenstahl, Gwen Ffrancon-Davies, Hartley Shawcross, Strom Thurmond, Sir Robert Mayer, Alf Landon, Dame Ninette De Valois

Featured on stamps

Michael Jackson (Tanzania)

Sir Elton John (Grenada and Australia)

Sir Mick Jagger (St Vincent)

Whitney Houston (Tanzania)

Cher (Grenada)

Jerry Seinfeld (US)

Elle Macpherson (Australia)

Ian Botham (St Vincent)

Arnold Schwarzenegger (Mali)

Clive Lloyd (Guyana)

Dolly Parton (Grenada)

Viv Richards (Antigua)

Frank Sinatra (St Vincent)

Jimmy Connors (Lesotho)

Carl Lewis (Niger)

Eddie Murphy (Tanzania)

Muhammad Ali (Liberia)

Baroness Thatcher (Kenya)

Nick Faldo (St Vincent)

Stevie Wonder (Tanzania)

Gladys Knight (Tanzania)

Bruce Springsteen (Grenada)

Barbra Streisand (St Vincent)

George Michael (St Vincent)

Robert De Niro (Gambia)

Boris Becker (Central African Republic)

Prince (St Vincent)

Tina Turner (Tanzania)

Björn Borg (Ivory Coast)

Paul Newman (The Maldives)

Elliott Gould (Gambia)

Gary Lineker (Gambia)

Pele (Brazil)

John McEnroe (Sierra Leone)

Martina Navratilova (Ivory Coast)

Kirk Douglas (Mali)

MADE PARACHUTE JUMPS

Jim Davidson, Phillip Schofield, Tom Baker, Ian Ogilvy, Matthew Kelly, Jeremy Beadle, Suzanne Dando, Sarah Kennedy, Tony Blackburn, Prince Charles, David Davis, Janet Ellis, Lorraine Chase, Alex Best, Alan Davies, Christian Califano, Matt LeBlanc, Billy Connolly, Jon Finch, David Hasselhoff

CAN COMMUNICATE IN SIGN LANGUAGE

Jane Fonda, Holly Hunter, William Hurt, Richard Griffiths, Hugh Grant, Sinéad O'Connor, Richard Dreyfuss, Louise Fletcher

LEARNED TO SWIM AS ADULTS

Frank Skinner, Dame Norma Major, Dame Shirley Bassey, Sir Paul McCartney, Tina Turner, Pablo Picasso, Sir Peter O'Sullevan, Donna D'Errico, Robin Williams, Sir David Frost, Adam Faith

PROFICIENT MAGICIANS

Prince Charles, Christo Van Rensburg, Muhammad Ali, General Norman Schwarzkopf, Michael Jackson, Arsenio Hall

Wrote children's books

Susannah York (*The Last Unicorn*)

Ian Fleming (*Chitty Chitty Bang Bang*)

David Byrne (*Stay Up Late*)

Roger McGough (*The Magic Fountain*)

Dame Elizabeth Taylor (*Nibbles And Me*)

Prince Charles (*The Old Man of Lochnagar*)

Terry Jones (*Lady Cottington's Pressed Fairy Book*)

Colonel Muammar Gaddafi (*The Village, The Village, The Earth, The Earth ... And The Suicide of The Spaceman*)

Lenny Henry (*Charlie And The Big Chill*)

Nanette Newman (*Spider The Horrible Cat*)

Jamie Lee Curtis (*Where Do Balloons Go?*)

Madonna (*The English Roses*)

INVENTORS

Jamie Lee Curtis ('baby wipe diaper')

Hedy Lamarr (a machine that helped the Americans target U-boats)

Julie Newmar (bottom-shaping tights and a bosom-firming bra)

Steve McQueen (low-slung bucket seat for racing cars)

Neil Young (portable exercise device)

Harry Connick Jr (computer program that allows musicians to follow the score on a screen)

Benjamin Franklin (the rocking chair)

HAD THEIR PAINTINGS EXHIBITED

Tony Curtis, David Hemmings, Joni Mitchell, Desmond Morris, Prince Charles, Anthony Quinn, Bryan Ferry, Ronnie Wood, Sylvester Stallone, Miles Davis, Sir Noel Coward, Adolf Hitler, Sir Paul McCartney, Rolf Harris, Jeff Bridges, David Bowie, Rod Stewart, Jennifer Aniston (at the Metropolitan Museum of Art in New York), Marilyn Manson, Dennis Hopper, Steve Kanaly, Artie Shaw, Elke Sommer, Red Skelton, Herve Villechaize, Donna Summer, e.e. cummings, Nelson Mandela

Pipe smokers of the year

2003: Stephen Fry

2002: Richard Dunhill

2001: Russ Abbot

2000: Joss Ackland

1999: Trevor Baylis

1998: Willie-John McBride

1997: Professor Malcolm Bradbury

1996: Sir Colin Davis

1995: Jethro

1994: Sir Ranulph Fiennes

1993: Rod Hull

1992: Tony Benn

1991: Sir John Harvey-Jones

1990: Laurence Marks

1989: Jeremy Brett

1988: Ian Botham

1987: Barry Norman

1986: David Bryant

1985: Jimmy Greaves

1984: Sir Henry Cooper

1983: Sir Patrick Moore

1982: Dave Lee Travis

1981: James Galway

1980: Edward Fox

1979: J.B. Priestley

1978: Magnus Magnusson

1977: Brian Barnes

1976: Sir Harold Wilson ('Pipeman of the Decade' – the only man to have won twice, this year and in 1965)

1975: Sir Campbell Adamson

1974: Fred Trueman

1973: Frank Muir

1972: No award

1971: Lord Shinwell

1970: Eric Morecambe

1969: Jack Hargreaves

1968: Peter Cushing

1967: Warren Mitchell

1966: Andrew Cruickshank

1965: Sir Harold Wilson

1964: Rupert Davis

NAMES OF THINGS YOU DIDN'T KNOW HAD NAMES

The holes in Swiss cheese are called 'eyes'.

'Mucophagy' is the medical term for 'snot-eating', the consumption of the nasal mucus obtained from nose-picking.

The technical term for snapping your fingers is 'fillip'.

A poem written to celebrate a wedding is called an 'epithalamium'.

A 'vamp' is the upper front part of a shoe.

The 'you are here' arrow on a map is called the 'IDEO locator'.

The S-shaped opening in a violin is called the 'f-hole'.

The little bumps on the surface of a table tennis paddle are called 'pips'.

The infinity symbol is a 'lemniscate'.

A holder for a cup or a mug without handles is called a 'zarf'.

The plastic covering on the end of a shoelace is an 'aglet'.

The word for having a gap between your teeth is 'diastema'.

The dot above the letter 'i' is called a 'tittle'.

The metal hoop a lampshade sits on is called a 'harp'.

Food that's spat out is 'chanking'

The white tip of the finger and toenail is called a 'lunula' because the end of the nail is rounded like the moon.

A pig's snout is called a 'gruntle'.

A puff of smoke, such as that produced when someone smokes a pipe, is called a 'lunt'.

A band worn around the arm is called a 'brassard'.

The thin line of cloud that forms behind an aircraft at high altitudes is called a 'contrail'.

The little finger or toe is called the 'minimus'.

The symbol # is called an 'octothorpe'.

Illegible handwriting is known as 'griffonage'.

The word for empty space between the bottle top and the liquid is called 'ullage'.

'Walla' is a sound engineer's term for room noise.

The act of stretching and yawning is 'pandiculation'.

1/100th of a second is called a 'jiffy'.

A 'dzo' is the offspring of a yak and a cow.

A cat's whiskers are called 'vibrissae'.

A 'geep' is the offspring of a sheep and a goat.

The little hole in the sink that lets water drain out instead of flowing over the side is called a 'porcelator'.

The ball on top of a flagpole is called the 'truck'.

The little lump of flesh just in front of the ear canal is called a 'tragus'.

The cap on the fire hydrant is called a 'bonnet'.

NB There is no single word for the back of the knee.

CODES USED BY LOVERS ON LETTER ENVELOPES

S.W.A.L.K. (Sealed with a loving kiss)

H.O.L.L.A.N.D. (Hope our love lasts and never dies)

E.G.Y.P.T. (Ever giving you pleasant thoughts)

T.T.F.N.D. (Ta ta for now, ducks)

Y.A.A.I.M.H. (You are always in my heart)

I.T.A.L.Y. (I trust and love you)

I.L.Y.W.A.M.H.D. (I love you with all my heart, darling)

O.O.L.A.A.K.O.E.W. (Oceans of love and a kiss on every wave)

B.O.L.T.O.P. (Better on lips than on paper)

R.P.R.L.H. (Run postman, run like hell)

INSURANCE: A CAUTIONARY TALE

A lawyer from Charlotte, North Carolina, bought a box of very expensive cigars, then insured them against fire. Within a month, having smoked every single one of them – and despite the fact that he hadn't yet paid his first premium – the lawyer filed a claim, declaring that the cigars had been lost 'in a series of small fires'. The insurance company refused to pay, for the obvious reason: the man had merely consumed the cigars correctly. Nevertheless, the lawyer won.

In handing out his ruling, the judge agreed with the insurance company that the claim was frivolous but stated that the lawyer held a policy from the company in which it had warranted that the cigars were insurable and also guaranteed that it would insure them against fire. It had not defined what was considered to be unacceptable fire, and therefore was obliged to pay the claim. The insurance company paid $15,000 to the lawyer for the loss of his cigars in the 'fires'.

After the lawyer cashed the cheque, however, the insurance company had him arrested on 24 counts of arson. With his own insurance claim used against him, the lawyer was convicted of intentionally burning his insured property and sentenced to 24 months in jail and a $24,000 fine.

This is a true story.

GENUINE THINGS WRITTEN BY DRIVERS ON INSURANCE FORMS

'I didn't think the speed limit applied after midnight.'

'I knew the dog was possessive about the car but I would not have asked her to drive it if I had thought there was any risk.'

'I consider that neither car was to blame, but if either one was to blame, it would be the other one.'

'I knocked over a man. He admitted it was his fault as he had been run over before.'

'I remember nothing after passing the Crown Hotel until I came to and saw PC Brown.'

'Coming home I drove into the wrong house and collided with a tree I don't have.'

'I collided with a stationary truck coming the other way.'

'In my attempt to kill a fly, I drove into a telephone pole.'

'The other car collided with mine without giving warning of its intentions.'

'I had been shopping for plants all day and was on my way home. As I reached an intersection, a hedge sprang up, obscuring my vision, and I did not see the other car.'

'I had been driving for forty years when I fell asleep at the wheel and had an accident.'

'I was on my way to the doctor with rear end trouble when my universal joint gave way causing me to have an accident.'

'My car was legally parked as it backed into the other vehicle.'

'As I approached the intersection a sign suddenly appeared in a place where no sign had ever appeared before, making me unable to avoid the accident.'

'I told the police I was not injured, but upon removing my hair, I found that I had a fractured skull.'

'I was sure the old fellow would never make it to the other side of the road when I struck him.'

'I saw a slow-moving, sad-faced old gentleman as he bounced off the roof of my car.'

'The indirect cause of the accident was a little guy in a small car with a big mouth.'

'I was thrown from my car as it left the road, and was later found in a ditch by some stray cows.'

'A pedestrian hit me and went under my car.'

'I thought my window was down, but I found out it was up when I put my head through it.'

'To avoid hitting the bumper of the car in front, I struck the pedestrian.'

'The guy was all over the road. I had to swerve a number of times before I hit him.'

'An invisible car came out of nowhere, struck my car and vanished.'

'The pedestrian had no idea which way to run, so I ran over him.'

'A lorry backed through my windscreen into my wife's face.'

'I pulled away from the side of the road, glanced at my mother-in-law, and headed over the embankment.'

'The accident happened because I had one eye on the lorry in front, one eye on the pedestrian and the other on the car behind.'

'I started to slow down but the traffic was more stationary than I thought.'

'I pulled into a lay-by with smoke coming from under the hood. I realized the car was on fire so took my dog and smothered it with a blanket.'

Question: 'Could either driver have done anything to avoid the accident?' Answer: 'Travelled by bus?'

The claimant had collided with a cow. Question: 'What warning was given by you?' Answer: 'Horn.' Question: 'What warning was given by the other party?' Answer: 'Moo.'

'I started to turn and it was at this point I noticed a camel and an elephant tethered at the verge. This distraction caused me to lose concentration and hit a bollard.'

'On approach to the traffic lights the car in front suddenly broke.'

'I was going at about 70 or 80 mph when my girlfriend on the pillion reached over and grabbed my testicles so I lost control.'

'First car stopped suddenly, second car hit first car and a haggis ran into the rear of second car.'

'Windscreen broken. Cause unknown. Probably Voodoo.'

'The car in front hit the pedestrian but he got up so I hit him again.'

'The telephone pole was approaching. I was attempting to swerve out of the way when I struck the front end.'

'The gentleman behind me struck me on the backside. He then went to rest in a bush with just his rear end showing.'

'I had been learning to drive with power steering. I turned the wheel to what I thought was enough and found myself in a different direction going the opposite way.'

'I was backing my car out of the driveway in the usual manner, when it was struck by the other car in the same place it had been struck several times before.'

'I blew my horn but it would not work as it had been stolen.'

'The accident happened when the right front door of a car came round the corner without giving a signal.'

'No one was to blame for the accident but it would never have happened if the other driver had been alert.'

'I was unable to stop in time and my car crashed into the other vehicle. The driver and passengers then left immediately for a vacation with injuries.'

'The pedestrian ran for the pavement, but I got him.'

'I saw her look at me twice. She appeared to be making slow progress when we met on impact.'

'The accident occurred when I was attempting to bring my car out of a skid by steering it into the other vehicle.'

'The accident was due to another man narrowly missing me.'

'When I saw I could not avoid a collision I stepped on the gas and crashed into the other car.'

'I left my Austin 7 outside, and when I came out later, to my astonishment, there was an Austin 12.'

'The water in my radiator accidentally froze at midnight.'

'I had to turn the car sharper than was necessary owing to an invisible lorry.'

'The other man altered his mind so I had to run into him.'

'There was no damage to the car, as the gatepost will testify.'

'The car occupants were stalking deer on the hillside.'

'I told the other idiot what he was and went on.'

'I can give no details of the accident as I was concussed at the time.'

'Wilful damage was done to the upholstery by rats.'

'Three women were talking to each other and when two stepped back and one stepped forwards I had to have an accident.'

'I unfortunately ran over a pedestrian and the old gentleman was taken to hospital much regretting the circumstances.'

'Cow wandered into my car. I was afterwards informed that the cow was half-witted.'

'A bull was standing near and the fly must have tickled him as he gored my car.'

'If the other driver had stopped a few yards behind himself the accident would not have happened.'

'She suddenly saw me, lost her head, and we met.'

'I bumped a lamppost which was obscured by pedestrians.'

'I ran into a shop window and sustained injuries to my wife.'

'I misjudged a lady crossing the street.'

'A dog on the road braked, causing a skid.'

'A lamp-post bumped the car, damaging it in two places.'

'I left my car unattended for a minute and, whether by accident or design, it ran away.'

ALLEGEDLY GENUINE RESPONSES GIVEN BY MOTHERS TO THE CHILD SUPPORT AGENCY IN THE SECTION ASKING FOR FATHERS' DETAILS

'Regarding the identity of the father of my twins, child A was fathered by [name given]. I am unsure as to the identity of the father of child B, but I believe that he was conceived on the same night.'

'I am unsure as to the identity of the father of my child as I was being sick out of a window when taken unexpectedly from behind. I can provide you with a list of names of men that I think were at the party if this helps.'

'I do not know the name of the father of my little girl. She was conceived at a party at [address given] where I had unprotected sex with a man I met that night. I do remember that the sex was so good that I fainted. If you do manage to track down the father can you send me his phone number? Thanks.'

'I don't know the identity of the father of my daughter. He drives a BMW that now has a hole made by my stiletto in one of the door panels. Perhaps you can contact BMW service stations in this area and see if he's had it replaced?'

'I have never had sex with a man. I am awaiting a letter from the Pope confirming that my son's conception was immaculate and that he is Christ risen again.'

'I cannot tell you the name of child A's dad as he informs me that to do so would blow his cover and that would have cataclysmic implications for the British economy. I am torn between doing right by you and right by the country. Please advise.'

'I do not know who the father of my child was as all squaddies look the same to me. I can confirm that he was a Royal Green Jacket.'

'[name given] is the father of child A. If you do catch up with him can you ask him what he did with my AC/DC CDs.'

'From the dates it seems that my daughter was conceived at EuroDisney. Maybe it really is the Magic Kingdom.'

'So much about that night is a blur. The only thing that I remember for sure is Delia Smith did a programme about eggs earlier in the evening. If I'd have stayed in and watched more TV rather than going to the party at [address given], mine might have remained unfertilized.'

'I am unsure as to the identity of the father of my baby. After all, when you eat a can of beans you can't be sure which one made you fart.'

RELATIVE VALUES

Whoopi Goldberg's first grandchild was born on her 35th birthday

Hilary Swank is Rob Lowe's sister-in-law

Zubin Mehta's first ex-wife is married to his brother

Norman Cook's father was responsible for introducing the bottle bank to Britain

Richard Blackwood's father used to be married to Naomi Campbell's mother

Alicia Silverstone filed for emancipation from her parents at the age of 15 so that she could work as an adult

Natalie Portman has never revealed her true surname as she wants to protect her family's privacy

Carol Vorderman's great-grandfather had two butterflies named after him

Jane Seymour used to be Nigel Planer's sister-in-law

Elizabeth Hurley's grandfather – a Mr Tit – used to be Tara Palmer-Tomkinson's milkman

Jeremy Clarkson's father-in-law won the VC

Peter Kay's school metalwork teacher was Steve Coogan's father

Kathleen Turner and Donna Karan are sisters-in-law

USE THEIR MOTHER'S MAIDEN NAME
Ryan Giggs (instead of Wilson)

Shirley MacLaine (Beaty)

Marilyn Monroe (Baker)

Lauren Bacall (Perske)

Shelley Winters (actually, her mother's maiden name was Winter)

Catherine Deneuve (Dorleac)

Ed Stewart (Mainwaring)

Kevin Spacey (Fowler)

Beck Hansen (Campbell)

Chris De Burgh (Davidson)

Elvis Costello (MacManus)

Marti Pellow (McLachlan)

Ivor Novello (Davies)

Patsy Palmer (Harris)

Sir Ian Holm (Cuthbert)

Klaus Maria Brandauer (Steng)

MEN WHO CAN USE ROMAN NUMERAL III AFTER THEIR NAMES

Loudon Wainwright, Ted Turner, Davis Love, Ted Danson, Alec Baldwin, Cliff Robertson, Luke Perry, Bill Gates, Eminem (Marshall Mathers III), Sam Shepard (born Samuel Shepard Rogers III)

People who adopted children

Ellen Burstyn, Tom Hanks, Angelina Jolie, Ilie Nastase, President Ronald Reagan, Lionel Richie, Marlon Brando, Bob Monkhouse, David Bellamy, Lord David Steel, Burt Reynolds & Loni Anderson, Linda Ronstadt, Sheena Easton, Steven Spielberg & Kate Capshaw, Burt Bacharach & Carole Bayer Sager, Jill Ireland & Charles Bronson, Ted Danson, Graham Chapman, Graham Gouldman, Magic Johnson, Prue Leith, Dora Bryan, Muhammad Ali, David Niven, Una Stubbs, Henry Fonda, Rosie O'Donnell, Isabella Rossellini, Robin Givens, Ella Fitzgerald, Kate Jackson, Kevin Lloyd, John Denver, Joan Crawford, George Burns, Patti LaBelle, Walt Disney, James Cagney, Bob Hope, Jerry Lewis, Paul Newman & Joanne Woodward, Bette Davis, Bernard Matthews, George Orwell, Josephine Baker, Imelda Marcos, Harpo Marx, Hugh Jackman

PEOPLE WITH FAMOUS STEP-PARENTS

Sally Field – Jock Mahoney

David Cassidy – Shirley Jones

Paloma Picasso – Jonas Salk

Mark Nicholas – Brian Widlake

Nicolette Sheridan – Telly Savalas

Christian Bale – Gloria Steinem

Cherie Blair – Pat Phoenix

Carlene Carter – Johnny Cash

Liv Tyler – Todd Rundgren

Bijou Phillips – Michelle Phillips

NB Gore Vidal shared a stepfather with Jacqueline Kennedy (his mother, Nina, married Jackie's stepfather, Hugh Auchincloss)

BABYSITTERS

Little Eva babysat for Carole King's children – which is how she came to sing Carole King's hit 'The Locomotion'

Lindsay Wagner babysat for Glen Campbell's children

Billy Crystal had Billie Holiday as a babysitter

Edward Norton had Betsy True as a babysitter

Vicki Michelle's au pair as a child was Elke Sommer

CAR ACRONYMS

Audi
Accelerates Under Demonic Influence
Always Unsafe Designs Implemented

BMW
Born Moderately Wealthy
Break My Windows
Bought My Wife

Buick
Big Ugly Indestructible Car Killer

Chevrolet
Car Has Extensive Valve Rattle On Long Extended Trips
Cheap, Hardly Efficient, Virtually Runs On Luck Every Time

Chevy
Cheapest Heap Ever Visioned Yet

Dodge
Dangerous On Days Gears Engage

Fiat
Failed Italian Automotive Technology
Failed In All Tests

Ford
Fix Or Repair Daily
Fails On Rainy Days
Fast Only Rolling Downhill

Honda
Had One – Never Did Again

Hyundai
Hope You Understand Nothing's Driveable And Inexpensive

Mazda
Most Always Zipping Dangerously Along

Mercedes
Many Expensive Repairs Can Eventually Discourage Extra Sales

Nissan
Needs Immediate Salvage So Abandon Now

Oldsmobile
Overpriced, Leisurely Driven Sedan Made Of Buick's Irregular Leftover
Equipment

Pontiac
Poor Old Nut Thinks It's A Cadillac

Porsche
Proof Only Rich Suckers Can Have Everything

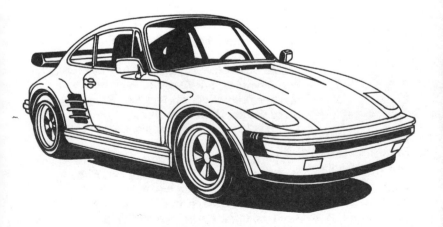

Rolls-Royce
Regarded Only as Luxury Life Style. Runs Over Your Current Expenses

Saab
Sad Attempt At Beauty
Send Another Automobile Back

Subaru
Screwed Up Beyond All Repair Usually

Toyota
Too Often Yanks Overprice This Auto

Volvo
Very Odd Looking Vehicular Object

HARLEY-DAVIDSON OWNERS

Arnold Schwarzenegger, Whitney Houston, Burt Reynolds, Eric Clapton, Sylvester Stallone, Billy Idol, Jon Bon Jovi, Wynonna, Nicky Clarke, Liam Neeson, Ian Wright, George Clooney, Bruce Willis, Damon Hill, Eddie Irvine, Chris Eubank, David Copperfield, Ronan Keating, Paul Young, Kurt Russell, Colin Farrell, Neil Fox, Steve McQueen, Jim Bowen, Errol Flynn, Elvis Presley, T.E. Lawrence, Bill Haley, George Sanders, Clark Gable, Howard Hughes, Viscount Linley, Midge Ure

SURVIVED A HELICOPTER CRASH

Christy O'Connor Jnr, Christie Brinkley, Sarah Greene, Mike Smith, Kirk Douglas, Joe Longthorne, Alessandro Nannini, Adam Faith, Leni Riefenstahl (at the age of 97)

Astronomy

Buzz Aldrin's mother's maiden name was Moon.

The Sun is 93 million miles from Earth, which is 270 times closer than the next nearest star.

When the Americans sent a man into space, they spent a million dollars developing a pen that could write upside down in conditions of zero gravity. The Russians used a pencil.

It would take about 2,000 years to walk to the Sun.

Since the Moon has no atmosphere, footprints left there by astronauts will remain visible for at least 10 million years.

All the planets in our solar system could be placed inside the planet Jupiter.

All the moons of the solar system are named after Greek and Roman mythology, except the moons of Uranus, which are named after Shakespearean characters.

If you take one pound of cobwebs and spread them out in one straight line, it will go twice around the Earth.

Neutron stars are so condensed that a fragment the size of a sugar cube would weigh as much as all the people on Earth put together.

A lightning bolt generates temperatures five times hotter than those found at the Sun's surface.

**A car travelling at 100mph would take
more than 29 million years to reach the nearest star –
but you could reach the Sun by car in a little over 106 years.**

If you were standing on Mercury, the Sun would appear 2.5 times larger than it appears on Earth.

It takes 8.5 minutes for light to get from the Sun to the Earth.

The Milky Way galaxy contains 5 billion stars larger than our Sun.

The Earth weighs approximately 6,588,000,000,000,000,000 tons.

10 tons of space dust fall on the Earth every day.

Every year the Sun loses 360 million tons.

The pressure at the Earth's inner core is 3 million times the Earth's atmospheric pressure.

Over one thousand planets the size of the Earth could fit inside the Sun.

The average modern home computer is more powerful than all of NASA's computers at the time of the Apollo moon landings put together.

In 1963, baseball pitcher Gaylord Perry remarked, 'They'll put a man on the moon before I hit a home run.' On 20 July 1969, a few hours after Neil Armstrong set foot on the moon, Gaylord Perry hit his first – and only – home run.

NB: The Mount of Jupiter and the Girdle of Venus are found on the palm of your hand.

Uranus is visible to the naked eye

NUMBER 142,857

142,857 is a cyclic number: when multiplied by a number up to 6, it will produce a number containing the same digits in the same order – albeit starting in a different place.

1 x 142,857 = 142,857

2 x 142,857 = 285,714

3 x 142,857 = 428,571

4 x 142,857 = 571,428

5 x 142,857 = 714,285

6 x 142,857 = 857,142

Look what happens when you multiply 142,857 by 7: it equals 999,999.

When 1 is divided by 7 it comes to 0.142857,142857,142857.

If you multiply 142,857 by 8, you get 1,142,856. If you take off the first digit (1) and add it to the last six digits, see what happens: 1 + 142,856 = 142,857.

Similarly, if you multiply 142,857 by – say – 17, you get 2,428,569. Now take off the first digit (2) and add it to the last six digits and see what happens: 2 + 428,569 = 428,571 – which is, of course, the original number in stage three of its cycle.

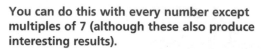

You can do this with every number except multiples of 7 (although these also produce interesting results).

If you take the number 142,857 and split it into two – 142 and 857 – and then add those two numbers, you get 999.

MORE NUMBERS

Japanese researchers have calculated pi to 1.2411 trillion places. If you need to remember pi, just count the letters in each word of the sentence: 'May I have a large container of coffee?' If you get the coffee and are polite say: 'Thank you,' and get two more decimal places: 3.141592653 …

The 772nd to 777th digits of pi are 999999.

For the ancient Greeks any number more than 10,000 was a 'myriad'.

In the carol 'Twelve Days of Christmas', the total number of gifts that 'my true love gave to me' is 364.

When 21,978 is multiplied by 4, the result is 87,912 – which is 21,978 reversed.

Any number, squared, is equal to one more than the numbers on either side of it multiplied together – 5x5=25 and 4x6=24; 6x6=36 and 5x7=35 etc.

The Roman numerals for 1666 are MDCLXVI (1000+500+100+50+10+5+1) – the only year featuring all the Roman numerals from the highest to the lowest.

One penny doubled every day becomes over £5 million in just 30 days.

37 x 3 = 111

37 x 6 = 222

37 x 9 = 333

37 x 12 = 444

37 x 15 = 555

37 x 18 = 666

37 x 21 = 777

If you add up the numbers 1–100 consecutively (1+2+3+4+5 etc.) the total is 5,050.

1961 was the most recent year that could be written both upside down and right side up and appear the same. The next year this will be possible will be 6009.

The smallest number with three letters is 1

… with four letters is 4

… with five letters is 3

… with six letters is 11

… with seven letters is 15

… with eight letters is 13

… with nine letters is 17

… with 10 letters is 24

The word INTERCHANGEABILITY contains the numbers THREE, EIGHT, NINE, TEN, THIRTEEN, THIRTY, THIRTY-NINE, EIGHTY, EIGHTY-NINE, NINETY and NINETY-EIGHT.

In English, the only number that has the same number of letters as its name is FOUR. Here are some other languages and the only numbers that contain precisely the same number of letters:

Basque BEDERATZI (9)

Catalan U (1)

Czech TRI (3)

Danish and Norwegian TO (2), TRE (3), FIRE (4)

Dutch VIER (4)

Esperanto DU (2), TRI (3), KVAR (4)

Finnish VIISI (5)

German VIER (4)

Italian TRE (3)

Pilipino APAT (4)

Polish PIATY (5)

Portuguese and Spanish CINCO (5)

Romanian CINCI (5)

Serbo-Croatian TRI (3)

Swedish TRE (3), FYRA (4)

Turkish DÖRT (4)

One thousand contains the letter A, but none of the words from one to nine hundred ninety-nine has an A.

Two of a Kind

OWNS A STUD FARM

Charlie Watts

Susan George

DIED IN AN APARTMENT OWNED BY HARRY NILSSON

Mama Cass Elliot

Keith Moon

SON OF DEAF PARENTS

Lon Chaney

Richard Griffiths

WROTE A BALLET

David Bellamy (*Heritage*)

Sir Patrick Moore (*Lyra's Dream*)

EYES OF DIFFERENT COLOURS

Jane Seymour (one green and one brown)

David Bowie (one green and one blue)

MARRIED A WOMAN CALLED KELLY PRESTON (NOT THE SAME WOMAN)

Lou Diamond Phillips

John Travolta

EX-*BLIND DATE* CONTESTANT

Jenni Falconer

Amanda Holden

MODELLED FOR TEEN PHOTO-ROMANCE STORIES

Hugh Grant

George Michael

HAD A SONG WRITTEN ABOUT HIM BY STING

Rod Stewart ('Peanuts')

Quentin Crisp ('An Englishman In New York')

HOLDER OF HGV LICENCE

Rowan Atkinson

Chris Eubank

ENDOWED A UNIVERSITY PROFESSORSHIP

Barbra Streisand (in Intimacy and Sexuality)

Sir Cameron Mackintosh (in Musical Theatre)

EX-BULLFIGHTER

Frederick Forsyth

Gabriel Byrne

THE CONTESTANTS IN *I'M A CELEBRITY … GET ME OUT OF HERE!* AND HOW THEY FARED

SERIES ONE (EIGHT CONTESTANTS, 25 AUGUST TO 8 SEPTEMBER 2002)

Tony Blackburn (winner)

Tara Palmer-Tomkinson (2nd)

Christine Hamilton (3rd)

Nell McAndrew (4th)

Rhona Cameron (5th)

Darren Day (6th)

Nigel Benn (7th)

Uri Geller (8th)

SERIES TWO (TEN CONTESTANTS, 29 APRIL TO 12 MAY 2003)

Phil Tufnell (winner)

John Fashanu (2nd)

Linda Barker (3rd)

Wayne Sleep (4th)

Antony Worrall Thompson (5th)

Toyah Willcox (6th)

Catalina Guirado (7th)

Chris Bisson (8th)

Sian Lloyd (9th)

Danniella Westbrook (retired between the evictions of Sian Lloyd and Chris Bisson)

SERIES THREE (TEN CONTESTANTS, 26 JANUARY TO 9 FEBRUARY 2004)

Kerry McFadden (winner)

Jennie Bond (2nd)

Peter Andre (3rd)

Lord Brocket (4th)

Jordan (5th)

Alex Best (6th)

Neil Ruddock (7th)

Diane Modahl (8th)

Mike Read (9th)

John Lydon (retired between the evictions of Neil Ruddock and Alex Best)

THE QUEEN

The Queen was the first (future monarch) to be born in a private house – 17 Bruton Street, London W1 – which is now the site of a bank. She was delivered by caesarean section on a Wednesday.

When she was born she was third in line to the throne (her father and her uncle David, later King Edward VIII, were ahead of her).

She learned to curtsey perfectly before the age of two and made her last curtsey in 1952, to her father's body in St George's Chapel, Windsor.

She's 5 feet 4 inches and weighs about 8 stones.

She and Prince Philip were related before they married. They're third cousins (through their descent from Queen Victoria) and second cousins once removed (through King Christian IX of Denmark).

The Queen has only once signed an autograph for a member of the public. In 1945, Sergeant Pat Hayes asked for her autograph and was given it.

Private Eye's nickname for her is 'Brenda'; her childhood nickname was 'Lilibet' which was the way she mispronounced her own name and is now the name by which her closest relatives know her; her grandmother, Queen Mary, called her 'the bambino'.

At the precise moment in 1952 when she acceded to the throne, she was wearing a shirt, a cardigan and a pair of slacks.

She's superstitious: she throws salt over her left shoulder if she accidentally spills any, she won't have 13 people at the dinner table and she's been known to touch wood before her horses run.

Whenever she travels abroad she always takes with her barley water, a specially formulated egg and lemon shampoo and her feather pillow.

As Queen, she can or could: drive without taking a driving test;

disobey the laws of the land because they are, of course, *her* laws; refuse to give evidence in court as the courts are *her* courts (she also can't be sued); declare war on another country (the armed forces are under her command); disband the army and sell all the Navy's ships; send letters without putting stamps on (her letters carry the Royal cipher); give as many honours – including peerages and knighthoods – as she likes; declare a State of Emergency (which she once did – on 31 May 1955 because of the railway strike); turn any parish in the country into a university; pardon any (or all) of the prisoners in *her* jails; dismiss the government, and get rid of the Civil Service.

The Queen's retinue includes: Keeper of the Queen's Swans, Mistress of the Robes, The Queen's Raven Master, The Clerk of the Closet, Lady of The Bedchamber, Woman of the Bedchamber, Hereditary Grand Falconer, Royal Bargemaster, The Queen's Racing Pigeon Manager and Grand Almoner.

The Queen loves: military march music, popular classical works and musicals, champagne, corgis, watching TV (favourite programmes include *Dad's Army*, *Brideshead Revisited* and *The Good Life*), horse racing, crossword puzzles, impersonations (she's also a gifted impressionist herself) and charades.

The Queen hates: dictating letters, garlic, cats, tennis, pomposity, the cold, smoking and any mention of King Edward VIII whose abdication pushed her father on to the throne, the stress of which (or so the Queen Mother always believed) caused his early death.

TITLES HELD BY PRINCE PHILIP

Privy Councillor, Knight of the Thistle, Admiral of the Royal Yacht Squadron, Grand Master of the Guild of Air Pilots and Air Navigators, Field-Marshal, Marshal of the RAF, Admiral of the Fleet, Knight of the Garter, Chancellor of the University of Cambridge.

KING EDWARD VIII

Edward had more names than any other king in history. He was baptized with the names Edward Albert Christian George Andrew Patrick David – a total of seven.

When he was a little boy, the nurse who looked after him (and his brothers) was determined to set his parents against him. She used to pinch him before he was sent in to see his parents so he'd walk in crying and be sent away in disgrace.

Whatever talents he had, billiards wasn't one of them. Once when playing with his father at Sandringham, he miscued and ripped the felt. His father banned him from the table for a year.

It wasn't only his father who was strict with him. Once he was eating with his grandfather, King Edward VII, and, on trying to talk to him, was told to wait for permission. When this permission was finally

granted, he said: 'It's too late now, Grandpa. There was a caterpillar on your lettuce but you've eaten it.'

Wallis wasn't the first married woman he fell for – in fact, all his lovers were married. When he set his sights on Freda Dudley Ward, he sent round a note – addressed to Mrs Dudley Ward – requesting an invitation to tea. To his shock, he found himself alone at tea with an elderly woman: Freda's mother-in-law, Mrs Dudley Ward!

On 1 January 1936, Sir Winston Churchill, commenting on the growing crisis caused by the relationship of Edward and Mrs Simpson, said, 'He falls instantly in and out of love. His present attachment will follow the course of all the others.' In fact, the relationship lasted until the duke's death in 1972 (at the age of 77 from throat cancer).

Looking back over his brief reign, Edward reckoned that all he'd done was introduce the King's Flight and end the rule that Beefeaters had to have beards.

He was an admirer of Adolf Hitler and Nazism. The reason he was sent off to the Bahamas during World War Two was because the establishment was bothered that he might be a focus for conciliation with the Germans in the event of an invasion. He once said to Diana Mosley (wife of British fascist leader Oswald), 'Every drop of blood in my veins is German.'

Edward liked to indulge in Americanisms such as 'hot-diggerty dog', 'makin' whoopee' and 'okey-dokey'.

As a result of Edward's abdication, the year 1936 saw three different kings on the throne: his father, George V, himself and his brother George VI. There are two other years when this has happened: 1066 (Edward The Confessor, Harold and William The Conqueror) and 1483 (Edward IV, Edward V and Richard III).

As Prince of Wales, he was a great fashion leader. At Oxford University, he wore plus-fours and made turned-up trousers fashionable. He introduced the bowler hat to America. He also invented the Windsor tie knot, which, along with his affected Cockney accent, annoyed his father, George V.

He had a tendency to monophobia, the morbid fear of being alone.

The legendary actress, Marlene Dietrich, took it into her head that she could persuade the King to give up Mrs Simpson and, to that end, she tried phoning him on many occasions, but he refused to take her calls. Eventually, she tried to see him in person but she was refused entry and decided to give up her quest.

King George V had no illusions about his children. He once said, 'I pray to God that my eldest son (Edward) will never marry and have children and that nothing will come between Bertie (George VI) and Lilibet (Elizabeth II) and the Throne.'

When he was Governor of the Bahamas, he used to make black people use the back door.

When the writer Harold Nicolson said to H.G. Wells that Edward had 'charm', Wells contradicted him: 'Glamour.'

Although he was King, he was never actually crowned. He abdicated in December 1936; his coronation had been arranged for the following May.

When he came to sign the instrument of abdication, he found there was 'no damned ink in the pot'.

Although his duchess spent money like a sailor on shore leave, the duke was much more frugal. For example, he always saved his half-smoked cigars from the evening before.

The duke and duchess had a code for when they wanted to leave uninteresting parties: one of them would refer to the 'bore hunt'.

THE WAY WE LIVE

90 per cent of women who walk into a department store immediately turn to the right. No one knows why.

Tuesday is the most productive day of the working week.

908,000 US one-dollar bills weigh exactly one ton.

The average woman uses about 6 pounds of lipstick during her lifetime.

It is estimated that at any one time 0.7 per cent of the world's population is intoxicated.

There has never been a sex-change operation performed in Ireland.

90 per cent of movies released in the United States are porn films.

Couples who marry in January, February or March have the highest divorce rate.

75 per cent of Japanese women own vibrators. The global average is 47 per cent.

The Christmas holidays are the busiest time in plastic surgeons' offices.

80 per cent of women wash their hands after leaving a public toilet; only 55 per cent of men do.

No, no – this way, Martha.

In Turkey the colour of mourning is violet. In most Muslim countries and in China it is white.

In China, the bride wears red.

40 per cent of people who come to a party in your home have a look in your medicine cabinet.

One in every eight boss–secretary romances ends in marriage.

25 per cent of all businesses in the US are franchises.

People who work at night tend to weigh more than people who work during the day.

On an average work day, a typist's fingers travel 12.6 miles.

One out of five pieces of the world's garbage is generated in the United States.

6 per cent of American men propose marriage by phone.

On average, Americans stand

There's an average of 178 sesame seeds on a Big Mac bun.

About 75 per cent of the people in the US live on 2 per cent of the land.

In the vast majority of the world's languages, the word for 'mother' begins with the letter 'm'.

Mexico City has more taxis than any other city in the world.

85 per cent of international phone calls are conducted in English.

The largest toy distributor in the world is McDonald's.

The average person drinks 70,000 cups of coffee in a lifetime.

After a three-week holiday, your IQ can drop by as much as 20 per cent.

In the course of a lifetime, the average person spends about two years on the phone.

14 inches apart when they converse.

The typical driver will honk their car horn 15,250 times during their lifetime.

The average British adult will eat 35,000 biscuits in their lifetime.

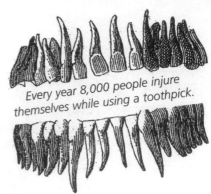

Every year 8,000 people injure themselves while using a toothpick.

In the USA 9 milligrams of rat droppings are allowed in a kilogram of wheat.

Every year the average person eats 428 bugs by mistake.

The average Briton is 38 years old.

One in every four Americans has appeared on television.

17,000 individual Smarties are eaten every minute in the UK.

Peanuts are one of the ingredients of dynamite.

If a statue in the park of a person on a horse has both front legs in the air, the person died in battle; if the horse has one front leg in the air, the person died as a result of wounds received in battle; if the horse has all four legs on the ground, the person died of natural causes.

30 per cent of all the non-biodegradable rubbish buried in American landfills is disposable nappies.

The stall closest to the door in a public toilet is the cleanest, because it is the least used.

People spend two weeks of their life kissing.

People spend more than five years of their lives dreaming.

A typist's left hand does 56 per cent of the work.

The average driver will be locked out of their car nine times during their lifetime.

When asked for a colour, three out of five people say red.

YOGA PRACTITIONERS

Geri Halliwell, Ali MacGraw, Gillian Anderson, Jerry Hall, Sting, Trudie Styler, Woody Harrelson, Goldie Hawn, Madonna, Gwyneth Paltrow, Raquel Welch, Brooke Shields, Michael Jackson, Patricia Arquette, Al Pacino, Flea, Courtney Love, Jemima Khan, Jodie Foster, Cindy Crawford, Ricky Martin, Peter Alliss, Dani Behr, Helen Hunt, Catrina Skepper, Zeinab Badawi, Jerry Seinfeld, Mel C, Kristin Davis, Tobey Maguire, Justin Timberlake, Sadie Frost, Reese Witherspoon, Rachel Weisz, Heather Graham

EYES CORRECTED BY LASER SURGERY

Sir Richard Branson, Simon Le Bon, Courteney Cox, Cilla Black, Tiger Woods, Brad Pitt, Julianne Moore, Lee Westwood, Sir Clive Woodward, Sharron Davies, Dennis Waterman, Padraig Harrington, Myleene Klass, Nicole Kidman, Adam Sandler, Sally Jessy Raphael

Used hrt (hormone replacement therapy)

Kate O'Mara, Marjorie Proops, Teresa Gorman, The Duchess of Kent, Joan Collins, Fay Weldon, Angela Thorne, Germaine Greer, Lizzie Webb, Jill Gascoine, Stephanie Beacham, Dr Miriam Stoppard, Isla Blair, Judy Finnigan, Anne Robinson

Had a vasectomy

Dean Martin, Richard Madeley, Faron Young, Paul Ross, Billy Eckstine, Abbie Hoffman, Michael Parkinson, Howard Hughes, George Melly, Neil Kinnock, Adrian Edmondson

Had a liver transplant

George Best, Larry Hagman, Jack Bruce, David Crosby, Jim Baxter, Rory Gallagher, Brian Clough

Had a kidney transplant

Lucy Davis (from her mother), Gary Coleman (two)

Flat feet

Stan Collymore, Linda Lusardi, Roger Black, Zoë Ball, Edwina Currie, Dame Alicia Markova, Newt Gingrich, Prince Charles, Cyndi Lauper, Stephen King, Robin Smith, Terence Stamp

HARD OF HEARING

George Melly, David Hockney, Eric Sykes, Lester Piggott, Bill Clinton, Norman Mailer, King Juan Carlos, Rob Lowe (deaf in his right ear), Luciano Pavarotti, Dominick Dunne, Sir John Mills, Stephanie Beacham, Sir George Martin, Brian Wilson (deaf in one ear and so has never heard his songs in stereo), Lucinda Lambton (deaf in her right ear), Halle Berry (lost 80 per cent hearing in her left ear after ex-lover beat her), Rodney Marsh (deaf in his left ear), Richard Thomas, Kate Adie, Des O'Connor (deaf in one ear)

NB Thomas Edison was completely deaf in his left ear and had limited hearing in his right ear

SURVIVED A STROKE

Dickie Davies, Raymond Blanc, Bill Maynard, Kirk Douglas, Charlie Drake, Sir John Harvey-Jones, Barbara Windsor, Boris Yeltsin, Keith Floyd, Sharon Stone

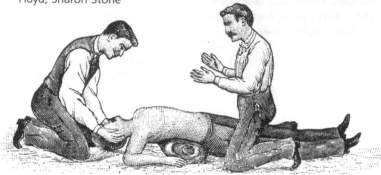

HAD KIDNEY STONES

Michael Heseltine, Edward Stourton, Sir Gary Sobers, Anne Diamond, Sir Ranulph Fiennes, Bob Dole, Letitia Dean, Montserrat Caballe, Henry Kelly, Michael Crawford, Lord Richard Attenborough, Steve Cram

HAD APPENDIX REMOVED

Dave Stewart (unnecessarily so – it was just wind), Dian Fossey (as a precaution before going into the jungle), Mel Gibson, Sir Steven Redgrave, Pope John Paul II, Isla Blair, Mika Hakkinen, Patsy Palmer, Sue Barker, Ann Widdecombe, Robert Powell, Steven Norris, Jeremy Beadle, Fidel Castro, Lisa Snowdon, Meg Mathews, Jenna Bush, Minnie Driver, Kelsey Grammer, Tim Allen, Glenda Jackson, Gavin Hastings, Vicky Entwistle, Jo O'Meara, Prince Charles, Kevin Costner, Gyles Brandreth, Dame Vera Lynn, Julia Volkova (of Tatu), Kate Beckinsale

HAD TONSILS REMOVED AS AN ADULT

David Coulthard, Ringo Starr, Bryan Ferry, Don Maclean (twice – as a child and as an adult when they'd grown back), Kelly Holmes, Kyran Bracken, Judy Simpson, Paul Way, Roger Cook, Drew Barrymore, Ben Okri, Rudolf Nureyev, Claire Richards, Graham Taylor, Billie Piper

HEART MURMUR

Judy Finnigan, Arnold Schwarzenegger, Bridget Fonda, Retief Goosen, Rachel Hunter, Evander Holyfield, Dame Elizabeth Taylor

HAS A HEART PACEMAKER

Sir Elton John, Dick Cheney, Sir Patrick Moore, James Major, Gareth Hale

HAD EPILEPTIC FITS

Julius Caesar, Alexander The Great, Cameron Sharp, François Pienaar, Lord Byron, Michael Miles, Vincent van Gogh, Julia Somerville, Edward Lear, Derek Bentley, Peter The Great, Max Clifford, Billy Idol, Neil Young, Ward Bond, Ian Curtis, Margaux Hemingway, Florence Griffith Joyner

SURVIVED MENINGITIS

Victoria Beckham, Jerry Lewis, Lee Sharpe, Queen Beatrix of the Netherlands, Steve Elkington, Peter Francisco, Dr Phil Hammond, Nick Conway, Maria Shriver, John Morris, Bruce Grobelaar, Johnny Rotten (Lydon), Ben Peyton

HAS SUFFERED FROM ASTHMA

Nick Hancock, Adam Woodyatt, Tony Robinson, Edwina Currie, Liz McColgan, Lee Hurst, Dewi Morris, Gerald Scarfe, Rodney Bewes, Ian Wright, Jason Donovan, Steven Seagal, Alan Freeman, Peter Sissons (had an asthma attack while reading the news), Wynonna, Stephen Fry, Joe Jackson (used to be put into oxygen tents in hospital), Kathleen Quinlan, Shirley Manson, Karen Pickering, Nikki Sanderson, Austin Healey, Paul Scholes

SUFFERED FROM ANOREXIA

Sinitta, Marina Ogilvy, Lena Zavaroni, Karen Carpenter, Patsy Palmer, Tracy Shaw, Patricia Cornwell, Kate Beckinsale, Davina McCall

Tinnitus sufferers

Russell Grant, Pete Townshend, Barbra Streisand, Julia McKenzie, Alan Bleasdale

Suffered from bulimia

Diana, Princess of Wales, Zina Garrison, Lysette Anthony, Uri Geller, Jane Fonda, Emma Thompson, Sir Elton John, Geri Halliwell, Kym Marsh, Linda Thorson, Adam Rickitt, Carre Otis

Parkinson's disease

Ray Kennedy, Michael J. Fox, Sir Michael Redgrave, Mao-Tse Tung, Sir John Betjeman, Muhammad Ali, Johnny Cash, Janet Reno, Deborah Kerr, Billy Graham

Suffered from manic depression

Axl Rose, Spike Milligan, Nicola Pagett, Sir James Goldsmith, Vincent van Gogh, Ted Turner, Vivien Leigh, Jeremy Brett, Freddie Starr, Jess Yates, Robert Schumann, Abbie Hoffman, Patricia Cornwell, Margot Kidder, Mario Lanza, Capucine, Dorothy Dandridge, Patty Duke

SUFFERED FROM CHILDHOOD POLIO

Alan Alda, Ian Dury, Lord Snowdon, Kerry Packer, Sir Walter Scott, Joni Mitchell, Sir Julian Critchley, Neil Young, Itzhak Perlman, Steve Harley, Joe Coral, Sir Harold Hobson, Wilma Rudolph, Ruskin Spear, Dinah Shore, Francis Coppola

DIABETICS

Gary Mabbutt, Bill Maynard, Bernard Manning, Lisa Harrow, Michael Barry, Luther Vandross, Mary Tyler Moore, Halle Berry, Wasim Akram, Sir Steven Redgrave, Mick Fleetwood, Sharon Stone, John Peel, Syd Barrett, B.B. King, George Lucas, Meat Loaf, Jack Wild

SURVIVED A HEART ATTACK

Edward Woodward, Sue Townsend, Martin Sheen, Kerry Packer, Michael Heseltine, Omar Sharif, Eddy Grant, Jerry Lee Lewis, Eddie Large, Paul O'Grady, Nigel Lythgoe

SUFFERS FROM ARTHRITIS

John Cleese, The Queen, Claire King, Tommy Smith, José Maria Olazabal, Dame Elizabeth Taylor, Prince Philip, Simon Geoghegan, Dermot Reeve, Jack Nicklaus, Lord Nigel Lawson, Malcolm Allison, Chris Broad, Joe Royle, Dame Julia Neuberger, Jo Durie, Barry Gibb

Survived a nervous breakdown

Emily Lloyd, David Helfgott, Honor Blackman, Bob Hoskins, Leslie Phillips, The Duchess of Kent, Yitzhak Rabin, Leslie Caron, Brian Wilson, Daniel Day-Lewis, Brian Blessed, Yves St Laurent, Kylie Minogue, Lee Evans, Roseanne, Tuesday Weld, Sarah Lancashire, Mariah Carey, Beyoncé Knowles, Kate Beckinsale, Norman Cook

Lost a finger

Jerry Garcia, Boris Yeltsin, James Doohan, Dr Alex Comfort, Telly Savalas, Daryl Hannah (wears a prosthetic fingertip), Admiral Isoroku Yamamoto (who planned attack on Pearl Harbor), Matt Perry (lost middle finger in kindergarten accident), Gary Burghoff (Radar from M*A*S*H – left hand always hidden by clipboard), Dave Allen (missing tip of one finger), Terry Nutkins (fingertip bitten off by an otter), Dustin Hoffman (lost the tip of his finger when a seat collapsed while filming *Neverland* in 2003)

BLIND

Stevie Wonder, David Blunkett, John Milton, Ray Charles, Louis Braille, Claude Monet, Helen Keller, Jose Feliciano, James Thurber, Joseph Pulitzer, Peggy Mount, George Shearing, Sue Townsend

LOST AN EYE

Gordon Banks, Sir Rex Harrison, Herbert Morrison, Joe Davis, James Thurber, Colin Milburn, John Ford, Moshe Dayan, Peter Falk, John Milton, Sammy Davis Jr, Sandy Duncan, Alan Jay Lerner, Raoul Walsh, Ry Cooder

NB Gordon Brown and Amanda Barrie are both blind in one eye

HAVE USED VIAGRA

Jim Carrey, Jerry Springer, Bob Dole, Hugh Hefner, Julio Iglesias, Ryan O'Neal, Johnnie Walker, Vidal Sassoon, Ben Affleck (once – 'all it did was make me sweat and feel dizzy. I felt no sexual effects whatsoever'), Kim Cattrall, Jack Nicholson, Ozzy Osbourne

PREGNANCY CRAVINGS

Catherine Zeta-Jones – beetroot (first child), Branston Pickle and curry (second child)

Lowri Turner – red meat

Fiona Phillips – cream and then mints

Mel B – peanut butter, cheesecake, ice cream and chips

Gloria Estefan – sweetened condensed milk

Victoria Beckham – gherkins

Kate Winslet – fizzy cola sweets, blackcurrant juice and tomatoes

Madonna – butternut squash

Zoë Ball – lettuce and fruit

Marie Osmond – grapefruit sorbet topped with sardines

Davina McCall – tabasco sauce and Coca-Cola (first child); radishes and Coca-Cola (second child)

Cate Blanchett – sardines

Natasha Hamilton – sweet puddings and fried breakfasts

Jade Goody – pickled onion Monster Munch dipped in hummus

Brooke Shields – extremely strong coffee and nutmeg

Ms Dynamite – strawberry flavour Ben and Jerry's ice cream

Ulrika Jonsson – digestive biscuits (third child)

Melinda Messenger – cucumber

NATURE

Millions of trees are accidentally planted by squirrels that bury nuts and then forget where they left them.

The smallest trees in the world are Greenland dwarf willows.

It snowed in the Sahara desert on 18 February 1979.

The canopy of a rainforest is so thick that only 1 per cent of sunlight reaches the ground.

An ordinary raindrop falls at about 7 miles per hour.

Lightning strikes the Earth about 200 times a second.

Heavy rain pours down at the rate of about 20 miles per hour.

The Siberian larch accounts for more than 20 per cent of the world's trees.

The giant water lily grows almost a foot a day.

Some bamboo plants grow 3 feet a day.

Oak trees do not produce acorns until they are at least 50 years old.

A cucumber is 96 per cent water.

There is cyanide in apple pips.

A notch in a tree will remain the same distance from the ground as the tree grows.

If you put a raisin in a glass of champagne, it will keep floating to the top and sinking to the bottom.

Almonds are part of the peach family.

There are more stars in the universe than grains of sand on all the beaches in the world.

There are 10 million bacteria in a litre of milk; that's equivalent to the population of Greece.

Cranberries are one of just three major fruits native to North America. Blueberries and Concord grapes are the other two.

A ripe cranberry will bounce.

Wheat is the world's most widely cultivated plant; grown on every continent except Antarctica.

All snow crystals are hexagonal.

The water we drink is 3 billion years old.

The average iceberg weighs 20 million tons.

You can figure out which way is south if you are near a tree stump. The growth rings are wider on the south side.

It is estimated that a plastic container can resist decomposition for as long as 50,000 years.

The most abundant metal in the Earth's crust is aluminium. The Chinese were using aluminium to make things as early as AD300. Western civilization didn't rediscover it until 1827.

The angle of the branches from the trunk of a tree is constant from one member to another of the same species.

The cashew is a member of the poison ivy family.

Strawberries are a member of the rose family.

Most orchids are bisexual.

SCIENCE

If you slowly pour a handful of salt into a totally full glass of water it will not overflow. In fact, the water level will go down.

Hot water freezes quicker than cold water.

Magnesium was used in early flash photography because it burns with a brilliant light.

A scientific satellite needs only 250 watts of power to operate.

The letter J does not appear on the periodic table of the elements.

Minus 40 degrees Celsius is exactly the same temperature as minus 40 degrees Fahrenheit.

Radio waves travel so much faster than sound waves that a broadcast voice can be heard sooner 18,000 km away than in the back of the room in which it originated.

Waves break when their height reaches more than 7/10ths of the depth of the water.

X-ray technology has shown that there are three different versions of the *Mona Lisa* under the one that's visible.

Because of the rotation of the earth, an object can be thrown farther

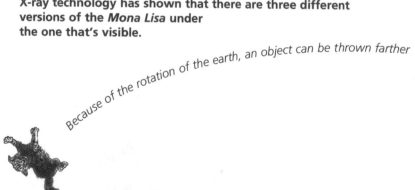

In an atom, the electron weighs 1/2000th the weight of the proton.

At the deepest point of the ocean (11.034 km), an iron ball would take more than an hour to sink to the ocean floor.

When scientists at Australia's Parkes Observatory began picking up radio waves, they thought they had proof of alien life. However, it transpired that the emissions came from a microwave oven in the building.

Only 13.5 per cent of scientists are women.

Sterling silver contains 7.5 per cent copper.

Hydrogen gas is the least dense substance.

Ocean waves can travel as fast as a jet plane.

Aspirin was the first drug offered as a water-soluble tablet, in 1900.

Mercury is the only metal that is liquid at room temperature.

In a scientific study, children were told to imagine that they were wearing heavy mittens. The temperature of their fingertips went up.

1/25th of the energy put out by a light bulb is light. The rest is heat.

No matter how high or low it flies, an aeroplane's shadow is always the same size.

if it is thrown west.

GUEST APPEARANCES IN TV PROGRAMMES

ABSOLUTELY FABULOUS

Germaine Greer, Richard E. Grant, Marianne Faithfull, John Wells, Jo Brand, Zandra Rhodes, Britt Ekland, Eleanor Bron, Marcella Detroit, Nicky Clarke, Christian Lacroix, Bruce Oldfield, Dora Bryan, Richard Madeley, Judy Finnigan, Stephen Gately, Anita Pallenberg, Dave Gorman, Dale Winton, Whoopi Goldberg, Debbie Harry, Fern Britton, Kristin Scott Thomas, Mariella Frostrup, Minnie Driver, Emma Bunton, Sir Elton John

BLACKADDER

Angus Deayton, Jim Broadbent, Rik Mayall, Miriam Margolyes, Tom Baker, Robbie Coltrane, Chris Barrie, Nigel Planer, Adrian Edmondson, Geoffrey Palmer

CHEERS

Glynis Johns, Dick Cavett, Sherilyn Fenn, Senator Gary Hart, Lisa Kudrow, Arsenio Hall, Bobby Hatfield, Mike Dukakis, Celeste Holm, Harry Connick Jr, Harvey Fierstein, Senator John Kerry, Johnny Carson

FILTHY RICH & CATFLAP

Midge Ure, Lynda Bellingham, David Baddiel, Stephen Fry, The Nolan Sisters, Barbara Windsor, Mel Smith, Hugh Laurie

GOODNIGHT SWEETHEART

John Motson, Timothy West, Bonnie Langford

M*A*S*H

Leslie Nielsen, Ron Howard, Loudon Wainwright III, Brian Dennehy

MEN BEHAVING BADLY

Hugo Speer, Ulrika Jonsson

RED DWARF

Koo Stark, Tony Slattery, Glynis Barber, Arthur Smith, Nicholas Ball, Jane Horrocks, Anita Dobson, Brian Cox, Geraldine McEwan

THE VICAR OF DIBLEY

Alistair McGowan, Dervla Kirwan, Stephen Tompkinson, Terry Wogan, Darcey Bussell, Richard Griffiths, Martyn Lewis

YES, MINISTER/YES, PRIME MINISTER

Bob McKenzie, Robert Dougall, Sue Lawley, Eleanor Bron, Graeme Garden, John Fortune, John Wells, Bill Bailey, John Bird

'PHONED UP' *FRASIER*

Mel Brooks, Rosemary Clooney, Jeff Daniels, Patty Hearst, Piper Laurie, Timothy Leary, John Malkovich, Henry Mancini, Joe Mantegna, Reba McEntire, Mary Tyler Moore, Christopher Reeve, Carl Reiner, Eric Stoltz, Garry Trudeau, Eddie Van Halen, Elijah Wood, Amy Madigan, Art Garfunkel, Ben Stiller, Beverly D'Angelo, Billy Crystal, Carrie Fisher, Cindy Crawford, Cyd Charisse, David Duchovny, Ed Harris, Eric Idle, Gillian

Anderson, Gloria Estefan, Halle Berry, Jay Leno, Jill Clayburgh, Joan Allen, JoBeth Williams, Jodie Foster, John Cusack, John Lithgow, John McEnroe, Kevin Bacon, Laura Dern, Lily Tomlin, Macaulay Culkin, Mary Elizabeth Mastrantonio, Matthew Broderick, Pia Zadora, Ron Howard, Sandra Dee, Shelley Duvall, Tom Hulce, Tommy Hilfiger, William H. Macy, Yo-Yo Ma

GUESTED IN *FRIENDS*

George Clooney (Dr Mitchell)

Julia Roberts (Susie Moss)

Elliott Gould (Jack Geller – Monica & Ross's father)

Noah Wyle (Dr Rosen)

Chris Isaak (Rob Donnen – children's library organizer)

Tom Selleck (Dr Richard Burke – Monica's boyfriend)

Morgan Fairchild (Nora Bing – Chandler's mother)

Brooke Shields (Erika Ford – Joey's stalker)

Jean-Claude Van Damme (as himself)

Charlie Sheen (Ryan – Phoebe's sailor)

Charlton Heston (as himself)

The Duchess of York (as herself)

Jennifer Saunders (Mrs Waltham – Emily's stepmother)

Tom Conti (Dr Waltham – Emily's father)

Sir Richard Branson (as himself)

Robin Williams (Thomas)

Billy Crystal (Tim)

David Arquette (Malcolm – Ursula's stalker)

Hank Azaria (David – Phoebe's scientist boyfriend)

Elle Macpherson (Janine Lacroix – Joey's roommate)

Sherilyn Fenn (Ginger, the girl with the wooden leg)

Helen Hunt (Jamie Buchanan)

Chrissie Hynde (Stephanie – a professional guitarist)

Ralph Lauren (as himself)

Jay Leno (as himself)

Rebecca Romijn-Stamos (Cheryl – Ross's girlfriend)

Isabella Rossellini (as herself)

Ben Stiller (Tommy, Rachel's boyfriend)

Bruce Willis (Paul Stevens – Elizabeth's father & Rachel's boyfriend)

Reese Witherspoon (Jill Greene – Rachel's sister)

Guest stars in *Doctor Who*

Jean Marsh (played Joanna in 1965. NB she was married to the future doctor, Jon Pertwee)

Julian Glover (played King Richard the Lionheart in 1965)

Kenneth Kendall (appeared as himself in 1966)

John Cleese (played an art critic in 1979)

Eleanor Bron (played an art critic in 1979 and Kara in 1985)

Martin Jarvis (making his TV debut played Captain Hilio in 1965; he went on to play Butler in 1974 and the Governor in 1985)

Hywel Bennett (making his TV debut played Rynian in 1965)

Hannah Gordon (played Kirsty in 1966–7)

Pauline Collins (Samantha Briggs in 1967; she was asked if she wanted to become one of the doctor's companions but turned it down because she didn't want to become typecast)

Nerys Hughes (Todd in 1982 – opposite the veteran British actor Richard Todd)

Tim Pigott-Smith (Harker in 1971 and then played Marco in 1976)

Carmen Silvera (Clara in 1966 and Ruth in 1974)

Kate O'Mara (the Rani in 1985 and in 1987)

Jason Connery (Jondar in 1985)

Alexei Sayle (the DJ in 1985)

William Gaunt (Orcini in 1985)

Ken Dodd (Tollmaster in 1987)

Richard Briers (the Chief Caretaker in 1987)

Windsor Davies (Toby in 1967)

Peter Sallis (Penley in 1967)

Brian Glover (Griffiths in 1985)

Susan Penhaligon (Lakis in 1972)

Gareth Hunt (Arak in 1974)

Keith Barron (Captain Striker in 1983)

Burt Kwouk (Lin Futu in 1982)

Beryl Reid (Captain Briggs in 1982)

Michael Gough (Councillor Hedin in 1983)

Liza Goddard (Kari in 1983)

Rodney Bewes (Stein in 1984)

Peter Wyngarde (Timanov in 1984)

Faith Brown (Flast in 1985)

Honor Blackman (Professor Lasky in 1986)

GUESTED IN *STAR TREK*

Joan Collins, Stephanie Beacham, Whoopi Goldberg, Teri Garr, Linda Thorson, Kelsey Grammer, Professor Stephen Hawking, Steven Berkoff, Mick Fleetwood, David Soul, Iggy Pop, King Abdullah of Jordan (had a cameo non-speaking role)

PRESENTED *TOP OF THE POPS*

Angus Deayton, The Spice Girls, Julia Carling, Chris Eubank, Dannii Minogue, Vic Reeves and Bob Mortimer, Frankie Dettori, Jarvis Cocker, Leo Sayer, Russ Abbot, Jack Osbourne, Davy Jones, Sir Elton John, Roger Daltrey, Sir Cliff Richard, Kevin Keegan, Lenny Henry, Mr Blobby, Meat Loaf, Jack Dee, Julian Clary, Malcolm McLaren, Steve Punt and Hugh Dennis, Kylie Minogue, Michelle Gayle, Lily Savage, Neneh Cherry, Damon Albarn, Gary Glitter, Keith Allen, Phill Jupitus, Whigfield, Dale Winton, Jo Brand, Mark Lamarr, Robbie Williams, Suggs, Louise, Ronan Keating, Stephen Gately, Björk, Lulu, Lee Evans, Ian Wright, Peter Andre, Nigel Kennedy, Ian Broudie, Rhona Cameron, Phil Daniels, Noddy Holder, Denise Van Outen

GREAT MISQUOTATIONS

'I never said I want to be alone, I only said I want to be left alone.'
(Greta Garbo)

'Alas, poor Yorick, I knew him well.'

'Alas poor Yorick! I knew him, Horatio.' (Hamlet in *Hamlet* by William Shakespeare)

'A little knowledge is a dangerous thing.'

'A little learning is a dangerous thing.' (Alexander Pope)

'Spare the rod, spoil the child.'

'He who spares the rod hates his son, but he who loves him is careful to discipline him.' (Bible, Proverbs 13:24)

'Money is the root of all evil.'

'For the love of money is the root of all evil.' (Bible, Timothy 6:10)

'Abandon hope, all ye who enter here.'

'Abandon all hope, you who enter.' (*The Divine Comedy* by Dante)

'Water, water everywhere, and not a drop to drink.'

'Water, water everywhere, nor any drop to drink.' (*Rime of the Ancient Mariner* by Samuel T. Coleridge)

'Hell hath no fury like a woman scorned.'

'Heaven has no rage, like love to hatred turned, Nor hell a fury, like a woman scorned.' (*The Mourning Bride* by William Congreve)

'Music has charms to soothe a savage beast.'

'Music has charms to soothe a savage breast.' (*The Mourning Bride* by William Congreve)

'Come up and see me sometime.'

'Why don't you come up sometime, and see me?' (Mae West to Cary Grant in *She Done Him Wrong*)

'Pride goes before a fall.'

'Pride goeth before destruction and an haughty spirit before a fall.' (Bible, Proverbs 16:18)

'My lips are sealed.'

'My lips are not yet unsealed.' (Stanley Baldwin)

'Nice guys finish last.'

'Nice Guys Finish Seventh.' (Brooklyn Dodgers manager Leo Durocher speaking in the days when the National League had seven teams so seventh was, in fact, last)

'Elementary, my dear Watson.'	'Elementary.' (Sherlock Holmes to Dr Watson in Sir Arthur Conan Doyle's stories)
'Hubble bubble, toil and trouble.'	'Double double, toil and trouble.' (The witches in *Macbeth* by William Shakespeare)
'Methinks the lady doth protest too much.'	'The lady does protest too much, methinks.' (Gertrude in *Hamlet* by William Shakespeare)
'To gild the lily.'	'To gild refined gold, to paint the lily.' (The Earl of Salisbury in *King John* by William Shakespeare)
'Me Tarzan, you Jane.'	Tarzan and Jane pointed at themselves and each said their own name in *Tarzan The Ape Man*
'He who hesitates is lost.'	'The woman that deliberates is lost.' (*Cato* by Joseph Addison)
'Et tu, Brutus?'	'Et tu, Brute?' (*Julius Caesar*. In the unlikely event that he said those words, Brutus would have taken the vocative)
'When in Rome do as the Romans do.'	'If you are at Rome, live after the Roman fashion; if you are elsewhere, live as they do there.' (St Ambrose)

'I disapprove of what you say but I will defend to the death your right to say it.'

'Think for yourselves and let others enjoy the privilege to do so too.' (Voltaire)

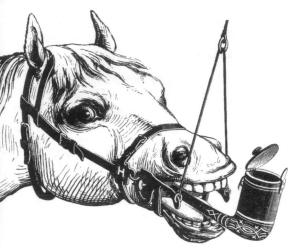

'Don't look a gift horse in the mouth.'

'Never inspect the teeth of a gift horse.' (original proverb)

'Discretion is the better part of valour.'

'The better part of valour is discretion.' (Falstaff in *King Henry IV, Part I* by William Shakespeare)

'There's method in his madness.'

'Though this be madness, yet there is method in't.' (Polonius in *Hamlet* by William Shakespeare)

'In the future, everybody will be famous for 15 minutes.'

'In the future, there won't be any more stars. TV will be so accessible that everybody will be a star for 15 minutes.' (Andy Warhol)

PEOPLE AND THE FILMS THEY DIRECTED

Norman Mailer – *Tough Guys Don't Dance* (1987)

Frank Sinatra – *None But The Brave* (1965)

Joan Rivers – *Rabbit Test* (1978)

Anthony Quinn – *The Buccaneer* (1958)

Rossano Brazzi – *The Christmas That Almost Wasn't* (1966)

James Clavell – *To Sir, With Love* (1967)

Arnold Schwarzenegger – *Christmas In Connecticut* (1992)

Michael Crichton – *Westworld* (1973)

Albert Finney – *Charlie Bubbles* (1968)

Patrick McGoohan – *Catch My Soul* (1973)

Timothy Leary – *Cheech And Chong's Nice Dream* (1981)

Sir Tom Stoppard – *Rosencrantz & Guildenstern Are Dead* (1990)

Michael Nesmith – *Doctor Duck's Super Secret All-Purpose Sauce* (1985)

Ringo Starr – *Born To Boogie* (1972)

Howard Hughes – *Hell's Angels* (1930)

Larry Hagman – *Son of Blob* (1972)

Richard Burton – *Dr Faustus* (1967)

Songs that inspired films

'Coward of The County': Kenny Rogers's 1980 hit about a supposed coward who eventually learns to fight became a 1981 film starring Mr Rogers himself as a preacher whose nephew is the 'coward'.

'Convoy': Back in 1976 at the height of the CB radio craze, C.W. McCall released 'Convoy', about a trucker trying to run a police blockade. Two years later, Sam Peckinpah directed a film based on the song starring Kris Kristofferson and Ali MacGraw.

'Torn Between Two Lovers': In 1977, Mary MacGregor had a Top Five hit with this ballad. In a 1979 film of the same name, Lee Remick is similarly torn between George Peppard and Joseph Bologna.

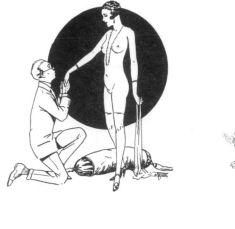

'Rock Around The Clock': Bill Haley and his Comets' hit record caused teenagers to rip up cinema seats when it was featured in the credits of the 1955 film *The Blackboard Jungle*. The following year, Bill and the boys starred in a cheap film named after their classic song.

'Mrs Brown, You've Got A Lovely Daughter': In 1965, Herman's Hermits had a US No. 1 with this song. Three years later, the lads were cast in a film of the same name, which attempted to cash in on the Swinging London phenomenon.

'Harper Valley PTA': In 1968, Jeannie C. Riley had a hit with this song about a woman who is ruled to be an unfit mother by her local PTA. The 1978 film of the same name – starring Barbara Eden – took this story and showed the heroine getting even by exposing the members of the PTA as hypocrites.

'Yellow Submarine': The 1966 Beatles song – the only single to feature Ringo on lead vocals – was the inspiration for the 1968 animated film (co-written by *Love Story* author, Erich Segal), which has become a cult classic.

'Ode To Billy Joe': In 1967, Bobbie Gentry released this song about a love affair that ends in suicide. In 1976, a film of the same title opened up the story of Billy Joe and his jump off the Tallahatchee Bridge.

'Lili Marlene': This extraordinary song's place in musical history was assured when it became the only song in World War Two to be adopted by both the Germans and the British. The song subsequently inspired a 1980 film of the same name starring Hanna Schygulla.

'White Christmas': The song 'White Christmas' – written by Irving Berlin – was so popular when Bing Crosby sang it in the 1942 film *Holiday Inn* that it was used as the title of a 1954 film – also starring Bing Crosby.

PEOPLE AND THE FILMS THEY APPEARED IN

Martin Amis – *A High Wind In Jamaica*

Björk – *Dancer In The Dark*

Salman Rushdie – *Bridget Jones's Diary*

Andrea Corr – *Evita*

Anna Kournikova – *Me, Myself And Irene*

Naomi Campbell – *Girl 6*

Simon Cowell – *Scary Movie 3*

Sergio Garcia – *Stuck On You*

Bruce Springsteen – *High Fidelity*

Gary Lineker – *Bend It Like Beckham*

Dani Behr – *Rancid Aluminium*

Sophie Dahl – *A Revenger's Tragedy*

Jackie Collins – *All At Sea*

Craig Stadler – *Tin Cup*

Herb Alpert – *The Ten Commandments*

Earl Spencer – *Another Country*

Magic Johnson – *Grand Canyon*

Ernest Hemingway – *The Old Man And The Sea*

Justin Timberlake – *Model Behavior*

Germaine Greer – *Universal Soldier*

John McEnroe – *Anger Management*

Christopher Isherwood – *Rich And Famous*

Pablo Picasso – *Life Begins Tomorrow*

Michael Parkinson – *Love Actually*

Leon Trotsky – *My Official Wife*

Saul Bellow – *Zelig*

Mark Twain – *A Curious Dream*

Graham Greene – *Day for Night*

**Sir David Frost –
*The VIPs***

Elle MacPherson – *Sirens*

Jean Shrimpton – *Privilege*

Sir Henry Cooper –
Royal Flash

**Yoko Ono –
*Satan's Bed***

WALT DISNEY

Born on 5 December 1901, Walt(er) Elias Disney first started drawing cartoons professionally in exchange for free haircuts.

When he was 16, Disney tried to enlist in the US Army but was refused admission because of his age. So he tried the Canadian Army – with the same result. Eventually, he went to France as a Red Cross ambulance driver.

While waiting to become an ambulance driver, he worked as a postal clerk in Chicago. When he returned from France, he worked as a postal clerk in Kansas City.

Disney started the Laugh-O-Gram Corporation, a vehicle for his animated fairy tales, in Kansas City in 1921 with $15,000 from investors. He went bankrupt two years later when his backers pulled out as a result of problems with New York distributors.

In 1923, he went to Hollywood to go into partnership with his brother Roy, taking all his worldly possessions: one jacket, one pair of trousers, one shirt, two sets of underwear and a few drawing materials.

For four years, Disney and his wife, the actress Lillian Bounds, lived in poverty until he had a (relative) success with *Oswald The Lucky Rabbit*.

The same year, Disney took inspiration from the mice that used to play in his studio and created Mickey Mouse. He originally called him 'Mortimer', but his wife thought 'Mickey' sounded better. Disney himself supplied the voice for Mickey in the 1928 hit talkie *Steamboat Willie*. Disney once said of his creation: 'I love Mickey more than any woman I've ever known.'

Disney's 1940 film *Pinocchio* is regarded as a classic, but Paulo Lorenzini, the nephew of the original author of *Pinocchio*, Carlo

Lorenzini, wanted the Italian government to sue Disney for making Pinocchio too American. He failed to persuade the authorities to launch a lawsuit.

When Disney set out to make his film of *Peter Pan*, he became stuck when it came to how Tinker Bell should be depicted. In the end, he decided to model her on the ideal American woman: Marilyn Monroe.

By the time of his death on 15 December 1966 at the age of 65, Disney had won more Oscars (32) than anyone else in history.

ALL THE WINNERS OF THE CECIL B. DEMILLE AWARD AT THE GOLDEN GLOBES

2003: Michael Douglas

2002: Gene Hackman

2001: Harrison Ford

2000: Al Pacino

1999: Barbra Streisand

1998: Jack Nicholson

1997: Shirley MacLaine

1996: Dustin Hoffman

1995: Sir Sean Connery

1994: Sophia Loren

1993: Robert Redford

1992: Lauren Bacall

1991: Robert Mitchum

1990: Jack Lemmon

1989: Audrey Hepburn

1988: Doris Day

1987: Clint Eastwood

1986: Anthony Quinn

1985: Barbara Stanwyck

1984: Elizabeth Taylor

1983: Paul Newman

1982: Sir Laurence Olivier

1981: Sidney Poitier

1980: Gene Kelly

1979: Henry Fonda

1978: Lucille Ball

1977: Red Skelton

1976: Walter Mirisch

1975: No Award

1974: Hal B. Wallis

1973: Bette Davis

1972: Samuel Goldwyn

1971: Alfred Hitchcock

1970: Frank Sinatra

1969: Joan Crawford

1968: Gregory Peck

1967: Kirk Douglas

1966: Charlton Heston

1965: John Wayne

1964: James Stewart

1963: Joseph E. Levine

1962: Bob Hope

1961: Judy Garland

1960: Fred Astaire

1959: Bing Crosby

1958: Maurice Chevalier

1957: Buddy Adler

1956: Mervyn LeRoy

1955: Jack L. Warner

1954: Jean Hersholt

1953: Darryl F. Zanuck

1952: Walt Disney

1951: Cecil B. DeMille

The award for 2004 will be given in 2005.

RELATIONSHIPS THAT STARTED ON FILM SETS

Tom Cruise & Nicole Kidman (*Days of Thunder*)

Tom Cruise & Penelope Cruz (*Vanilla Sky*)

Meg Ryan & Dennis Quaid (*Innerspace*)

Gwyneth Paltrow & Brad Pitt (*Seven*)

Gwyneth Paltrow & Ben Affleck (*Shakespeare In Love*)

Sadie Frost & Jude Law (*Shopping*)

Ethan Hawke & Uma Thurman (*Gattaca*)

Julia Roberts & Daniel Moder (*The Mexican*)

Jeff Goldblum & Laura Dern (*Jurassic Park*)

William Hurt & Marlee Matlin (*Children of A Lesser God*)

Humphrey Bogart & Lauren Bacall (*To Have And Have Not*)

Warren Beatty & Madonna (*Dick Tracy*)

Laurence Olivier & Vivien Leigh (*Fire Over England*)

Steve McQueen & Ali MacGraw (*The Getaway*)

Paul Hogan & Linda Koslowski (*Crocodile Dundee*)

Richard Burton & Elizabeth Taylor (*Cleopatra*)

THINGS ROBERT DE NIRO HAS DONE TO 'FIND' HIS CHARACTERS

The Godfather Part 2 (1974) It was for this role, as the young Vito Corleone, that De Niro won his first Oscar. To get into character and play the part with conviction, De Niro learned to speak Sicilian Italian.

Taxi Driver (1976) For this role, De Niro was obliged to lose weight – some two and a half stones. He also worked as a taxi-driver. Once he picked up a fare who, recognizing him, said, 'You're the actor, aren't you? Guess it's hard to find steady work.'

New York, New York (1977) Most actors when required to portray musicians settle for a rough approximation of pretending to play their instruments. Not De Niro. Cast as a saxophonist, he learned to play the saxophone. His playing was still dubbed over by a professional but his finger-placement earned him praise from the experts.

The Deer Hunter (1978) In this film, De Niro played a steelworker, so he went to live in a steelworking community for a few weeks before starting to film. He also performed his own stunts – including one where he has to jump from a helicopter into the river.

Raging Bull (1980) For his Oscar-winning role as boxer Jake La Motta, De Niro learned how to box – training with La Motta for six months and breaking the caps on the ex-boxer's teeth. La Motta later said that if De Niro tired of acting he could earn a living as a boxer. For the film's scenes where his character becomes fat, De Niro gained 60 pounds, which he later shed.

True Confessions (1981) One of De Niro's less memorable movies. He played a priest who gets caught up in a murder case involving his policeman brother. Once again, De Niro learnt a language for a role – this time, Latin.

The Untouchables (1987) For his brief but brilliant portrayal of Al Capone, De Niro put on weight and inserted plugs into his nose to make him look and sound more like the infamous gangster. He also wore silk underwear bought from the firm that had supplied Capone.

Midnight Run (1988) In this comedy-thriller, De Niro played a bounty hunter. To prepare for the role, he went out on the road with a real bounty hunter to see how the job is done. He also learned how to pick a lock for one scene and managed to do it so well that the scene had to be dropped for fear that children would learn the technique from it.

Cape Fear (1991) The actor trained for eight months to get his body fat down to just 3 per cent for his role as Max Cady.

A Bronx Tale (1993) This was De Niro's first film as a director and he was determined that it would be absolutely accurate. He was also playing a part himself – as a bus driver. He trained and then took the New York bus drivers' exam, passing second time round.

ACCOMPLISHED ROLLER-BLADERS

Tom Cruise, Lady Helen Taylor, Janet Jackson, Dustin Hoffman, Warren Beatty, Tiggy Legge-Bourke, Peter Gabriel, Emilio Estevez, Nicole Kidman, Annabel Croft, Robbie Williams, Phillip Schofield, Cher, Viscount Linley, Daryl Hannah, Bruce Willis, Madonna, Sarah Michelle Gellar, Charisma Carpenter, Lisa Scott-Lee

KEEN ANGLERS

Dame Diana Rigg, Chris Tarrant, Jack Charlton, Jeremy Paxman, Steve Guppy, Jack Cunningham, Sean Wilson, Nick Faldo, Robert Redford, Nicholas Soames, Prince Charles, Michael Atherton, Paul Gascoigne, Bernard Cribbins, Anton Rodgers, Barry Hearn, Michael Chang, Fiona Armstrong, Geoff Capes, Michael Barrymore, Robson Green, Paul Young, Kate Groombridge, Tiger Woods, Eric Clapton, Pierce Brosnan, Liam Neeson

KEEN DIVERS

Nick Ross, Nicholas Lyndhurst, Loyd Grossman, John Simpson, Richard E. Grant, David Jason, Jeff Probyn, Chris De Burgh, John Prescott, Sid Owen, Gillian Anderson, Mariella Frostrup, Esther McVey, Catrina Skepper, Nick Carter, Patrick Duffy, Jason Statham (was a professional), Kathleen Quinlan

Adept at needlepoint

Elizabeth Hurley, Dillie Keane, Katie Boyle,
Nanette Newman, Dame Joan Sutherland,
Elizabeth Jane Howard, Wendy Richard, Sian
Phillips, Lea Salonga, Judy Parfitt, Sam West,
Loretta Swit

Keen chess players

**Madonna, Guy Ritchie, Sting, Bono, Jude Law, Ewan McGregor,
Arnold Schwarzenegger, Jennifer Lopez, Stephen Fry, Jonathan
Edwards, Loyd Grossman, Roger Lloyd Pack, Greta Scacchi,
James Galway, Sir Patrick Moore, Martin Amis, Joe Bugner,
Michael Jayston, Dane Bowers, Boris Becker, Al Pacino, Dennis
Quaid, Lennox Lewis, Steve Davis, Keith Allen**

Keen skiers

Ruthie Henshall, Michel
Roux, Jane Asher, Jeremy
Irons, Melanie Griffith, Angus
Deayton, Sandi Toksvig, Patsy Kensit,
Sarah, Duchess of York, Michael
Brandon, Mike Oldfield, Sir Richard
Branson, Elaine Paige, Prince Charles,
David Gower, Sir Roger Moore, Kim
Wilde, Don Johnson, Nick Ross,
Jeremy Paxman, Jason Donovan,
Patsy Palmer, Nicky Clarke,
Tamzin Outhwaite, Jurgen
Prochnow

KEEN WATERSKIERS

Nicky Clarke, Esther McVey, Prince William, Sophie, Countess of Wessex, Minnie Driver, Ruthie Henshall, Richard Dunwoody, David Emanuel, Ian Woosnam, Susan Hampshire, Mark Pitman

KARATE BLACK BELTS

John Fashanu, Sharon Stone, Chris Silverwood, Nigel Mansell, Taki, Phil Spector, Jean Jacques Burnel, Chuck Norris, Glen Murphy, Jennifer James, Gail Porter, Guy Ritchie, Dane Bowers, Danny Grewcock, John Saxon

NB: Emma Bunton's mother is a karate instructor and has taught her daughter to a high standard

REAL-TENNIS PLAYERS

David Gower, Sally Jones, David Troughton, Martina Navratilova, Prince Edward, Gabriela Sabatini, Alan Alda

FENCERS

Marcel Marceau, Neil Diamond, Anita Harris, Bryan Mosley, Sir Rocco Forte, Gene Wilder, J.P. Donleavy, David Acfield, Mick Fleetwood, Bruce Dickinson, Ioan Gruffudd, Antonio Banderas, Sylvester Stallone, Robson Green, Sir Christopher Bland (also fenced in the Olympics), Catherine Zeta-Jones, Elijah Wood

ADEPT AT JUDO

Laetitia Casta (Brown belt)

Tony Slattery (Black belt)

Honor Blackman (Brown belt)

Tony Bullimore (Black belt)

David Lee Roth (Black belt)

Kelly Holmes (Blue belt)

Manuel Noriega (Black belt)

Nigel Mansell (Black belt)

Vladimir Putin (Black belt)

Dawn Airey (Black belt)

James Cagney (Black belt)

KEEN HORSERIDERS

Charisma Carpenter, Kate Moss, Shane Filan, Kylie Minogue, Frazer Hines, Liza Goddard, Keith Chegwin, Jimmy Hill, Cybill Shepherd, Jane Seymour, Janet Jackson, Angela Rippon, Tracy Edwards, Prue Leith, Alan Coren, Lynn Redgrave, Alan Titchmarsh, Joe Brown, Michael Kitchen, Sir Chay Blyth, Patsy Kensit, Tracey Ullman, Lucy Speed, David Emanuel, Michael Brandon, Jeremy Irons, Sue Carpenter

POLO PLAYERS

Kenny Jones, Prince Charles, Kerry Packer, Trevor Eve, William Devane, Stacy Keach, Stefanie Powers, Rory Bremner, Jodie Kidd, Prince William, Ginger Baker, Prince Harry

GOOD AT DIY

Nick Faldo, Harrison Ford (a former carpenter), Courteney Cox, Brad Pitt, Jennifer Lopez, David Beckham, Jeremy Irons, Colin Montgomerie, Liza Tarbuck, David Jason

POKER PLAYERS

Brad Pitt, Steve Davis, Jimmy White, David Mamet, Bill Gates, Martin Amis, Matt Damon, Stephen Hendry, Keith Allen, Raj Persaud, Patrick Marber, Ben Affleck, David Schwimmer

KEEN KNITTERS

Julia Roberts, Cameron Diaz, Russell Crowe, Uma Thurman, Winona Ryder, Goldie Hawn, Naomi Campbell, Julianne Moore, David Duchovny, Kate Beckinsale, Bridget Fonda, Sandra Bullock, Anjelica Huston, Kate Moss, Eva Herzigova, Ulrika Jonsson, Craig Charles, David Arquette, Geri Halliwell, Madonna, Iman, Hilary Swank, Daryl Hannah, Sarah Jessica Parker

CARTOONISTS/CARICATURISTS

David Beckham, Moby, Patricia Cornwell, Will Self, George Clooney

RELIGION

Psalm 117 (O praise the LORD, all ye nations: praise him, all ye people. For his merciful kindness is great toward us: and the truth of the LORD endureth for ever. Praise ye the LORD) is the shortest chapter in the Bible: it is also the centre chapter in the Bible. However, the middle two *verses* of the Bible are in Psalm 118.

49 different kinds of food are mentioned in the Bible.

The religion of the Todas people of southern India forbids them to cross any kind of bridge.

On 1 July 2003, the First Baptist Church in Forest, Ohio was struck by lightning just as the visiting evangelist was telling the congregation that 'God's voice often sounds like thunder'.

Some saints in the Middle Ages were dirty because they thought it would bring them closer to God.

During the First Crusade, a band of religious hysterics marched behind a goose they believed was filled with the Holy Spirit.

Belief in the existence of vacuums used to be punishable by death under church law.

Playing music containing augmented 4th chords was avoided because it was thought to invoke the Devil.

There's a temple in Sri Lanka dedicated to a tooth of the Buddha.

In 1654, Bishop Ussher of Ireland, having analysed all the 'begats' in Genesis, concluded that planet Earth had been created at 9 a.m. on 26 October 4004BC, a Thursday.

St John was the only one of the 12 apostles to die a natural death.

Most of the villains in the Bible have red hair.

David is the most common name in the Bible. Jesus is second.

Pope Paul IV was so outraged when he saw the naked bodies on the ceiling of the Sistine Chapel that he ordered Michelangelo to paint garments on them.

The term 'devil's advocate' comes from the Roman Catholic Church. When considering whether someone should be created a saint, a devil's advocate was appointed to give an alternative view.

The word Sunday is not in the Bible.

A GUIDE TO DIFFERENT RELIGIONS

Taoism: Shit happens.

Zen: What is the sound of shit happening?

Hinduism: This shit's happened before.

Buddhism: If shit happens, it isn't really shit.

Islam: If shit happens, it's the will of Allah.

Protestantism: Shit happens because we don't work hard enough.

Catholicism: Shit happens because we are bad.

Christian Fundamentalism: Shit happens because the Bible says so.

Jehovah's Witness: Knock, knock. 'Shit happens.'

Judaism: Why does shit always happen to us?

Agnosticism: We don't know shit.

Atheism: No shit.

Hare Krishna: Shit happens – rama rama ding ding.

Rastafarianism: Let's smoke this shit.

SCIENTOLOGISTS

Tom Cruise, Chick Corea, John Travolta, Priscilla Presley, Kirstie Alley, Isaac Hayes, Anne Archer, Kelly Preston, Mimi Rogers, Sharon Stone

PRACTISING BUDDHISTS

Uma Thurman, Stephanie Beacham, Keanu Reeves, Cindy Crawford, Susan Sarandon, Sandie Shaw, Woody Harrelson, Tina Turner, Courtney Love, Harrison Ford, Richard Gere, Koo Stark, Oliver Stone, Pamela Stephenson, Claudia Schiffer, Lulu, Annie Lennox, Jim Carrey, Björk

ROMAN CATHOLICS

Christina Aguilera, Farrah Fawcett, Eddie Van Halen, Nick Nolte, Rosie O'Donnell, Regis Philbin, Celine Dion, Rupert Everett, Ben Affleck, Jean-Claude Van Damme, Antonio Banderas, Martin Scorsese, Nicolas Cage, Camille Paglia, Brigitte Bardot, Sylvester Stallone, Pierce Brosnan, Pele, Lara Flynn Boyle, Sir Paul McCartney, Catherine Deneuve, Faye Dunaway, Mel Gibson, Martin Sheen, Liam Neeson, Madonna, Cyndi Lauper, Arnold Schwarzenegger, Brooke Shields, Sean Penn, Bianca Jagger, Al Pacino, Robert De Niro, John McEnroe, Anne Bancroft, Bill Murray, Luciano Pavarotti, Sophia Loren, Alanis Morissette, Natalie Imbruglia, Heather Graham, Tommy Hilfiger, Claudia Schiffer,

Gabriel Byrne, Danny DeVito, Jim Carrey, Martin Short, Joe Pesci, Catherine Zeta-Jones, Jennifer Lopez, Salma Hayek, John Cusack, Haley Joel Osment, Matt Dillon, Rachel Hunter, Kelsey Grammer, Lucy Lawless, Chris O'Donnell, Gwen Stefani, Alyssa Milano, Noel & Liam Gallagher, Patsy Kensit, Brendan Fraser, Juliette Binoche, Ray Liotta, Mira Sorvino, Elvis Costello, Mary Tyler Moore, Mia Farrow, Alan Alda, Meg Ryan, Melissa Joan Hart, Tom Clancy, Dan Aykroyd, Aidan Quinn, Jack Nicholson, Denise Richards, J.D. Salinger, Charlotte Church, Minnie Driver, Joey Fatone, Lea Salonga, Jon Bon Jovi, Pete Postlethwaite, Judy Davis, Victoria Principal, Mandy Moore, Anne Robinson, Michael Crawford, Christy Turlington, Gloria Estefan, Axl Rose, Tracy Shaw, Ann Widdecombe, Cherie Blair, Julian Clary, Jodie Foster, Ray Liotta, Anna Nicole Smith, Diego Maradona, Belinda Carlisle, Gary Lineker, Cilla Black, Jimmy Tarbuck, Jimmy Saville, Pat Cash, Goran Ivanisevic, Franz Beckenbauer, Elijah Wood, Bruce Springsteen, Delia Smith, Chris De Burgh, Whoopi Goldberg, Johnny Vaughan

JEWS

Alicia Silverstone, Gwyneth Paltrow, David Copperfield, William Shatner, Randy Newman, Yasmine Bleeth, Ben Stiller, Jerry Seinfeld, Harrison Ford, Natalie Portman, Sarah Jessica Parker, Joel Stransky, Gary Kasparov, Calvin Klein, Debra Winger, Geraldo Rivera, David Blaine, Rodney

Dangerfield, Artie Shaw, Dame Elizabeth Taylor (convert), Harvey Keitel, Leonard Nimoy, Tony Curtis, Gene Simmons, Barry Manilow, Hank Azaria, Barbra Streisand, Neil Diamond, Manfred Mann, Leonard Cohen, Adam Sandler, Sacha Baron Cohen, Vidal Sassoon, Herb Alpert, Lauren Bacall, Dyan Cannon, Peter Green, Cyd Charisse, Gloria Steinem, Jerry Springer, Marcel Marceau, Carly Simon, Roman Polanski, Phil Spector, Mel Torme, Jody Scheckter, Larry King, Howard Stern, Felicity Kendal (convert), Neil Sedaka, Norman Mailer, James Caan, Lou Reed, Paul Simon, Art Garfunkel, Bette Midler, Billy Crystal, Billy Joel, Geraldo Rivera, Henry Winkler, Goldie Hawn, Rachel Stevens, Winona Ryder, Carole King, Bob Dylan, Noah Wyle, Burt Bacharach, Helen Reddy, Ruth Prawer Jhabvala, Dame Alicia Markova, Barbara Walters

JEHOVAH'S WITNESSES

Hank B. Marvin, Venus & Serena Williams, The Jacksons (although Michael joined the Nation of Islam in December 2003), Prince, Geri Halliwell (raised as one by her mother), Dwight Eisenhower (raised as one), Roy Harper, Mickey Spillane, Viv Nicholson

LUTHERANS

Loni Anderson, Beau Bridges, Jeff Bridges, David Hasselhoff, William Hurt, William H. Macy, Ann-Margret, David Soul, Sally Struthers, Liv Ullman, Bruce Willis, Gary Larson, Theodore Geisel (aka Dr Seuss), Elke Sommer, Dana Carvey, Johann Sebastian Bach, John Woo, General Norman Schwarzkopf, Edwin Meese, William Rehnquist, Kris Kristofferson, Lyle Lovett, John Mellencamp, Dag Hammarskjöld, Soren Kierkegaard, Dr Albert Schweitzer, Dietrich Bonhoeffer, Martin Niemoeller, Lou Gehrig, Andy North, Duffy Waldorf, Garrison Keillor

MORMONS

Rick Schroeder, Matthew Modine, Robert Walker, The Osmonds, Gladys Knight, Randy Bachman

QUAKERS

Dame Judi Dench, Sheila Hancock, Paul Eddington, Joel Cadbury, Margaret Drabble, Richard Nixon, James Michener, Anna Wing, A.S. Byatt, Herbert Hoover, David Lean, Cheryl Tiegs, Bradley Whitford

BAPTISTS

Britney Spears, John Bunyan, Warren G. Harding, Harry S. Truman, Bill Clinton, Clarence Thomas, Newt Gingrich, Al Gore, Martin Luther King,

Jesse Jackson, Payne Stewart, Jonathan Edwards, Glen Campbell, Donna Summer, Jessica Simpson, Otis Redding, Aretha Franklin, John Grisham, Chuck Norris, Billy Graham

CONVERTED TO ISLAM

Michael Jackson, Muhammad Ali, Jemima Khan, Mike Tyson, Malcolm X, Gérard Depardieu (although he later converted back to Christianity), Art Blakey, Cat Stevens, Chris Eubank

CHRISTIAN SCIENTISTS

John Simpson, Joyce Grenfell, Ginger Rogers, Jim Henson, Dame Gwen Ffrangcon-Davies, H.R. Haldeman, Sir Harold Hobson, Dame Edith Evans, Doris Day, Carol Channing, Lady Nancy Astor, Robert Duvall, Joan Crawford, Val Kilmer

NB The parents of Sir V.S. Pritchett, Dame Elizabeth Taylor, Peter Barkworth, Jean Harlow, Ellen DeGeneres and Dudley Moore were all Christian Scientists

BORN-AGAIN CHRISTIANS

Mandy Smith, David Suchet, Jason Robinson, Charlene Tilton, Alvin Stardust, Glenn Hoddle, Andre Agassi, Marcus Gayle, Rosemary Conley, Cyrille Regis, Tommy Cannon, Bobby Ball, Samantha Fox, Tiffany, Gina G, Cuba Gooding Jr, Jane Russell

INTO KABBALAH

Madonna, Guy Ritchie, Demi Moore, Sir Elton John, Sir Mick Jagger, Jeff Goldblum, Naomi Campbell, Dame Elizabeth Taylor, Barbra Streisand, Courtney Love

LAY PREACHERS

Sir David Frost, David Blunkett, George Foreman, Dr Brian Mawhinney, Peter Pollock, Jimmy Armfield, Alan Beith, Paul Daniels, Frank Williams (the vicar in *Dad's Army*), Sir James Anderton, Nigel Benn

CHILDREN OF LAY PREACHERS

Frank Bruno, David Bellamy, Baroness Thatcher, Brian Moore, John Poulson, Jonah Lomu, Alistair Cooke, James Baldwin, Paula Jones, Herol Graham, Mark Thomas

CONSIDERED BECOMING PRIESTS

Joseph Stalin, David Alton, Christopher Marlowe, Ben Vereen, Morten Harket, Alan Bennett, Charles Darwin, Kenny Everett, Mike McShane, Bob Guccione, Bernhard Langer, Gabriel Byrne, Nigel Pivaro, Roberto Benigni, Tom Cruise (aged 14, he enrolled in a seminary but dropped out after a year), John Woo, Johnny Vegas (trained to be a priest but quit after getting drunk on the clerics' sherry), Stephen Tompkinson, Pete Postlethwaite

CONSIDERED BECOMING RABBIS

Gene Simmons, Ian Mikardo, Leonard Bernstein

NB Jackie Mason was a rabbi

MIGHT HAVE BECOME NUNS

Heather Graham (her parents had ambitions for her to become one)

Kristin Scott Thomas (at 16, she enrolled in a convent school with a view to becoming a nun)

Cher ('There was a time when I nearly became a nun myself, but it didn't last long')

Zoë Wanamaker ('Despite being born Jewish …')

Francesca Annis
(wanted to be
a nun)

AGNOSTICS

Brian Sewell, Martin Amis, Uma Thurman, Michael Palin, Ken Livingstone, Nicky Campbell, Esther Rantzen, David Bowie, Professor Stephen Hawking, Carrie Fisher, James Taylor, Sean Penn, Larry King, Roman Polanski, Matt Groening, Al Stewart

ATHEISTS

Dr David Starkey, Sir John Mortimer, Paul McKenna, Raymond Briggs, Dave Allen, Billy Bragg, Dame Mary Peters, Robin Cook, Bill Gates, Claire Rayner, Woody Allen, Sir Richard Branson, Arthur C. Clarke, Amanda Donohoe, Patrick Duffy, Larry Flynt, Dario Fo, Jodie Foster, Debbie Harry, Margot Kidder, Clive Barker, Alex Cox, David Cronenberg, Brian Eno, John Fowles, Kinky Friedman, Janeane Garofalo, Roy Hattersley, Björk, John Carpenter, Fidel Castro, Harvey Fierstein, Angelina Jolie, Neil Jordan, Neil Kinnock, John Malkovich, Barry Manilow, Warren Mitchell, Desmond Morris, Camille Paglia, Steven Soderbergh, Gore Vidal, James Watson, Nick Mason, Sir Ian McKellen, Terry Pratchett, Howard Stern, Michael Stipe, Tom Lehrer, Mike Leigh, Alexander McQueen, Arthur Miller, Randy Newman, Jack Nicholson, Gary Numan, James Randi, Christopher Reeve, Griff Rhys Jones, Captain Sensible, Donald Sutherland, Julia Sweeney

FLAGS

The state flag of Alaska was designed by a 13-year-old boy.

Egypt, Dominica, Mexico, Fiji, Zambia and Kiribati all have birds on their flags.

Texas is the only US state allowed to fly its state flag at the same height as the US flag.

The Dominican Republic has the only national flag with a bible on it.

Cyprus has its outline on its flag.

Nepal is the only country without a rectangular flag.

Libya has the only flag that's one colour (green) with nothing else on it.

BANISHED WORDS

Since 1976, Lake Superior State University in Michigan, USA, has been publishing its annual list of 'Words Banished from the Queen's English for Mis-use, Over-use and General Uselessness'.

THE 2004 LIST

Metrosexual – An urban male who pays too much attention to his appearance.

X – As in the 'Generation-X demographic, X-files, Xtreme, Windows XP and X-Box.

Punked – As in bamboozled, duped, flimflammed, hornswoggled.

Place stamp here – Can we [the US] legitimately claim to be a superpower if we need to be reminded to put a stamp on an envelope?

Companion animals – They're called PETS.

Bling or **bling-bling** or any of its variations – Street slang for items of luxury.

LOL and other abbreviated 'e-mail speak', including the symbol '@' when used in advertising and elsewhere.

Embedded journalist – As used in the Iraq War.

Smoking gun – Another one that came from Iraq, but is widely used elsewhere.

Shock and awe – Still another from Iraq.

Captured alive – Well, what other way are you going to be captured? Maybe 'found dead' or 'discovered dead' but never 'captured dead'.

Shots rang out – Shots don't 'ring' unless you are standing too close to the muzzle, and in that case you don't need the reporter telling you about it.

Ripped from the headlines – TV shows are often described as being 'ripped from the headlines'. Kicking and screaming, no doubt.

In harm's way – Who is he, and why would you want to get in his way?

Sweat like a pig – Pigs do not have sweat glands; that is why they roll in mud to cool themselves.

Handcrafted latte – To apply 'handcrafted' to the routine tasks of the modern-day equivalents of soda jerks cheapens the whole concept of handicraft.

Sanitary landfill – What happened to the county or city dump?

SOME OF THE BANISHED WORDS FROM 1976–2003 IN ALPHABETICAL ORDER

24/7 **2000**

Academically fragile **2001**

Academically ineligible **1993**

Active possibility **1977**

Actual facts **1991**

Adults over 21 **1988**

Afterfeel **1987**

Alcohol-related drunk driving **1989**

All except **1990**

All-time record **1982**

Almost exactly **1990**

Alternative lifestyle **1988**

Always consistent **1994**

Armed and dangerous **1996**

Armed gunman **1993**

As if **1997**

As per **2003**

At risk **2000**

At this point in time **1976**

Awesome **1984**

Babyboomers **1989**

Ballpark figure **1980**

Bare naked **1985**

Basically **1984, 1986, 1993**

Been there, done that **1996**

Begs the question **2001**

Best-kept secret **1990**

Big time **1992**

Bill Clinton & Monica Lewinsky **1999**

The bottom line **1979, 1992**

Brainstorm/brainstorming **2002**

'Bring them to justice' or 'Bring the evil-doers to justice' **2002**

Build-down **1984**

The bullet went all the way through the body **1983**

By and large **1987**

Campaign rhetoric **1981**

Car-jacking **2002**

Cautiously optimistic **1992**

Ceremonialization **1984**

Chad **2001**

Chill out **1980**

Classic **1982, 1989**

Clearly ambiguous **1994**

Close proximity **1990**

Close to everything **1991**

Closure **1996**

Community **1992**

Completely empty **1993**

Conceptualize **1983**

Connect or hook up **1992**

Consumer confidence **1995**

Conventional wisdom **1993**

Courtesy call **1999**

Cult classic **1989**

Cutting edge **1988**

Cyber **1996**

Dead meat **1991**

Dead serious **1994**

Definite possibilities **1993**

De-install **1987**

Delay due to an earlier accident **2002**

De-plane **1981**

Docudrama **1989**

Doing the _____ thing **1997**

Don't (even) go there **1997**

Done deal **1996**

Done in good taste **1986**

Dot.com **2001**

Downsizing **1993**

Down time **1997**

Drug czar **1990**

Dude **2001**

Dysfunctional **1994**

'E'-anything **2000**

Each and every one of you **1996**

Eh **1979**

Enclosed please find **1985, 1989**

End result **1991**

Exact same **1981, 1990**

Extreme **2003**

Faith-based **2002**

False pretenses **1991**

Family values **1995**

Filmed before a live studio audience **1983, 1987, 1990**

Final destination **2001**

First time ever **1982, 1983**

Forced relaxation **1989**

Foreign imports **1987**

Foreseeable future **2002**

Free gift **1988**

Fresh frozen **1989**

Friendly fire **2002**

Gathered together **1994**

Get a life **1997**

Giving 110 per cent **1998**

Grass roots **1993**

Gridlock **1993**

Gun control **1994**

Gut feeling **1983**

Hands-on participatory experience **1987**

Happy camper **1993**

Have a good one! **2001**

Having said that **2003**

He/she **1994**

The health care delivery system/industry **1987**

Hello!? **1999**

High tech **1984**

The honest truth **1991**

Hopefully **1978**

Humanitarian **1995**

I feel your pain **1995**

I know where I'm coming from **1978**

But I don't know where you're coming from **1978**

I see what you are saying **1992**

If ____ then the terrorists win **2002**

I'm 150 per cent behind you **1995**

I'm like **1997**

I'm talkin ____ here **1987**

In my humble opinion **1992**

In terms of **1982**

In the public interest **1980**

In the wake of … **2002**

In your face **1993**

Incentivize, -vizing, -vized **1983**

Information superhighway **1995**

Infotainment **1986, 1989**

Input **1976**

Interface **1980**

Issues **2000**

It's the pits **1980**

Jumbo shrimp **1995**

Large size petites **1990**

Let's do lunch **1986**

Level playing field **1992**

Like (see also 'I'm like') **1997**

Like I said **1986**

Listen up **1983**

Living in poverty **1988**

Longer hours **1991**

Managing terrorism **1989**

Mandate **1985**

Manual recount by hand **2001**

Material breach **2003**

Mc(anything) **1986**

Mean-spirited **1995**

Meaningful dialogue **1976**

Millennium **2000**

Mission statement **1996**

Mopping-up operation **1991**

Moral majority **1981**

More importantly **1992**

More than happy **1994**

The more you buy, the more you save **1990**

Most complete **1993**

Mother of all ____ **1994**

Multi-tasking **1997**

Must-see TV **2003**

Near miss **1985**

Negative growth **2001**

Neonatal unit **1987**

Networking **1988**

New innovation **1990**

New kid on the street/block **1984**

Nine-eleven (9-11) **2002**

No-brainer **2002**

No problem **1980**

Not **1993**

Now, more than ever **2003**

On a _____ basis **1991**

On a roll **1984, 1988**

On the ground **2003**

Ongoing **1984, 1986, 1993**

Online **1996**

Out-sourcing **1997**

Overview **1992**

Parenting skills **1991**

Past experience **1994**

Past history **1981**

The patient did not fulfill his wellness potential **1987**

Paying my dues **1981**

Peacekeeping force **1996**

Peel-and-eat shrimp **2003**

Percent pure **1995**

Perfectly candid **1977**

Perimeters/parameters **1979**

Political reality **1983**

Political strongman **1990**

Politically correct **1994**

Post-consumer products **1995**

Post-modern **1984**

Potential hazard **1987**

Pre-board **1980**

Pre-plan **1983**

Pre-planning **1989**

Prequel **1985**

Preventative maintenance **1987**

Prioritize **1978**

Proactive **1991, 1993**

Process **1978**

Pushing the envelope **1995**

Quality of life **2000**

Quality time **1985**

The race card **1996**

Read my lips **1989**

Reaffirm **1988**

Reaganomics **1983**

Reality TV **2002**

Really **1979**

The reason is because **1985**

Refusenik **1988**

Rename it something else **2002**

Reverse discrimination **2003**

Road rage **2000**

Rocket scientist **1991**

Rush hour **1990**

Safe haven **1993**

Safe sex **1988**

Same difference **1987**

Sanction **1992**

Scenario **1976, 1991**

Sea change **2000**

Secluded privacy **1988**

Senseless murder **1984**

Serves no useful purpose **1981**

Signage **1987**

Situation **1978**

Sketchy details **1994**

Slight glitch **1995**

So **1999**

Somewhere down the road **1979**

Sound bite **1989**

Speaks to **2001**

Spearhead **1994**

Spin doctor **1989**

State of the art **1983**

Step up/step it up **1999**

Stun **1999**

Sucks **1995**

Supermarket-fresh **1989**

Superstar **1984**

Surely if we can send a man to the moon we can ____ **1980**

Surgical strike **2002**

Surrounding environs **1992**

Sworn affidavit **2002**

Synergy **2002**

A tad **1987**

Talk to the hand **1998**

Take it to the next level **1998**

Target audience **1995**

Task **1988**

That said **2003**

There you go **1987**

Thinking outside the box **2000**

This program was recorded before a live audience **1983**

Time frame **1980**

To be perfectly honest with you **1992**

To die for **1995**

To liaison with **1982**

Too right **1989**

Total capacity of this room limited to 100 persons **1989**

Totally unique **2002**

Touch base **1996**

Track record **1991**

Trained professional **1993**

Turned up missing **1987**

Two twins **1991**

Undisclosed, secret location **2003**

Unplugged **1996**

Unprecedented new **2002**

Unrequested leave of absence **1991**

Untimely death **2003**

Up front **1992**

Up to speed **1985**

Use only as directed **1988**

User friendly **1984**

Utilize **1987**

Vast majority **1995**

Very unique **1983, 2002**

Viable **1976**

Viable alternative **1979, 1992**

Victimless crime **1993**

Virtual reality **1996**

Vision statement **1996**

Visual view **1986**

Visually eyeball the runway **1985**

Void where prohibited **1988**

Wake-up call **2000**

We must focus our attention **1983**

Weapons of mass destruction **2003**

Went ballistic **1993**

What are you into? **1979**

Whatever **1997**

Whatsup? **1998**

Win-win **1993**

Window of opportunity **1991**

Working mother **1983**

World class **1982, 1993**

Y2K **1999**

Yadda yadda yadda **1998**

Yes **1985**

Yo **1990**

You go, girl **1997**

You got it **1985**

You'd better believe **1978**

Your call is very important to us **1996**

Yuppie **1986**

Zero-percent increase **1991**

LENNON AND MCCARTNEY SONGS NEVER RELEASED BY THE BEATLES (APART FROM ON THE ANTHOLOGIES)

'Bad To Me' (Billy J. Kramer and the Dakotas)

'Nobody I Know' (Peter and Gordon)

'Like Dreamers Do' (The Applejacks)

'Tip Of My Tongue' (Tommy Quickly)

'Step Inside Love' (Cilla Black)

'That Means A Lot' (P.J. Proby)

'A World Without Love' (Peter and Gordon)

'I'm In Love' (The Fourmost)

'One And One Is Two' (The Strangers with Mike Shannon)

'It's For You' (Cilla Black)

'Hello Little Girl' (The Fourmost)

'I'll Keep You Satisfied' (Billy J. Kramer and the Dakotas)

COVERS OF BEATLES SONGS

'Got To Get You Into My Life' (Joe Pesci)

'Something' (Telly Savalas)

'Lucy In The Sky With Diamonds' (William Shatner)

'I Am The Walrus' (Jim Carrey)

'Love Me Do' (The Brady Bunch)

'A Hard Day's Night' (Peter Sellers)

'Blackbird' (Kevin Spacey)

'I Want You (She's So Heavy)' (Donald Pleasence)

'We Can Work It Out' (George Burns)

'Come Together' (Robin Williams)

'When I'm 64' (Jon Pertwee)

'All My Loving' (Alvin and the Chipmunks)

'Hey Jude' (Tottenham Hotspur FC)

'Yellow Submarine' (Milton Berle)

'Ob-La-Di Ob-La-Da' (Jack Wild)

'I Want To Hold Your Hand' (Metal Mickey)

'Maxwell Silver Hammer' (Jessica Mitford)

'Mean Mr Mustard' (Frankie Howerd)

'Can't Buy Me Love' (Pinky and Perky)

BEATLES SONGS AND THEIR WORKING TITLES

'Hello Goodbye' – Hello Hello

'A Day In The Life' – In The Life Of

'Yesterday' – Scrambled Eggs

'It's Only Love' – That's A Nice Hat

'Think For Yourself' – Won't Be There With You

'Flying' – Aerial Tour Instrumental

'Eleanor Rigby' – Miss Daisy Hawkins

'Thank You Girl' – Thank You Little Girl

'Love You To' – Granny Smith

'I Saw Her Standing There' – Seventeen

ACTS SIGNED TO APPLE RECORDS

Mary Hopkin, Badfinger, James Taylor, The Black Dyke Mills Band, Hot Chocolate, Ronnie Spector, Billy Preston, Jackie Lomax

SONGS ABOUT THE BEATLES

'All I Want For Christmas Is A Beatle' (Dora Bryan)
The most successful Beatles' tribute record in the UK – it reached No. 20 in 1963.

'We Love You Beatles' (The Carefrees)
The most successful Beatles' tribute song in the US – it reached No. 39 in 1964.

'My Girlfriend Wrote A Letter To The Beatles' (The Four Preps)
And guess what? They didn't write back.

'I Wanna Be A Beatle' (Gene Cornish and the Unbeatables)
Soon after recording this they changed their name to The Young Rascals (and had hits including 'Groovin'').

'Ringo I Love You' (Bonnie Jo Mason)
Bonnie Jo Mason was a pseudonym for Cher.

'A Beatle I Want To Be' (Sonny Curtis)
Sonny was one of Buddy Holly's Crickets – and the Fab Four had named themselves after The Crickets.

'I Hate The Beatles' (Allan Sherman)
Sherman was an American humorous singer whose only British hit was 'Hello Muddah, Hello Faddah'.

'Get Back Beatles' (Gerard Kenny)
Kenny later wrote the song 'New York New York' (not the Sinatra one but the one that goes 'New York New York, so good they named it twice') and also the music for the theme song for *Minder*.

'I'm Better Than The Beatles'
(Brad Berwick and the Bugs) History would suggest otherwise …

'The Beatles' Barber' (Scott Douglas)
About a man who has been put out of work because
the Fabs never have their mop tops cut. Or something.

'Ringo For President'
(Rolf Harris) American presidents have to be American – which might
explain why the song bombed.

ARTISTS WHO HAD BIGGER HITS WITH LENNON AND MCCARTNEY SONGS THAN THE BEATLES DID

Billy J. Kramer and the Dakotas: 'Do You Want To Know A Secret?'

The Overlanders: 'Michelle'

Joe Cocker: 'With A Little Help From My Friends'

Marmalade: 'Ob-La-Di Ob-La-Da'

Earth Wind And Fire: 'Got To Get You Into My Life'

Steve Harley and Cockney Rebel: 'Here Comes The Sun'

Emmylou Harris: 'Here There And Everywhere'

Kenny Ball and his Jazzmen: 'When I'm 64'

Billy Bragg: 'She's Leaving Home'

SINGERS WHO REFER TO THEMSELVES BY NAME IN SONGS

'The Universal' (The Small Faces – Steve Marriott on vocals 1968)

'I Feel For You' (Chaka Khan 1984)

'Blue Motel Room' (Joni Mitchell 1976)

'My Name Is Prince' (Prince 1992)

'Sweet Baby James' (James Taylor 1970)

'Strong Persuader' (Robert Cray 1986)

'Creeque Alley' (The Mamas and the Papas – Mama Cass Elliot on vocals 1967)

'The Mind of Love' (k.d. lang 1992)

'Float On' (The Floaters – all of them individually 1977)

'Wannabe' (The Spice Girls – all of them individually 1996)

'Brooklyn Roads' (Neil Diamond 1976)

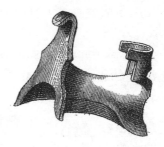

DUETS

Madeline Kahn & Frankie Laine on 'Blazing Saddles' in 1973

Catherine Zeta-Jones & David Essex on 'True Love Ways' 1994

Rock Hudson & Rod McKuen on 'Love Of The Common Celebrities' 1970

Peter Sellers & Sophia Loren on 'Goodness Gracious Me' 1959

Don Johnson & Barbra Streisand on 'Till I Loved You' (Love Theme From Goya) 1988

Beavis and Butt-Head & Cher on 'I Got You Babe' 1994

Bruce Willis & The Pointer Sisters on 'Respect Yourself' 1987

Ewan McGregor & Nicole Kidman on 'Come What May' 2001

Michael J. Fox & Joan Jett on 'Light of Day' 1986

Victoria Principal & Andy Gibb on 'All I Have To Do Is Dream' 1981

Joan Collins & Bing Crosby on 'Let's Not Be Sensible' 1962

Alain Delon & Shirley Bassey on the album *Shirley Bassey & Alain Delon* 1984

PEOPLE IMMORTALIZED IN SONG TITLES

Smokey Robinson – 'When Smokey Sings' (ABC 1987)

Spencer Tracy – 'He Looks Like Spencer Tracy Now' (Deacon Blue 1988)

Grigori Rasputin – 'Rasputin' (Boney M 1978)

Buddy Holly – 'I Feel Like Buddy Holly' (Alvin Stardust 1984)

Otis Redding – 'Ode To Otis Redding' (Mark Johnson 1968)

Elvis Presley – 'Elvis Presley And America' (U2 1984)

Dolly Parton – 'Dolly Parton's Guitar' (Lee Hazlewood 1977)

Jackie Wilson – 'Jackie Wilson Said' (Van Morrison 1972)

Bo Diddley – 'The Story Of Bo Diddley' (The Animals 1964)

Hank Williams – 'The Night Hank Williams Came to Town' (Johnny Cash 1986)

Sir Michael Caine – 'Michael Caine' (Madness 1984)

Dickie Davies – 'Dickie Davies Eyes' (Half Man Half Biscuit 1986)

Benito Mussolini – 'Do The Mussolini' (Cabaret Voltaire 1978)

Robert De Niro – 'Robert De Niro's Waiting' (Bananarama 1984)

Bonnie Parker & Clyde Barrow – 'Ballad of Bonnie And Clyde' (Georgie Fame 1967)

James Callaghan – 'Jim Callaghan' (Mr John Dowie 1977)

Sean Penn – 'Sean Penn Blues' (Lloyd Cole and the Commotions 1987)

Christine Keeler – 'Christine Keeler' (The Glaxo Babies 1979)

Kaiser Wilhelm II – 'I Was Kaiser Bill's Batman' (Whistling Jack Smith 1967)

Aretha Franklin – 'Aretha, Sing One For Me' (George Jackson 1971)

Michael Jackson – 'Dear Michael' (Kim Fields 1984)

Lee Remick – 'Lee Remick' (The Go-Betweens 1978)

Bette Davis – 'Bette Davis Eyes' (Kim Carnes 1981)

John Wayne – 'John Wayne Is Big Leggy' (Haysi Fantayzee 1982)

Tom Baker – 'Tom Baker' (Human League 1980)

Linda Evans – 'Linda Evans' (The Walkabouts 1987)

Vincent van Gogh – 'Vincent' (Don McLean 1972)

Andy Warhol – 'Andy Warhol' (David Bowie 1971)

Graham Greene – 'Graham Greene' (John Cale 1973)

Jim Reeves – 'Tribute To Jim Reeves' (Larry Cunningham 1964)

Marvin Gaye – 'Marvin' (Edwin Starr 1984)

Nerys Hughes – 'I Hate Nerys Hughes' (Half Man Half Biscuit 1985)

Pure trivia

It is physically impossible for pigs to look up into the sky.

The man who invented FM radio was Edwin Armstrong. The first men to use FM radio to communicate with Earth from the Moon's surface were Edwin 'Buzz' Aldrin and Neil Armstrong.

Iceland consumes more Coca-Cola per capita than any other nation.

Camel-hair brushes are made from squirrel hair.

Genghis Khan's original name was Temujin. He started out as a goatherd.

The Lazy Susan is named after Thomas Edison's daughter. He invented it to impress a gathering of industrialists and inventors.

Mickey Mouse's ears are always turned to the front, no matter which direction his nose is pointing.

Cows give more milk when they listen to music.

Mozart never went to school.

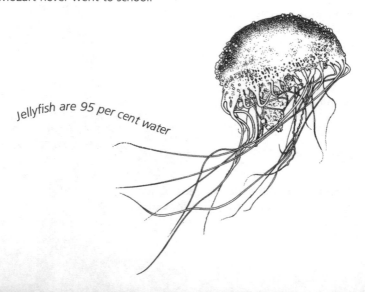

Jellyfish are 95 per cent water

Nanotechnology has produced a guitar no bigger than a blood cell. The guitar, 10 micrometres long, has strings which can be strummed.

7 per cent of the entire Irish barley crop goes into the making of Guinness.

To see a rainbow, you must have your back to the sun.

Rubber bands last longer when refrigerated.

South Africa used to have two official languages. Now it has eleven.

On 29 March 1848, Niagara Falls stopped flowing for 30 hours because of an ice jam blocking the Niagara river.

The national anthem of Greece is 158 verses long.

The original Guinness Brewery in Dublin has a 6,000-year lease.

Since 1896, the beginning of the modern Olympics, only Greece and Australia have participated in every games.

Thomas Edison, the inventor of the light bulb, was afraid of the dark.

The Albanian language, one of Europe's oldest, isn't derived from any other language.

Abraham Lincoln's Gettysburg Address was just 267 words long.

Men of the Walibri tribe of central Australia greet each other by shaking each other's penis instead of each other's hand.

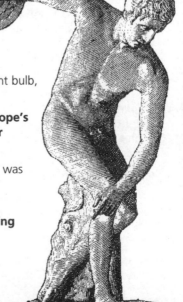

Huge wine jugs were often used by the ancient Greeks as coffins.

Wade Morrison, the inventor of Dr Pepper, named the drink after Dr Charles Pepper who had given him his first job.

Bugs Bunny was originally called 'Happy Rabbit'.

Mao Tse-Tung never brushed his teeth but washed his mouth with tea instead.

The average four-year-old child asks over 400 questions a day.

The oldest living thing in the world is a creosote bush in south-western California, which is more than 11,000 years old.

The average ratio of yellow kernels to white kernels in a bag of popcorn is 9:1.

The expression 'second string', meaning replacement or back-up, comes from the Middle Ages. An archer always carried a second string in case the one on his bow broke.

Counting how many times a cricket chirps in 15 seconds and then adding 40 to that number will tell you roughly what the outside temperature is in Fahrenheit.

Studies indicate that weightlifters working out in blue gyms can handle heavier weights.

Pepper was sold in individual grains during Elizabethan times.

215 pairs of jeans can be made with one bale of cotton.

ALL THE WINNERS OF THE GRAMMY FOR BEST NEW ARTIST

2003: Evanescence

2002: Norah Jones

2001: Alicia Keys

2000: Shelby Lynne

1999: Christina Aguilera

1998: Lauryn Hill

1997: Paula Cole

1996: LeAnn Rimes

1995: Hootie & The Blowfish

1994: Sheryl Crow

1993: Toni Braxton

1992: Arrested Development

1991: Marc Cohn

1990: Mariah Carey

1989: Awarded to Milli Vanilli but later withdrawn

1988: Tracy Chapman

1987: Jody Watley

1986: Bruce Hornsby and the Range

1985: Sade

1984: Cyndi Lauper

1983: Culture Club

1982: Men At Work

1981: Sheena Easton

1980: Christopher Cross

1979: Rickie Lee Jones

1978: A Taste Of Honey

1977: Debby Boone

1976: Starland Vocal Band

1975: Natalie Cole

1974: Marvin Hamlisch

1973: Bette Midler

1972: America

1971: Carly Simon

1970: The Carpenters

1969: Crosby Stills & Nash

1968: Jose Feliciano

1967: Bobbie Gentry

1966: No award

1965: Tom Jones

1964: The Beatles

1963: The Swingle Sisters

1962: Robert Goulet

1961: Peter Nero

1960: Bob Newhart

1959: Bobby Darin

The award for 2004 will be given in 2005.

Appeared in pop videos

Denise Van Outen – 'Proper Crimbo' by Avid Merrion

Jennifer Lopez – 'That's The Way Love Goes' by Janet Jackson

Elijah Wood – 'Ridiculous Thought' by The Cranberries

Wesley Snipes – 'Bad' by Michael Jackson

Neil Kinnock – 'My Guy' by Tracey Ullman

Phill Jupitus – 'Happy Hour' by The Housemartins

Sir Ian McKellen – 'Heart' by The Pet Shop Boys

Naomi Campbell – 'I'll Tumble For Ya' by Culture Club

French and Saunders – 'That Ole Devil Called Love' by Alison Moyet

Chevy Chase – 'You Can Call Me Al' by Paul Simon

Tamzin Outhwaite – 'Even Better Than The Real Thing' by U2

Frances Tomelty – 'Sister Of Mercy' by The Thompson Twins

Mike Tyson – 'Bad Boy 4 Life' by Sean (P Diddy) Combs

Donald Sutherland – 'Cloudbusting' by Kate Bush

Robert Bathurst & Claudia Schiffer – 'Uptown Girl' by Westlife

Diana Dors – 'Prince Charming' by Adam and the Ants

Kirsten Dunst – 'I Knew I Loved You' by Savage Gardens

Joss Ackland – 'Always On My Mind' by The Pet Shop Boys

Carmen Electra – 'We Are All Made Of Stars' by Moby

Michelle Collins – 'Up The Junction' by Squeeze

Danny DeVito – 'When The Going Gets Tough'
by Billy Ocean

**Frankie Howerd – 'Don't Let Me Down'
by The Farm**

Michelle Pfeiffer – 'Gangsta's Paradise' by
Coolio (she was also in the horn section
for B.B. King's 'In The Midnight Hour')

**Angelina Jolie – 'Rock & Roll
Dreams Come Through'
by Meat Loaf**

George Clooney – 'She's Just
Killin' Me' by ZZ Top

**Daryl Hannah – 'Feel'
by Robbie Williams**

A GUIDE TO ABBA

In the Bible, 'Abba', meaning 'father', is used to refer to God.
In Sweden, Abba is the name of a fish-canning company.

**Abba made their name by winning the 1974 Eurovision
Song Contest with 'Waterloo', but they were originally
going to do a song called 'Hasta Mañana', which
featured a lead vocal by Agnetha. In they end, they
chose 'Waterloo' because it was a group song.**

Abba's former name was 'Festfolk'. It was under this name that
the foursome of Björn, Benny, Agnetha and Anni-Frid made
their debut in a Gothenberg restaurant in November 1970.

**When Abba played the Royal Albert Hall in February
1977, they were the first Swedish artistes to perform
there for over a hundred years.**

'Fernando' is the biggest-selling single in Australian chart history – having spent 15 weeks at No. 1 there. It was also featured, along with other Abba songs, in the Australian film *Muriel's Wedding*.

Abba's only No. 1 single in the US is 'Dancing Queen', although they have had other Top 10 hits – starting with 'Waterloo', which was the first Eurovision Song Contest song to reach the US Top 10.

Benny owns a riding stables and has named some of his horses after guitars – e.g. 'Burns', 'Gretch' and 'Rickenbacker'.

Lasse Hallström (*Cider House Rules*, *Chocolat*) directed almost every one of Abba's music videos – as well as *Abba: The Movie*.

Abba's distinctive vocal-harmony sound was invented by their engineer Michael B Tretow, who, inspired by Phil Spector, found a way to alter the speed slightly between overdubs.

DRUMMERS

Rick Astley (Give Way – also drummed in a band with Gary Barlow)

Jim Davidson (various bands)

Madonna (The Breakfast Club)

Mark King (various holiday camp bands)

David Essex (The Everons)

Andrew Neil (various bands)

Joe Cocker (The Cavaliers)

Russ Abbot (The Black Abbots)

Richard Desmond (various bands)

Frank Zappa (The Black-outs)

Richard Hannon (The Troggs)

Greg Knight (Dime – and once drummed with The Four Seasons)

Jamie Oliver (Scarlet Division)

Billy Bob Thornton (Tres Hombres, a ZZ Top covers band)

John Altman (Resurrection – also plays guitar)

Mel Brooks (various bands)

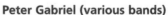

Peter Gabriel (various bands)

Rageh Omaar (The Swindlers – at prep school)

Peter Sellers (in dance bands)

APRIL FOOLS' DAY PRANKS

Probably the most famous British April Fools' Day prank was the Spaghetti Harvest on BBC TV's *Panorama* in 1957. Its presenter was the venerable Richard Dimbleby, definitely *not* a prankster, and millions of people were taken in when he told them about the spaghetti harvest and showed them the spaghetti 'growing' and being 'dried' in the sun.

In 1976, Patrick Moore told radio listeners that while Pluto passed behind Jupiter there would be a decrease in gravitational pull. He said that if people were to jump in the air they would feel as though they were floating. Several people rang up to say that they had enjoyed doing just that.

In 1994, Mars took out full-page advertisements in newspapers announcing their 'New Biggest Ever Mars Bar'. The 'Emperor'-sized Mars Bar was 32lb of 'thick chocolate, glucose and milk'. It was 'on sale' for only one day. April 1.

In 1977, the *Guardian* produced a supplement on the island of San Seriffe. Many readers were taken in by the authentic nature of the words and pictures. In fact, it was a fine spoof with plenty of clues – mostly relating to printing terms – for sharper minds.

In 1979, London's Capital Radio announced that because of all the constant changing between British Summertime and Greenwich Mean Time, we had gained an extra 48 hours, which would have to be lost by the cancellation of 5 April and 12 April. Readers phoned in wondering what would happen to birthdays, anniversaries and other such things.

Not to be outdone, in 1980, the BBC World Service told its listeners that Big Ben's clock-face would be replaced by a digital face. Since the World Service is treated with a lot of reverence, many people were taken in – only to be relieved by discovering the truth.

In 1992, a joker fitted a huge sign onto the roof of the stand at the Hollywood Park racetrack reading 'WELCOME TO CHICAGO'. This was visible to all passengers on flights coming into Los Angeles and caused no little consternation.

In 1983, the German car firm BMW ran a full-page advertisement for 'The first open-top car to keep out the rain even when it's stationary' (supposedly something to do with 'artificial airstreams'). Other years have produced gems such as 'A BMW you need never wash again', 'WARNING: are you driving a genuine BMW?' and, in 1993, a TV commercial introducing an 'anti-tracking device for secret lovers everywhere'.

In 1973, a Dr Ronald Clothier gave a serious-sounding lecture on Radio 3 about Dutch elm disease in which he 'revealed' that rats that had been exposed to the disease had developed a resistance to the human cold. It was eventually revealed that Dr Clothier was, in fact, Spike Milligan.

PEOPLE WHO DROPPED THEIR SURNAMES

Angelina Jolie (born Angelina Jolie Voight)

Richard E. Grant (Richard Grant Esterhuysen)

Richmal Crompton (Richmal Crompton Lamburn)

Bela Lugosi (Bela Lugosi Blasko)

John Leslie (John Leslie Stott)

Sam Shepard (Samuel Shepard Rogers III)

Tom Cruise (Thomas Cruise Mapother IV)

Roger Vadim (Roger Vadim Plemmiankov)

Fiona Apple (Fiona Apple Maggart)

Ray Charles (Ray Charles Robinson)

Bonnie Bedelia (Bonnie Bedelia Culkin)

Eddie Albert (Edward Albert Heimberger)

David Blaine (David Blaine White)

Joe Louis (Joseph Louis Barrow)

DERBY FIRSTS

The first Derby was held on 4 May 1780 and won by Diomed.

The first Earl of Derby to win the race was Edward Stanley, who won in 1787 with his horse, Sir Peter Teazle.

The first dead-heat was in 1828 and the two horses concerned raced again later that afternoon. (There was a second in 1884: the two jockeys met in the weighing room and decided to share the prize money.)

In 1895, The Derby became the first horse race to be filmed.

The Derby became the first horse race to be televised in 1932.

1949 saw the first Derby to be decided by a photo finish.

Starting stalls were used for the first time in the 1967 Derby.

The first winning horse to be owned by a reigning monarch was Minoru in 1909.

In 1801, Eleanor became the first filly to win both The Derby and, the following day, The Oaks.

In 1894, Earl Rosebery became the first prime minister to be the owner of a Derby winner.

WON OXBRIDGE BLUES

Hugh Laurie (Rowing)

Lord Jeffrey Archer (Athletics & Gymnastics)

Kris Kristofferson (Boxing)

Howard Jacobson (Table Tennis). NB 'Minor' sports such as table tennis attract Half Blues rather than Full Blues

Frank Bough (Soccer)

Lord Colin Moynihan (Rowing & Boxing)

Lord Snowdon (Rowing)

Lord James Douglas-Hamilton (Boxing)

Ian Balding (Rugby Union)

Sir Adrian Cadbury (Rowing)

John Gosden (Athletics)

WONDERFULLY NAMED (GENUINE) SOCCER FANZINES

Linesman You're Rubbish (Aberystwyth Town)

***Only The Lonely* (Airdrie)**

Shots In The Dark (Aldershot)

***Up The Arse!* (Arsenal)**

The Ugly Duckling (Aylesbury United)

***Revenge of The Killer Penguin* (Bath City)**

Where's The Vaseline? (Billericay Town)

***4,000 Holes* (Blackburn Rovers)**

Our Flag's Been To Wembley (Braintree Town)

Beesotted (Brentford)

And Smith Must Score (Brighton & Hove Albion)

Addickted (Charlton Athletic)

Super Dario Land (Crewe Alexandra)

Mission Impossible (Darlington)

The Gibbering Clairvoyant (Dumbarton)

It's Half Past Four … And We're 2–0 Down (Dundee)

One Team In Dundee (Dundee United)

Away From The Numbers (East Fife)

We'll Score Again! (Exeter City)

There's Only One F In Fulham (Fulham)

Brian Moore's Head Looks Uncannily Like The London Planetarium (Gillingham)

Sing When We're Fishing (Grimsby Town)

Crying Time Again (Hamilton Academicals)

Monkey Business (Hartlepool Town)

Still Mustn't Grumble (Hearts)

From Hull To Eternity (Hull City)

The Keeper Looks Like Elvis (Kidderminster Harriers)

To Elland Back (Leeds United)

Where's The Money Gone? (Leicester City)

Another Wasted Corner (Liverpool)

Mad As A Hatter (Luton Town)

Bert Trautmann's Helmet (Manchester City)

Dial M For Merthyr (Merthyr Tydfil)

No One Likes Us (Millwall)

Waiting For The Great Leap Forward (Motherwell)

Once Upon A Tyne (Newcastle United)

What A Load Of Cobblers (Northampton Town)

Frattonise (Portsmouth)

The Memoirs of Seth Bottomley (Port Vale)

Ooh, I Think It's My Groin! (QPR)

Exceedingly Good Pies (Rochdale)

Get A Grip, Ref! (Scunthorpe United)

The Ugly Inside (Southampton)

A View To A Kiln (Stoke City)

It's The Hope I Can't Stand! (Sunderland)

Nobody Will Ever Know (Swansea City)

Friday Night Fever (Tranmere Rovers)

Moving Swiftly On ... (Walsall)

Flippin' Heck Ref, That Was A Foul Surely! (Waterlooville)

Winning Isn't Everything (Welling United)

The Sheeping Giant (Wrexham)

She Fell Over (Yeovil Town)

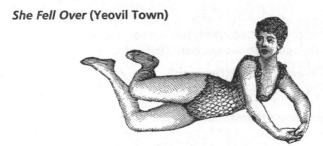

A GUIDE TO SNOOKER

The game was started in India in 1875 by Colonel Sir Neville Chamberlain (no, not that one) as a hybrid of pyramids, black pool and billiards. The game was brought over to England some ten years later.

The name 'snooker' came from the nickname given to cadets at the Royal Military Academy in Woolwich.

The well-known saying about skill at snooker being the sign of a misspent youth comes from Herbert Spencer, the Victorian social philosopher, who said to an opponent: 'A certain dexterity in games of skill argues a well-balanced mind, but such dexterity as you have shown is evidence, I fear, of a misspent youth.'

As every snooker fan knows, 147 is the magic number – it's the maximum break (15 reds each followed by the black and then all the colours). With free balls after a foul shot, 155 is technically the highest score possible, but the highest break ever recorded was 151 by Cliff Thorburn, who achieved his score with the benefit of a foul shot from his opponent.

The first officially ratified 147 break was made by Joe Davis in 1955. Davis is clearly the surname to have if you want to become a snooker champion: Joe, his brother Fred and Steve (no relation) have all managed it.

Snooker was at the height of its popularity in the 1980s when a survey was conducted which proved conclusively that Steve Davis was seen on TV more often than either the Queen or Margaret Thatcher.

'Whispering' Ted Lowe was the greatest of all snooker commentators but even he put his foot in it sometimes. Two of his best are: 'Fred Davis, the doyen of snooker, now 67 years of age and too old to get his leg over, prefers to use his left hand', and 'And for those of you watching this in black-and-white, the pink sits behind the yellow'.

GOALKEEPERS WHO SCORED GOALS

Peter Schmeichel (Aston Villa v. Everton 2001)

Steve Sherwood (Watford v. Coventry City 1984)

Steve Ogrizovic (Coventry City v. Sheffield Wednesday 1986)

Ray Cashley (Bristol City v. Hull City 1973)

Peter Shilton (Leicester City v. Southampton 1967)

Iain Hesford (Maidstone United v. Hereford United 1991)

Pat Jennings (Tottenham Hotspur v. Manchester United 1967)

Andy Goram (Hibernian v. Morton 1988)

RAN THE LONDON MARATHON

Gordon Ramsay, Babs Powell, Jasper Carrott, Dennis Canavan, Brenda Blethyn, Rhodri Morgan, Charlie Dimmock, Patrick Kielty, Jonathan Aitken, Sir Jimmy Savile, Susan Tully, Eric Morley, Peter Duncan, Stephanie Lawrence, Graham Taylor, John Conteh, Gavin Campbell, Alan Minter, Nigel Dempster, Simon Thomas, Steve Cram, Julia Carling, Steve Rider, Jeremy Bates, Jerome Flynn, Chris Chittell, Chris Kamara, Graham Gooch, Frank Bruno, Nick Gillingham, Niamh Cusack, Jason Flemyng, Jonny Lee Miller, John Gregory, Floella Benjamin, Alastair Campbell, Lucy Benjamin, Mark Hughes

FOOTBALL DIRECTORS

Jim Davidson: AFC Bournemouth 1981–1982

Delia Smith: Norwich City 1996–

Michael Grade: Charlton Athletic 1997–

Arthur English: Aldershot 1981–1990

Jasper Carrott: Birmingham City 1979–1982

Sir Elton John: Watford 1976–1990; 1991–

Tommy Cannon: Rochdale 1986–1987

Sir Richard Attenborough: Chelsea 1969–1982

Sir Norman Wisdom: Brighton & Hove Albion 1970–1978

Steve Davis: Leyton Orient 1997–

Fred Dinenage: Portsmouth 1995–

Sean Bean: Sheffield United 2002–

FORMER BOXERS

Bob Hope, Kris Kristofferson, Chris Isaak, Colin Moynihan, Eamonn Andrews, Terence Trent D'Arby, Berry Gordy, Sir Norman Wisdom, Billy Joel, Mark McManus, Liam Neeson, Chuck Berry, Michael Flatley

DID THE CRESTA RUN

David Gower, Errol Flynn, Emma Freud, the Duke of Kent, Hugh Grant

A GUIDE TO GOLF

In the 13th century, the Dutch used to play a game known as 'Spel metten colve' ('Game played with a club'). This became just 'colve', then 'colf' and, eventually, 'golf'.

A golfer is defined as 'one who shouts "fore", takes five and writes down three', while a golfing beginner is 'one who moves heaven and earth to get a game and then moves heaven and earth while playing'.

Robin Williams reckoned: 'Golf is a game where white men can dress up as black pimps and get away with it.'

Sir Winston Churchill described golf as 'an ineffectual attempt to direct an uncontrollable sphere into an inaccessible hole with instruments ill-adapted to the purpose'.

The first recorded hole-in-one was by the great Tom Morris in 1868.

Bing Crosby died immediately after playing a round of golf.

When someone told Gary Player that he was 'lucky', the great golfer replied: 'That's funny, the more I practise, the luckier I get.'

Michael Green's definition of the 'coarse golfer': one who has to shout 'fore' when he putts.

Golf spelt backwards is 'flog'. Another thing to consider is that golf carts are better than caddies because golf carts can't count.

Nick Faldo and his caddie Fanny Sunneson were lining up a shot at the Scottish Open when the commentator said: 'Some weeks Nick likes to use Fanny, other weeks he prefers to do it by himself.'

More people die playing golf than any other sport – from heart attacks and lightning, etc.

A GUIDE TO WACKY RACES

THE ELEVEN RACERS WERE:

00: Dick Dastardly & Muttley (The Mean Machine)

01: The Slag Brothers (Boulder Mobile)

02: The Gruesome Twosome (Creepy Coupe)

03: Prof. Pat Pending (Convert-A-Car)

04: The Red Max (Crimson Haybailer)

05: Penelope Pitstop (Compact Pussycat)

06: Sarge & Pvt. Pinkley (Army Surplus Special)

07: The Ant Hill Mob (Bulletproof Bomb)

08: Luke & Blubber Bear (Arkansas Chugabug)

09: Peter Perfect (Turbo Terrific)

10: Rufus Ruffcut & Sawtooth (Buzzwagon)

THE FINAL RANKINGS WERE:

Boulder Mobile 28 points

Buzzwagon 25 points

Bulletproof Bomb 24 points

Compact Pussycat 21 points

Creepy Coupe 21 points

Crimson Haybailer 20 points

Arkansas Chugabug 18 points

Convert-A-Car 18 points

Turbo Terrific 18 points

Army Surplus Special 11 points

Dick Dastardly & Muttley 0 points

THINGS SAID BY GROUCHO MARX

'Quote me as saying I was misquoted.'

'I've had a perfectly wonderful evening. But this wasn't it.'

'I was married by a judge. I should have asked for a jury.'

'Now that I think of it, I wish I had been a hell-raiser when I was thirty years old. I tried it when I was fifty but I always got sleepy.'

'This would be a better world for children if parents had to eat the spinach.'

'I've been around so long I can remember Doris Day before she was a virgin.'

'From the moment I picked your book up until I laid it down I was convulsed with laughter. Someday I intend reading it.'

'Military justice is to justice what military music is to music.'

'A man's only as old as the woman he feels.'

'I must say that I find television very educational. The minute somebody turns it on, I go to the library and read a book.'

'Women should be obscene and not heard.'

'Time wounds all heels.'

'Behind every successful man is a woman, behind her is his wife.'

'Outside of a dog, a book is man's best friend. Inside of a dog, it's too dark to read.'

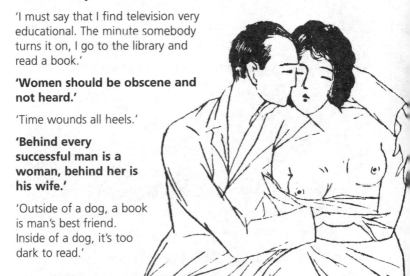

'Age is not a particularly interesting subject. Anyone can get old. All you have to do is live long enough.'

'I sent the club a wire stating, "Please accept my resignation. I don't care to belong to any club that will accept me as a member."'

'It isn't necessary to have relatives in Kansas City in order to be unhappy.'

'Money frees you from doing things you dislike. Since I dislike doing nearly everything, money is handy.'

'Go, and never darken my towels again.'

'Humour is reason gone mad.'

'I chased a girl for two years only to discover that her tastes were exactly like mine: We were both crazy about girls.'

'Here's to our wives and girlfriends … may they never meet.'

'I remember the first time I had sex – I kept the receipt.'

'The secret of life is honesty and fair dealing. If you can fake that, you've got it made.'

'When I was young I was amazed at Plutarch's statement that the elder Cato began at the age of eighty to learn Greek. I am amazed no longer. Old age is ready to undertake tasks that youth shirked because they would take too long.'

'I didn't like the play, but then I saw it under adverse conditions – the curtain was up.'

'The husband who wants a happy marriage should learn to keep his mouth shut and his chequebook open.'

'Paying alimony is like feeding hay to a dead horse.'

'Well, art is art, isn't it? Still, on the other hand, water is water! And east is east and west is west and if you take cranberries and stew them like applesauce they taste much more like prunes than rhubarb does. Now, you tell me what you know.'

'I'm going to Iowa for an award. Then I'm appearing at Carnegie Hall, it's sold out. Then I'm sailing to France to be honoured by the French government. I'd give it all up for one erection.'

'Those are my principles. If you don't like them, I have others.'

The ultimate college application

Hugh Gallagher, now a leading author, wrote the following as a high school essay, which won first prize in the humour category of the 1990 Scholastic Writing Awards and was published in *Harper's* magazine.

3A Essay: In order for the admissions staff of our college to get to know you, the applicant, better, we ask that you answer the following question:

Are there any significant experiences you have had, or accomplishments you have realized, that have helped to define you as a person?

I am a dynamic figure, often seen scaling walls and crushing ice. I have been known to remodel train stations on my lunch breaks, making them more efficient in the area of heat retention. I translate ethnic slurs for Cuban refugees, I write award-winning operas, I manage time efficiently. Occasionally, I tread water for three days in a row.

I woo women with my sensuous and godlike trombone playing, I can pilot bicycles up severe inclines with unflagging speed, and I cook Thirty-Minute Brownies in twenty minutes. I am an expert in stucco, a veteran in love, and an outlaw in Peru.

Using only a hoe and a large glass of water, I once single-handedly defended a small village in the Amazon Basin from a horde of ferocious army ants. I play bluegrass cello, I was scouted by the Mets, I am the subject of numerous documentaries. When I'm bored, I build large suspension bridges in my yard. I enjoy urban hang-gliding. On Wednesdays, after school, I repair electrical appliances free of charge.

I am an abstract artist, a concrete analyst, and a ruthless bookie. Critics worldwide swoon over my original line of corduroy evening wear. I don't perspire. I am a private citizen, yet I receive fan mail. I have been caller number nine and have won the weekend passes. Last summer I toured New Jersey with a traveling centrifugal-force demonstration. I bat 400. My deft floral arrangements have earned me fame in international botany circles. Children trust me.

I can hurl tennis rackets at small moving objects with deadly accuracy. I once read *Paradise Lost*, *Moby Dick*, and *David Copperfield* in one day and still had time to refurbish an entire dining room that evening.

I know the exact location of every food item in the supermarket. I have performed several covert operations for the CIA. I sleep once a week; when I do sleep, I sleep in a chair. While on vacation in Canada, I successfully negotiated with a group of terrorists who had seized a small bakery.

The laws of physics do not apply to me. I balance, I weave, I dodge, I frolic, and my bills are all paid. On weekends, to let off steam, I participate in full-contact origami. Years ago I discovered the meaning of life but forgot to write it down. I have made extraordinary four-course meals using only a mouli and a toaster oven. I breed prizewinning clams. I have won bullfights in San Juan, cliff-diving competitions in Sri Lanka, and spelling bees at the Kremlin. I have played Hamlet, I have performed open-heart surgery, and I have spoken with Elvis.

But I have not yet gone to college.

THINGS INVENTED BY WOMEN

Bulletproof vest, fire escape, windscreen wiper, laser printer, cotton gin, sewing machine, alphabet block, underwater telescope, cotton sewing thread (awarded the very first US patent), brassiere, jockstrap, cordless phone, pulsar (discovered rather than invented), condensed milk, space suit, AIDS drugs AZT and protease inhibitors, TV dinner, Jell-O, Barbie, chocolate-chip cookie, circular saw, dishwasher, disposable nappy, electric hot water heater, ironing board, crash helmet, life raft, medical syringe, rolling pin, rotary engine, Scotchgard fabric protector.

THE ONLY PEOPLE TO HAVE RECEIVED HONORARY US CITIZENSHIP GRANTED BY ACT OF CONGRESS

Sir Winston Churchill (1963), Raoul Wallenberg (1981), William and Hannah Penn (1984), Mother Teresa (1996)

THE SIMPSONS

The characters of Homer, Marge, Lisa and Maggie were given the same first names as Simpsons creator Matt Groening's real-life father, mother and two sisters.

On *The Simpsons* monopoly board, TYRE YARD is the equivalent of Old Kent Road and BURNS MANOR is the equivalent of Mayfair.

In an episode of *The Simpsons*, Sideshow Bob's criminal number is 24601 – the same as Jean Valjean's prison number in *Les Misérables*.

'APPEARED' ON *THE SIMPSONS*

Danny DeVito (Herb Powell)

Jack Lemmon (Frank Ormand, the Pretzel Man)

Donald Sutherland (Hollis Hurlbut)

Joe Mantegna (Fat Tony)

Willem Dafoe (Commandant)

Tracey Ullman (Emily Winthrop)

Johnny Cash (Coyote)

Kirk Douglas (Chester J. Lampwick)

Rodney Dangerfield (Larry Burns)

Anne Bancroft (Dr Zweig)

Penny Marshall (Ms Botz)

Harvey Fierstein (Karl)

Glenn Close (Mother Simpson)

Gillian Anderson (Scully)

David Duchovny (Mulder)

Jackie Mason (Rabbi Krustofski)

Beverly D'Angelo (Lurleen Lumpkin)

Kelsey Grammer (Sideshow Bob)

Michelle Pfeiffer (Mindy Simmons)

Sam Neill (Molloy)

Kathleen Turner (Stacy Lovell)

Winona Ryder (Allison Taylor)

Meryl Streep (Jessica Lovejoy)

Patrick Stewart (Number One)

Susan Sarandon (The Ballet Teacher)

Mandy Patinkin (Hugh Parkfield)

Albert Brooks (Hank)

Jeff Goldblum (MacArthur Parker)

Dustin Hoffman (Mr Bergstrom)

Cloris Leachman (Mrs Glick)

Dame Elizabeth Taylor (Baby Maggie)

John Waters (John)

James Earl Jones (The Narrator)

Ed Asner (Editor of *The Springfield Shopper*)

John Goodman (Meathook)

Henry Winkler (Ramrod)

Tim Robbins (Jim Hope)

Lisa Kudrow (Alex Whitney)

Robert Englund (Freddy Krueger)

Isabella Rossellini (Astrid Weller)

Michael McKean (Jerry Rude)

Martin Sheen (Sergeant Seymour Skinner)

Helen Hunt (Renée)

Rod Steiger (Captain Tenille)

Steve Martin (Ray Patterson)

Drew Barrymore (Sophie)

Patrick McGoohan (Prisoner no. 6)

Michael Keaton (Jack)

Pierce Brosnan (Computer)

Ben Stiller (Garth Motherloving)

Reese Witherspoon (Greta Wolfcastle)

Eric Idle (Desmond)

Professor Frink Senior (Jerry Lewis)

PLAYED THEMSELVES ON *THE SIMPSONS*

Buzz Aldrin, Paul Anka, Tony Bennett, Ernest Borgnine, Mel Brooks, James Brown, Johnny Carson, David Crosby, Dennis Franz, Joe Frazier, George Hamilton, Hugh Hefner, Bob Hope, Magic Johnson, Tom Jones, Tom Kite, Linda McCartney, Sir Paul McCartney, Bette Midler, Bob Newhart, Leonard Nimoy, Luke Perry, Linda Ronstadt, Mickey Rooney, Brooke Shields, Ringo Starr, Sting, Dame Elizabeth Taylor, James Taylor, Adam West, Barry White, James Woods, Professor Stephen Hawking, Britney Spears, Mel Gibson, Mark McGwire, Tom Arnold, Lucy Lawless, Dick Clark, Ron Howard, Penn & Teller, Butch Patrick, Gary Coleman, Bachman Turner Overdrive, Betty White, Ed McMahon, Regis Philbin, Kathie Lee Gifford, Jerry Springer, Alec Baldwin, Kim Basinger, The Moody Blues, Cyndi Lauper, Rupert Murdoch, Dolly Parton, Ed Begley Jr, Sir Elton John, Joe Namath, Jay Leno, U2, Elvis Costello, Sir Mick Jagger, Keith Richards, Lenny Kravitz, Tom Petty, Mark Hamill, Kid Rock, Willie Nelson, Pete Townshend, Roger Daltrey, Stephen King, Richard Gere, Elvis Costello, Little Richard, Tony Blair, J.K. Rowling, Sir Ian McKellen

FLOWERS

The chrysanthemum is never grown in the Japanese city of Himeji because of a legend about a girl called O-Kiku ('Chrysanthemum Blossom') who drowned, leaving behind a troubled spirit that could be settled only if the people of Himeji didn't grow the flower of her name.

The tiger lily in Lewis Carroll's *Through The Looking-Glass* claims that flowers talk 'when there's anybody worth talking to' but that 'in most gardens they make the beds too soft, so that the flowers are always asleep'.

When a fan tried to present the great Italian conductor Toscanini with flowers at the end of a performance, he said, 'They are for prima donnas or corpses: I am neither.'

Dame Iris Murdoch on the subject of flowers: 'People from a planet without flowers would think we must be mad with joy the whole time to have such things about us.'

What William Wordsworth said about daffodils:
'I wandered lonely as a cloud
That floats on high o'er vales and hills,
When all at once I saw a crowd,
A host, of golden daffodils.'

WILD PLANT NAMES

Baldmoney, Bastard Balm, Bloody Crane's-Bill, Butcher's Broom, Creeping Jenny, Devil's Bit Scabious, Enchanter's Nightshade, Fairy Foxglove, Fat-Hen, Fool's Parsley, Good-King-Henry, Hairy Violet, Hemlock Water-Dropwort, Hogweed, Hound's Tongue, Jack-by-the-Hedge, Jacob's Ladder, Lady's Bedstraw, Lady's Tresses, Lamb's Ear, Leopard's Bane, Lords-and-Ladies, Love-in-a-Mist, Mind-Your-Own-Business, Purple Loosestrife, Red-Hot Poker, Scarlet Pimpernel, Shepherd's Purse, Solomon's Seal, Stinking Hellebore, Traveller's Joy, Twiggy Spurge, Venus's Looking Glass, Viper's Bugloss, Wavy Hair Grass

PEOPLE WHO HAD A FLOWER OR PLANT NAMED AFTER THEM

Madonna (gladiolus)

Dame Edna Everage (gladiolus)

Emma Bunton (bergamot)

Frank Bruno (carnation)

Carol Vorderman (fuchsia – named 'Countdown Carol')

Charlie Dimmock (fuchsia)

Alan Titchmarsh (dianthus, lupin and fuchsia)

Audrey Hepburn (fuchsia)

Elvis Presley (sempervivum)

Ricky Martin (orchid – Renaglottis Ricky Martin is yellow and crimson and produces lasting flowers all year)

Whoopi Goldberg (rose)

Vegetarians

Jude Law, Leonardo DiCaprio, Danny DeVito, Charlie Watts, Belinda Carlisle, Dustin Hoffman, Christie Brinkley, Billy Idol, Kim Basinger, Damon Albarn, Seal, Billy Connolly, Gwyneth Paltrow, Ted Danson, Daryl Hannah, Richard Gere, Julie Christie, Candice Bergen, Rosanna Arquette, Brooke Shields, Paul Newman, Peter Gabriel, Boy George, Martina Navratilova, Sir Ian McKellen, LaToya Jackson, Prince, John Peel, Ringo Starr, Terence Stamp, Michael Jackson, Whitney Houston, Michael Bolton, Imelda Staunton, Morrissey, Chrissie Hynde, Lenny Kravitz, Ricki Lake, Vanessa Williams, Don McLean, Ozzy Osbourne, Sir Peter Hall, Yasmin Le Bon, Stevie Nicks, Sir Paul McCartney, Tony Blackburn, Victoria Wood, Gaby Roslin, Kate Bush, Elvis Costello, Bob Dylan, Yoko Ono, Twiggy, Jerry Seinfeld, Penelope Cruz, Tobey Maguire, Shania Twain (during her impoverished childhood, she made gins and snares to catch rabbits for the family to eat)

Lapsed vegetarians

Anthea Turner, Paul Weller, Jeanette Winterson, Liv Tyler

PURE TRIVIA

An artist from Chicago named Dwight Kalb created a statue of Madonna made out of 180 pounds of ham.

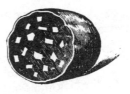

About 10 million bacteria live in 1 gram of soil.

The record for finishing the Rubik's cube is 16.5 seconds.

Nintendo was established in 1889 and started out making playing cards.

Himalaya means 'home of snow'.

The range of a medieval longbow was 220 yards.

The steepest street in the world is Baldwin Street in Dunedin, New Zealand, with an incline of 38 per cent.

Watermelons, which are 92 per cent water, originated from the Kalahari Desert in Africa.

Goat meat contains up to 45 per cent less saturated fat than chicken meat.

The sound made by the Victoria Falls in Zimbabwe can be heard 40 miles away.

Pumpkins were once recommended for removing freckles.

Aoccdnrig to a rscheearhc at Cmabgride Uinevrtisy, it deson't mtater waht oerdr the ltteres in a wrod are – so lnog as the frist and lsat ltteer are in the crorcet pclae. Tihs is bcuseae we dno't raed ervey lteter but the wrod as a wlohe.

Americans eat approximately 20 billion pickles every year.

In Belgium, there is a strawberry museum.

Sheep buried in snowdrifts can survive for up to two weeks.

Worldwide, grapes are grown more than any other fruit.

The mongoose was brought to Hawaii to kill rats but the project failed because rats are nocturnal while the mongoose hunts during the day.

Rhode Island is the smallest US state but it has the longest official name: Rhode Island and Providence Plantations.

If you were locked in a completely sealed room, you'd die of carbon dioxide poisoning before you'd die of oxygen deprivation.

There are 556 officially recognized Native American tribes.

The last time American green cards were actually green was 1964.

Harvard uses 'Yale' brand locks on its buildings.

The (American) football huddle originated in the 19th century at Gallaudet University, Washington DC, when the deaf football team found that opposing teams were reading their signed messages and intercepting plays.

Charles Lindbergh took just four

In the 1994 World Cup the entire Bulgarian team had surnames ending with the letters 'ov'.

Carnivorous animals will not eat another animal that has been hit by a lightning strike.

A mule is the offspring of a female horse and a male donkey but the offspring of a male horse and a female donkey is called a hinny.

Sir Isaac Newton was an ordained priest in the Church of England.

Dalmatian dogs are born pure white and only get their spots when they're a few days old.

Heroin is the brand name of morphine once marketed by Bayer.

The tango originated as a (practice) dance between two men.

Ben and Jerry's send their waste to local pig farmers to use as feed. Pigs love all the flavours except Mint Oreo.

sandwiches with him on his famous transatlantic flight.

Politics

'A government which robs Peter to pay Paul can always depend on the support of Paul.' (George Bernard Shaw)

'Politics is the art of looking for trouble, finding it everywhere, diagnosing it incorrectly and applying the wrong remedy.' (Groucho Marx)

'Politicians are the same all over. They promise to build a bridge even where there's no river.' (Nikita Khrushchev)

'A politician is an arse upon which everyone has sat except a man.' (e.e. cummings)

'Democracy must be something more than two wolves and a sheep voting on what to have for dinner.' (James Bovard)

'Giving money and power to government is like giving whiskey and car keys to teenage boys.' (P.J. O'Rourke)

'Just because you do not take an interest in politics doesn't mean politics won't take an interest in you.' (Pericles in 430BC)

'Suppose you were an idiot. And suppose you were a member of Congress. But I repeat myself.' (Mark Twain)

'I believe that all government is evil, and that trying to improve it is largely a waste of time.' (H.L. Mencken)

'The inherent vice of capitalism is the unequal sharing of the blessings. The inherent blessing of socialism is the equal sharing of misery.' (Sir Winston Churchill)

People who stood (unsuccessfully) for parliament

Sir Robin Day (Liberal)

Ted Dexter (Conservative)

Jonathan King (Royalist)

Pamela Stephenson (Blancmange Thrower)

David Bellamy (Referendum)

Vanessa Redgrave (Workers' Revolutionary)

Dennis Potter (Labour)

Cynthia Payne (Payne and Pleasure)

John Arlott (Liberal)

Lindi St Clair (Corrective)

A GUIDE TO DIFFERENT POLITICAL SYSTEMS

Communism: You have two cows. The government takes both and gives you a little sour milk.

Fascism: You have two cows. The government takes both, hires you to take care of them, and sells you the milk.

Bureaucracy: You have two cows. To register them, you fill in twenty-three forms in triplicate and don't have time to milk them.

Socialism: You have two cows. The government takes one of them and gives it to your neighbour.

Feudalism: You have two cows. Your lord takes some of the milk.

Democracy: You have two cows. A vote is held, and the cows win.

Environmentalism: You have two cows. The government bans you from milking or killing them.

Libertarianism: Go away. What I do with my cows is none of your business.

Capitalism: You have two cows. You sell one and buy a bull.

NB Surrealism: You have two porcupines. The government invites you to take cello lessons.

THINGS YOU DIDN'T KNOW ABOUT US PRESIDENTS

Before winning the 1860 US presidential election, Abraham Lincoln had lost eight elections for various offices.

Every US president with a beard has been Republican.

Abraham Lincoln's mother died when the family dairy cow ate poisonous mushrooms and Mrs Lincoln drank the milk.

Robert Todd Lincoln, son of Abraham Lincoln, was present at the assassinations of three US presidents: Lincoln, Garfield and McKinley.

There are more handwritten letters in existence by George Washington (1789–97) than there are by John F. Kennedy (1961–3).

In 1849, David Atchison became president of the United States for just one day (most of which he spent sleeping).

John Quincy Adams (1825–9) owned a pet alligator, which he kept in the east room of the White House. He swam in the Potomac River every morning – naked. His wife, Louisa Adams, was the first (and only) foreign-born First Lady of the US; she was born in London.

John F. Kennedy (1961–3) and Warren Harding (1920–3) were both survived by their fathers.

Lyndon Johnson's (1963–8) family all had the initials LBJ: Lyndon Baines Johnson, Lady Bird Johnson, Linda Bird Johnson and Lucy Baines Johnson. His dog was called Little Beagle Johnson.

Theodore Roosevelt's (1901–12) wife and mother died on the same day.

On New Year's Day 1907, Theodore Roosevelt shook hands with 8,150 people at the White House.

Since World War Two, every US president who has addressed the Canadian House of Commons in his first term of office has been re-elected to a second term. Eisenhower, Nixon, Reagan and Clinton all did so, while Kennedy, Johnson, Ford, Carter and Bush Snr didn't.

Franklin Pierce (1853–7) was the first president to have a Christmas tree in the White House.

When Franklin D. Roosevelt (1933–45) was five years old, he visited the White House and was told by the then president, Grover Cleveland (1885–9): 'My little man, I am making a strange wish for you: it is that you may never be president of the United States.' It is also worth noting that Roosevelt's mother dressed him exclusively in dresses until he was five.

Another president meeting a future president was in 1963 when Bill Clinton (1993–2001) shook hands with John F. Kennedy (1961–3) at a White House reception for members of Boys' Nation.

Richard Nixon's (1969–74) mother, who named her son after King Richard the Lionheart, originally wanted him to be a Quaker missionary.

William Henry Harrison (1841) was the first president to die in office.

Richard Nixon's mother wanted him to be a Quaker missionary

Martin Van Buren (1837–41) was the first president to be born a US citizen.

Gerald Ford (1974–7) was the only president never to have been elected as either president or vice-president.

Grover Cleveland (1885–9; 1893–7) was the only president elected to two non-consecutive terms.

Zachary Taylor (1849–50) moved around the country so much that he kept being unable to register to vote. He reached 62 before he voted.

John Tyler (1841–50) was the first president to marry in office.

James A. Garfield (1881) is the only man in US history to be simultaneously a congressman, a senator-elect and a president-elect.

Gerald Ford (1974–7) and Bill Clinton (1993–2001) were both adopted as children.

George Washington was the only president not to belong to a political party. He was also the only president to be elected unanimously. In the 1820 election, James Monroe (1817–25) would have got every electoral vote except that a New Hampshire delegate didn't want Washington to lose this distinction and so didn't vote for Monroe.

James Madison (1809–17) was the first president to wear long trousers; all the previous presidents had worn knee breeches.

NB Daniel Webster, a 19th-century US congressman, wanted to be president. He was offered the vice-presidency by William Henry Harrison, but turned it down. Then Harrison died in office. Again Webster was offered the vice-presidency, by Zachary Taylor, but turned it down. Taylor too died in office and Webster never did become president.

US PRESIDENTS WHO WON WITH LESS THAN HALF THE POPULAR VOTE

1824 John Quincy Adams (Democratic-Republican: 30.5%) beat Andrew Jackson (Democratic-Republican: 43.1%), Henry Clay (Democratic-Republican: 13.2%) and William H. Crawford (Democratic-Republican: 13.1%)

1844 James K. Polk (Democrat: 49.58%) beat Henry Clay (Whig 48.12%) and James G. Birney (Liberty: 2.3%)

1848 Zachary Taylor (Whig: 47.33%) beat Lewis Cass (Democrat: 42.54%) and Martin Van Buren (Free Soil: 10.13%)

1856 James Buchanan (Democrat: 45.32%) beat John C. Fremont (Republican: 33.13%) and Millard Fillmore (American: 21.55%)

1860 Abraham Lincoln (Republican: 39.83%) beat Stephen A. Douglas (Democrat: 29.46%), John C. Breckinridge (Southern Democrat: 18.1%) and John Bell (Constitutional Union: 12.61%)

1876 Rutherford B. Hayes (Republican: 48.03%) beat Samuel J. Tilden (Democrat: 51.06%)

1880 James A. Garfield (Republican 48.3%) beat Winfield S. Hancock (Democrat: 48.28%) and James B. Weaver (Greenback-Labor: 3.32%)

1884 Grover Cleveland (Democrat: 48.52%) beat James G. Blaine (Republican: 48.27%), Benjamin F. Butler Greenback (Labor/Anti-Monopoly: 1.74%) and John P. St. John (Prohibition: 1.47%)

1888 Benjamin Harrison (Republican: 47.86%) beat Grover Cleveland (Democrat: 48.66%), Clinton B. Fisk (Prohibition: 2.2%) and Anson J. Streeter (Union Labor: 1.29%)

1892 Grover Cleveland (Democrat: 46.08%) beat Benjamin Harrison (Republican: 42.99%), James B. Weaver (People's: 8.5%) and John Bidwell (Prohibition: 2.25%)

1912 Woodrow Wilson (Democrat: 41.85%) beat Theodore Roosevelt (Progressive: 27.39%), William H. Taft (Republican: 23.19%), Eugene V. Debs (Socialist: 5.99%) and Eugene W. Chafin (Prohibition: 1.38%)

1916 Woodrow Wilson (Democrat: 49.33%) beat Charles E. Hughes (Republican: 46.2%), A. L. Benson (Socialist: 3.19%) and J. Frank Hanly (Prohibition: 1.19%)

1948 Harry S. Truman (Democrat: 49.56%) beat Thomas E. Dewey (Republican: 45.07%), Strom Thurmond (States' Rights Democrat: 2.41%) and Henry Wallace (Progressive: 2.37%)

1960 John F. Kennedy (Democratic: 49.94%) beat Richard M. Nixon (Republican: 49.77%)

1968 Richard M. Nixon (Republican: 43.43%) beat Hubert H. Humphrey (Democrat: 42.73%) and George C. Wallace (American Independent: 13.54%)

1992 Bill Clinton (Democrat: 43.02%) beat George Bush (Republican: 37.46%) and H. Ross Perot (Independent: 18.91%)

1996 Bill Clinton (Democrat: 49.15%) beat Robert Dole (Republican: 40.86%), H. Ross Perot (Independent: 8.48%), Ralph Nader (Green: 0.63%) and Harry Browne (Libertarian: 0.5%)

2000 George W. Bush (Republican: 47.87%) beat Al Gore (Democrat: 48.38%) and Ralph Nader (Green: 2.74%)

NB Where the percentages total less than 100% it is because of unlisted minor party candidates who polled fewer than 1%.

PRIME MINISTERS WHO COMMITTED ADULTERY

The Duke of Grafton, The Earl of Bute, David Lloyd George, Lord Melbourne, Lord John Russell, Lord Grey, George Canning, The Duke of Devonshire, The Duke of Wellington, Lord Palmerston, Benjamin Disraeli, Sir Robert Walpole, Ramsay MacDonald, Herbert Asquith, John Major

THE HOUSE OF COMMONS

MPs can wave their order papers and shout 'hear hear' to signal approval of a speech but they're not allowed to clap.

Electronic voting equipment is not used: MPs must still walk through the 'Aye' and 'No' lobbies.

If an MP wants to empty the public galleries he only has to say, 'I spy strangers.'

When Black Rod comes to the House of Commons (for the state opening of Parliament), he is traditionally refused admission. This dates back to King Charles I and his attempts to curb the power of parliament.

MPs are not allowed to mention the House of Lords. Like superstitious actors referring to Macbeth as 'the Scottish play', they call the House of Lords 'the other place'.

There are yeomen dressed in Tudor uniform who ritually search the cellars of the House of Commons for gunpowder.

The Serjeant-at-Arms, whose office dates back to King Richard II, wears a cocked hat, cutaway coat, knee breeches, a lace ruffle, black stockings and silver buckled shoes.

MPs must not mention other MPs by name. Instead, they must refer to them by their constituencies (e.g. 'The member for …').

The Speaker of the House of Commons is obliged to show extreme reluctance on taking office.

MAYORS

Frank Carson – Balbriggan in Ireland

Clint Eastwood – Carmel, California

Sonny Bono – Palm Springs, California

Richard Whiteley – Wetwang, Yorkshire

Liz Dawn – given the title Lady Mayoress of Leeds – thanks to her fundraising for cancer sufferers in Yorkshire

Sir Anthony Hopkins – Pacific Palisades (suburb of Los Angeles), California

BEN & JERRY'S TOP TEN FLAVOURS

Cherry Garcia Ice Cream

Chocolate Chip Cookie Dough Ice Cream

Chocolate Fudge Brownie Ice Cream

New York Super Fudge Chunk Ice Cream

Chunky Monkey Ice Cream

Half Baked! Ice Cream

Phish Food Ice Cream

Cherry Garcia Frozen Yogurt

Peanut Butter Cup Ice Cream

Chocolate Fudge Brownie Frozen Yogurt

CHARLES DICKENS

Dickens's father was a navy pay clerk who was made redundant and ended up in debtors' prison. Young Charles worked in a blacking factory to help the family's finances.

Dickens used his father as the inspiration for Mr Micawber, the ever-optimistic character from *David Copperfield*. W.C. Fields played the part of Micawber in the Hollywood film version and, when told that Dickens hadn't written anything about Micawber juggling, replied, 'He probably forgot.'

Later, Dickens became a journalist – working first as a court reporter and eventually graduating to editor.

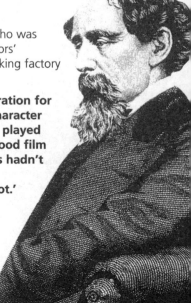

Dickens was prone to fainting fits. He gave dramatic readings of his books and sometimes worked himself up into such a state of excitement that he keeled over.

Dickens was an insomniac. He was also a little neurotic about his insomnia – always making sure that his bed pointed due north and that he was positioned in the absolute centre of it.

In his letters to his wife Kate, Dickens called her his 'dearest mouse' and his 'darling pig'.

Dickens fell 'deeply and intimately' in love with his wife's sister, Mary, when she came to live with them. Mary died at the age of 17 and Dickens wore her ring for the rest of his life. He asked to be buried next to her but was buried in Westminster Abbey instead.

After Mary, Dickens fell for another of his wife's sisters – Georgina – who came to live with them. When Dickens and his wife separated after 22 years of marriage (and ten children), Georgina stayed with him.

PEOPLE WHO HAD BOOKS DEDICATED TO THEM

Christopher Isherwood (*Myra Breckinridge* by Gore Vidal)

Brigid Brophy (*The Good Apprentice* by Iris Murdoch)

Robert Bolt (*Second Fiddle* by Mary Wesley)

Diana Mosley (*Vile Bodies* by Evelyn Waugh)

Philip Larkin (*Lucky Jim* by Kingsley Amis)

Kingsley Amis (*XX Poems* by Philip Larkin)

Robert Conquest (*Hearing Secret Harmonies* by Anthony Powell)

William Makepeace Thackeray (*Jane Eyre* by Charlotte Brontë)

Iris Murdoch (*The Sweets of Pimlico* by A.N. Wilson)

Ivy Compton-Burnett (*The Spoilt City* by Olivia Manning)

WRITE POETRY

Damon Albarn, Bob Hoskins, Eric Cantona, Jack Dee, Paul Gascoigne, Susan George, Ray Davies, Bobby Ball, Steven Berkoff, Nigel Planer, David Carradine, Patti D'Arbanville, Robert Downey Jr, Woody Harrelson, Traci Lords, Judd Nelson, Michael J. Pollard, Carl Reiner, Robbie Williams, Charisma Carpenter, Mark Lamarr (started off as a poet), Tara Palmer-Tomkinson, Pamela Anderson, Denzel Washington, Tionne Watkins, Brandy, Courtney Love & Russell Crowe (together), Christina Aguilera, Val Kilmer (for Michelle Pfeiffer), Kate Moss, Viggo Mortensen

Leap years

February 29 occurs once every four years because instead of precisely 365 days in a year there are approximately 365 and a quarter. That is, it takes the earth 365 1/4 days to go round the sun and complete an astronomical year. The extra day every four years allows the man-made calendar to catch up with the astronomical calendar.

Leap years occur in any year that is divisible by 4, except those divisible by 100, though the 100-rule doesn't apply to those divisible by 400. So although 1900 was divisible by 4 it wasn't a leap year, but 2000 was. Thought: if there are 52 weeks in the year and 7 days in a week, why aren't there 364 days in the year?

Leap years are so called because with 365-day years, a day of the month falling on Monday in one year will fall on a Tuesday in the next and on Wednesday in the third, but when the fourth year comes along with its extra day, it will 'leap' over the Thursday to fall instead on the Friday.

On a Leap Year's Day in 1956, a Mrs Christine McDonnell of Church Street, Dublin, gave birth to a set of twins. On the next Leap Year Day, in 1960, she gave birth to another set of twins.

On Leap Year's Day in 1984, Lisa Dluchik of Swindon was born. Her mother Suzanne was also born on Leap Year Day (1956). The odds against a mother and a daughter both being born on February 29 have been calculated as 2,000,000–1.

On Leap Year's Day in 1996, bachelors fled to Leicester's Stapleford Park Hotel for a men-only break to avoid marriage proposals.

Things that have happened on Leap Year's Day in history: in 1960, the Moroccan city of Agadir was devastated by an earthquake followed by a tidal wave which killed more than 12,000 people. In 1956, Pakistan became an Islamic republic. In 1960, Hugh Hefner opened his first Playboy Club (in Chicago). In 1984, John Francome rode the 1,000th winner of his career.

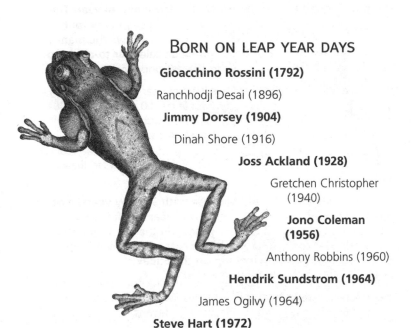

Born on leap year days

Gioacchino Rossini (1792)

Ranchhodji Desai (1896)

Jimmy Dorsey (1904)

Dinah Shore (1916)

Joss Ackland (1928)

Gretchen Christopher (1940)

Jono Coleman (1956)

Anthony Robbins (1960)

Hendrik Sundstrom (1964)

James Ogilvy (1964)

Steve Hart (1972)

CHAT-UP LINES

'You don't know me but I dreamt about you last night.'

'Did it hurt when you fell from heaven?'

'If I could rearrange the alphabet, I'd put U and I together.'

'Can I buy you a drink or do you just want the money?'

'Do you believe in love at first sight or shall I walk past you again?'

'How do you like your eggs? Fertilized?'

'Get your coat, love, you've pulled.'

'Is that a ladder in your tights or the stairway to heaven?'

'This body leaves in five minutes, be on it.'

'Your clothes would look great on my bedroom floor.'

'Can I have your picture so I can show Santa what I want for Christmas?'

'I may not be the best-looking bloke in the room but I'm the only one talking to you.'

'You're a thief: You've stolen my heart!'

'You remind me of someone I'd like to know.'

'Can I borrow your mobile? I told my parents I'd phone them when I met the girl of my dreams.'

'Is it me or do you always look this good?'

'I need a map because I'm lost in your eyes.'

'The word "beautiful" wouldn't be the same without U.'

MIGRAINE CURES

Pills without prescription: aspirin, paracetamol and ibuprofen – available either in generic form or as branded drugs.

Prescription drugs: sumatripan – manufactured under the brand name Imigran – which boosts the effect of the 5-HT chemical that helps transmit messages within the brain; the beta-blocker Propranolol; Ergotamine, which constricts dilated blood vessels in the head.

Regular exercise This will help *prevent migraines*. Also make sure blood pressure is under control, and don't smoke.

Diet Eat regular meals – every two hours if possible. Never miss breakfast. Eat a diet rich in carbohydrate. Avoid red wine, chocolate, cheese and citrus fruits.

Acupuncture In Denmark, doctors found that acupuncture was almost as effective as drugs against migraine but without any of the side effects.

Regular sleep Too little or, interestingly, too much sleep can cause migraines. This is why a lot of people suffer from migraines on a Sunday when they've had a long lie-in.

Special rose-tinted spectacles, initially developed for children In tests, the average number of migraine attacks suffered by children aged 8 to 14 fell from 6.2 to 1.6 per month when they wore these glasses. According to the head of the retina department of Birmingham's Eye Hospital, 'The spectacles are just as effective in preventing migraine in grown-ups as they are in children.'

Mental well-being Hypertension, stress, suppressed anger, anxiety and depression are all causes/contributory factors of migraines. If your migraines are frequent, try to alleviate the states of mind that might be causing them.

Medigen A gadget that emits minute electromagnetic impulses, which increase the brain's alpha waves.

Work Controversially, there are neurologists who believe that *not* giving in to a migraine, if possible, will see it off. A study of doctors who had worked through their migraines indicated that 'work suppressed their migraine … although once they reached home they took to bed'.

Botox injections People who've been to a botox clinic have found their migraines have mysteriously disappeared. Now people have the treatment for this reason.

UNCONSUMMATED MARRIAGES

Mary, Queen of Scots & Prince Francis of France

Stanley Spencer & Patricia Preece

Sir J.M. Barrie & Mary Ansell

Ronnie Kray & Kate Howard

George Bernard Shaw & Charlotte Townsend

Eva Bartok & William Wordsworth

Burt Lancaster & June Ernst

Zsa Zsa Gabor & Burhan Belge

Marie Stopes & Reginald Ruggles Gate

Prince Arthur (King Henry VIII's older brother) & Catherine of Aragon

Jean Harlow & Paul Bern

John Ruskin & Euphemia Gray (he was shocked to discover on their wedding night that she had pubic hair; she eventually left him for the artist John Millais, with whom she had eight children)

Rudolph Valentino & Jean Acker

Rudolph Valentino & Natasha Rambova

King Henry VIII & Anne of Cleves

Peter Tchaikovsky & Antonina Milyukova

Catherine & Peter The Great

Andre Gide & Madeleine Rondeaux

Fanny Brice & Frank White

Judy Garland & Mark Herron

Giuseppe Garibaldi & Giuseppina Raimondi

Zsa Zsa Gabor & Count Felipe de Alba

Note also that it took Marie Antoinette & King Louis XVI seven years to consummate their marriage.

MARRIED THEIR CHILDHOOD SWEETHEARTS

Ardal O'Hanlon, Jamie Oliver, Terry Wogan, Dick Cheney, Andrea McLean, Robbie Fowler, Perry Como, Ray Winstone, John Higgins, Colin McRae, Seve Ballesteros, Justine Henin-Hardenne, George Segal, Robert Smith, Ron Howard, Jon Bon Jovi, Tom Jones, Bono, George Carey, ex-Archbishop of Canterbury, Michael Parkinson, Bruce Rioch, Stephen Hendry, Nick Berry, Sir Ranulph Fiennes, Stephen King, Jeff Daniels, David Ginola, Al Gore, Gareth Edwards, Kevin Keegan, Carol Channing, Padraig Harrington, Rachel Griffiths, Martin Keown, Russell Watson

MARRIED AND DIVORCED THEIR CHILDHOOD SWEETHEARTS

Glenn Hoddle, Les Dennis, Bradley Walsh, Eamonn Holmes, Nigel Benn, David Blunkett, Harrison Ford, Sally Field, Michael Bolton, Angela Rippon, Sam Torrance, Gerhard Schröder, Sean Bean, Eminem, Richard Burton, Alan Cumming

WHO THEY CHOSE AS THEIR BEST MAN

GROOM	BEST MAN
Ronald Reagan	William Holden
Sir Paul McCartney	**Mike McGear (both times)**
Spike Milligan	Sir George Martin
Bryan Forbes	**Sir Roger Moore**
Jack Nicholson	Harry Dean Stanton
William Shatner	**Leonard Nimoy**
Vincente Minnelli	Ira Gershwin
Dougray Scott	**Ewan McGregor**
Patrick Stewart	Brent Spiner
David Gest	**Michael Jackson**
Larry Fortensky	Michael Jackson
David Beckham	**Gary Neville**
Julian Holloway	Sir Albert Finney
Ossie Clarke	**David Hockney**
Kevin Kennedy	Michael Le Vell
Rowan Atkinson	**Stephen Fry**
Peter Sellers	David Lodge
Nicholas Soames	**Prince Charles**
Mick Jagger	Lord Patrick Lichfield
Jake La Motta	**Sugar Ray Robinson**
Josef Goebbels	Adolf Hitler
Christopher Hitchens	**Martin Amis**
Martin Amis	Christopher Hitchens
Rory Bremner	**Graham Cowdrey**

ENGAGEMENTS THAT DIDN'T LEAD TO MARRIAGE

Michelle Pfeiffer & Fisher Stevens

Ronan Keating & Vernie Bennett

Martine McCutcheon & Gareth Cooke

Van Morrison & Michelle Rocca

Olivia Newton-John & Bruce Welch

Thomas Muster & Mariella Theiner

Dervla Kirwan & Robert Caldwell

Shane Richie & Dawn Rodger

Stan Collymore & Lotta Farley

Samantha Fox & Peter Foster

Tania Bryer & Count Gianfranco Cicogna

James Gilbey & Lady Alethea Savile

Phil Tufnell & Jane McEvoy

Shannen Doherty & Dean Factor

Bobby Davro & Zoë Nicholas

Axl Rose & Stephanie Seymour

Julie Goodyear & Jack Diamond

Adam Sandler & Margaret Ruden

Neil Morrissey & Elizabeth Carling

Laura Dern & Billy Bob Thornton

Martine McCutcheon & Jonathan Barnham

Eriq LaSalle & Angela Johnson

Sinitta & Simon Cowell

Robbie Williams & Nicole Appleton

Heath Ledger & Naomi Watts

Ben Affleck & Gwyneth Paltrow

Pamela Anderson & Kid Rock

Lenny Kravitz & Adriana Lima

Sophie Anderton & Simon Rubel

Fred Couples & Tawnya Dodd

Sinitta & Thomas Arklie

Nicholas Lyndhurst & Gail Parr

Carole Landis & Busby Berkeley

Sir David Frost & Karen Graham

Tessa Dahl & Angus Gibson

Emma Samms & Marvin Hamlisch

Malandra Burrows & Jonathan Armstead

Princess Stephanie of Monaco & Jean-Yves LeFur

Charlie Sheen & Kelly Preston (later married to John Travolta)

Jonathan Cake & Olivia Williams

Nicole Appleton & Darren Brodin

Dodi Fayed & Kelly Fisher

David Coulthard & Andrea Murray

Victoria Adams (now Beckham) & Mark Wood

Sharon Stone & Michael Benasra

Alan Cumming & Saffron Burrows

Yasmine Bleeth & Ricky Paull Goldin

Tamara Beckwith & Michael Stone (Sharon's brother)

VIRGINS ON THEIR WEDDING DAY

Shirley Temple, Katy Hill, Lisa Kudrow, Donny Osmond, Dame Elizabeth Taylor, Gwen Taylor, Priscilla Presley, Marthe Bibesco, Marjorie Proops, Gloria Hunniford, Ava Gardner, Loretta Lynn, Raquel Welch, Catherine The Great, William Gladstone, Dorothy Dandridge, Mark Twain, Vivien Leigh, Gloria Swanson, Mrs Patrick Campbell, Colette, Hedda Hopper, Mary Martin, Paul Muni

MARRIAGES THAT DIDN'T LAST

Zsa Zsa Gabor & Felipe De Alba (one day)

Britney Spears & Jason Alexander (one day)

Ethel Merman & Ernest Borgnine (four days)

Dennis Rodman & Carmen Electra (nine days)

Dennis Rodman & Annie Banks (twelve days)

Burt Lancaster & June Ernst (one month)

Henry Fonda & Margaret Sullavan (two months)

Aaliyah & R. Kelly (three months – annulled because she was just 15)

Janet Jackson & James DeBarge (four months)

Natasha Henstridge & Damian Chapa (five months)

Drew Barrymore & Tom Green (five months)

Fanny Cradock & Arthur Chapman (a few months)

Elton John & Renate Blauel (a few months)

Don Johnson & Melanie Griffith (the first marriage – a few months)

Arthur C. Clarke & Marilyn Mayfield (six months)

Patsy Palmer & Nick Love (six months)

Christie Brinkley & Ricky Taubman (seven months)

Axl Rose & Erin Everly (seven months)

Dennis Wilson & Karen Lamm (seven months the first time; two weeks the second time)

Jean Harlow & Hal Rosson (eight months)

Kelsey & Leanne Grammer (eight months)

Dodi Fayed & Suzanne Gregard (eight months)

Emma Samms & Bansi Nagji (eight months)

Judy Garland & David Rose (eight months)

Jennifer Lopez & Cris Judd (eight months)

Marilyn Monroe & Joe DiMaggio (nine months)

Sheena & Sandi Easton (nine months)

Suzanne Pleshette & Troy Donahue (nine months)

Jim Carrey & Lauren Holly (ten months)

Ellen Terry & George Watts (ten months)

Alyssa Milano & Cinjun Tate (ten months and 19 days)

Jim Davidson & Sue Walpole (eleven months)

Paul Simon & Carrie Fisher (eleven months)

Helen Hunt & Hank Azaria
(eleven months)

Sarah Bernhardt & Aristides Damala (less than a year)

Whoopi Goldberg & Dave Claessen (less than a year)

Sheena Easton & Timothy Delarm (less than a year)

NAMED AS CO-RESPONDENTS IN DIVORCE CASES

Warren Beatty (in the divorce of Sir Peter Hall and Leslie Caron)

Anthea Turner (Grant and Della Bovey)

Mick Jagger (Marianne Faithfull and John Dunbar)

Anthony Booth (David Elliott and Stephanie Buckley)

George Weidenfeld (Cyril Connolly and Barbara Skelton)

Cyril Connolly (George Weidenfeld and Barbara Skelton)

> NB This was the order in which this remarkable true-life soap occurred.

Olivia Newton-John (Bruce and Ann Welch)

Jessie Matthews (Evelyn Laye and Sonnie Hale)

John Osborne (Dr Roger and Penelope Gilliatt)

Dorothy Squires (Roger Moore and Doorn van Steyn)

Georgie Fame (The Marquess and Marchioness of Londonderry)

Glenn Hoddle (Jeffrey and Vanessa Shean)

W. Somerset Maugham (Henry and Syrie Wellcome)

James Hewitt (David and Sally Faber)

Ross Kemp (Lucien Taylor and Helen Patrick)

SEXUAL OFFERS THAT WERE TURNED DOWN

Marianne Faithfull turned down Bob Dylan and Jimi Hendrix

Marlon Brando turned down Tallulah Bankhead and Anna Magnani

Carol White turned down James Caan

Veronica Lake turned down Errol Flynn

Olivia de Havilland turned down Errol Flynn and Leslie Howard

Marlene Dietrich turned down Ernest Hemingway and Adolf Hitler (after approaches to her were made by Goebbels and Von Ribbentrop on his behalf)

Britt Ekland turned down Ron Ely

Ava Gardner turned down Howard Hughes

Mary Pickford turned down Clark Gable

Greta Garbo turned down Aristotle Onassis

Evelyn Keyes turned down Harry Cohn

Katharine Hepburn turned down Douglas Fairbanks Jnr and John Barrymore

Jean Simmons turned down John F. Kennedy and Howard Hughes

Lord Laurence Olivier turned down Merle Oberon

Angela Baddeley turned down Lord Laurence Olivier

Lana Turner turned down Mickey Rooney

Joan Collins turned down Daryl F. Zanuck and Richard Burton

Liam Gallagher turned down Paula Yates (she once asked him to make love to her in a loo but he refused because, as he told friends, 'she's way too old')

Tallulah Bankhead turned down John Barrymore

Jean Harlow turned down Louis B Mayer

Clara Bow turned down Al Jolson

Zizi Jeanmaire turned down Howard Hughes (this was after he'd brought over the entire ballet company for a film – purely to seduce her)

Gina Lollobrigida turned down Howard Hughes

Janet Leigh turned down Howard Hughes

Vaslav Nijinsky turned down Isadora Duncan

Gertrude Stein turned down Ernest Hemingway

Ava Gardner turned down George C. Scott

Jaclyn Smith turned down Warren Beatty

Bette Davis turned down Joan Crawford (according to Hollywood legend – although their lifelong enmity is equally likely to be due to the fact that Davis had an affair with Franchot Tone while he was married to Crawford)

Marilyn Monroe turned down Joan Crawford

Anthony Perkins turned down Ingrid Bergman

Jacqueline Susann turned down Coco Chanel

Rita Hayworth turned down Harry Cohn

Bette Davis turned down Miriam Hopkins

Merle Oberon turned down Stewart Granger

Tyrone Power turned down Norma Shearer

Grace Kelly turned down Bing Crosby

Paul McCartney turned down Little Richard

Mrs Patrick Campbell turned down George Bernard Shaw

John Wayne turned down Marlene Dietrich

Barbara Windsor turned down Warren Beatty

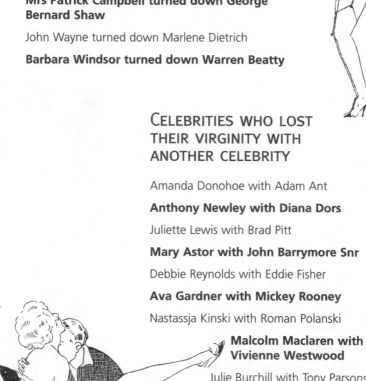

CELEBRITIES WHO LOST THEIR VIRGINITY WITH ANOTHER CELEBRITY

Amanda Donohoe with Adam Ant

Anthony Newley with Diana Dors

Juliette Lewis with Brad Pitt

Mary Astor with John Barrymore Snr

Debbie Reynolds with Eddie Fisher

Ava Gardner with Mickey Rooney

Nastassja Kinski with Roman Polanski

Malcolm Maclaren with Vivienne Westwood

Julie Burchill with Tony Parsons

Brigitte Bardot with Roger Vadim

Cecil Beaton with Adele Astaire

Elliott Gould with Barbra Streisand

Brooke Shields with Dean Cain

Priscilla Beaulieu with Elvis Presley

Gloria Swanson with Wallace Beery

MEMBERS OF THE MILE-HIGH CLUB

Bill Clinton

Joe McGann

Georgina Hale

Frances Ruffelle

Mel B

Julia Roberts & Jason Patric

Alan Whicker ('my safari suit got quite crumpled')

Tori Spelling

Dennis Rodman (on Concorde)

Samantha Fox

Pamela Anderson Lee & Tommy Lee (in a toilet on a flight from LA to New York. She said: 'It was fantastic. When we came out everyone clapped and cheered')

John Travolta & Kelly Preston (on the private jet back to America from France where they were married)

John Cusack

Danniella Westbrook & Brian Harvey

The Maharaja of Baroda

Leonardo DiCaprio (hired an executive jet, served a girl strawberries and ice cream and then made love looking at the stars)

Kelsey Grammer (with his then wife)

Sid Owen

Saeed Jaffrey (with an American woman on a flight from London to Edinburgh)

Kylie Minogue (with Michael Hutchence – in first class, just a few seats away from the Australian PM)

Carmen Electra ('The craziest place I made love was in an aeroplane, in the bathroom. I thought it was hot, I loved it')

Note also that Björn Borg says he did so with first wife Mariana on a flight from Copenhagen to New York, but the stewardess looking after them said that Björn spent the time reading Mickey Mouse comics

Men who lost their virginity with prostitutes

Henry Fonda, David Niven (with a London girl nicknamed Nessie), Clifford Irving, Uri Geller (a Greek-Cypriot girl called Lola), Anton Chekhov, Chris De Burgh (a French girl), Simon Raven, Tony Mortimer, The Duke of Windsor, Napoleon Bonaparte, James Boswell, James Joyce, John F. Kennedy (the girl charged $3), Benito Mussolini, Stendhal, Leo Tolstoy, H.G. Wells, Groucho Marx, Mike Tyson, Sir Richard Branson

NB Ian Fleming's James Bond loses his virginity in Paris at the age of 16 with a prostitute called Martha Debrant.

AGE AT WHICH THEY LOST THEIR VIRGINITY

AGED 13

Curt Smith, Peter Andre, Lennie Bennett, Justin Hayward (with a girl of 20)

AGED 14

David Chokachi, David Niven, James Joyce, Larry Adler, Derek Jameson

AGED 15

John Barrymore (with his stepmother), Shelley Winters, Peter O'Toole, Art Buchwald, Bobby Davro, Burt Reynolds, Tina Turner, Jack London (with a girl who 'came with' a boat he bought), Uri Geller, Sophie Anderton (a week before her 16th birthday), Angela Griffin, Paul Ross, Sting, Tony Mortimer, Damon Albarn, Lisa Marie Presley (with a 24-year-old drug dealer), Sally Field

AGED 16

Georgina Hale, Nell McAndrew, Benito Mussolini, Grigori Rasputin, Leo Tolstoy, Jean Harlow, Claire King (in the back of a Mini), Dorothy Squires, Samantha Janus, Carmen Electra ('It was in Cincinnati in the back seat of a car. It was not very glamorous and I don't remember it being such a great experience'), Mel C, Sir Richard Branson, Chris De Burgh, Richard Harris, Dean Gaffney, Teri Hatcher, Dani Behr, Raquel Welch, Shirley MacLaine, Ursula Andress, David Baddiel, Robert Burns, Sean Maguire, Shelley Duvall, Groucho Marx, Barbara Hutton, Jayne Mansfield, Mike Tyson

AGED 17

Ginger Rogers, Barry Newman, Alexander Dumas Snr, Steven Spielberg, Cyndi Lauper, Keith Chegwin, Erica Jong, Carrie Fisher, Dyan Cannon, Betty Boo, Mary Astor, Chris Evans, Samantha Fox, Bel Mooney, Alicia Silverstone, Bernard Manning, Donna D'Errico (in a car), Julie Burchill, Mark Lamarr, John Leslie (at a fancy dress party with a girl wearing a wedding dress with L-plates attached), Ronnie Biggs, Cathy Shipton, Liz Kershaw, Dr Ruth Westheimer, Shaw Taylor

AGED 18

Charles Baudelaire (on which occasion he contracted the venereal disease that would kill him 27 years later), Matt Goss, Baroness Issy Van Randwyck, Anthony Edwards, Brian Glover, Jancis Robinson, Patti Boulaye, Irma Kurtz, Zoë Ball, Victoria Principal, Emma Noble, Lisa Riley, Margi Clarke, Vivien Leigh, Tony Robinson (with the woman who became his wife), Susan Hayward

AGED 19

Lillian Hellman, Gerald Kingsland, Pattie Coldwell, 'Dr' Neil Fox, Alison Steadman, Carol Drinkwater

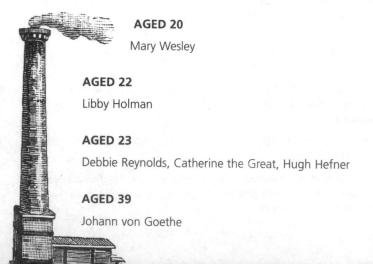

AGED 20

Mary Wesley

AGED 22

Libby Holman

AGED 23

Debbie Reynolds, Catherine the Great, Hugh Hefner

AGED 39

Johann von Goethe

THINGS SAID ABOUT SEX

'I believe that sex is a beautiful thing between two people. Between five, it's fantastic …' (Woody Allen)

'When women go wrong, men go right after them.' (Mae West)

'My father told me all about the birds and the bees. The liar – I went steady with a woodpecker till I was 21.' (Bob Hope)

'Sex is one of the nine reasons for reincarnation – the other eight are unimportant.' (Henry Miller)

'Conventional sexual intercourse is like squirting jam into a doughnut.' (Germaine Greer)

'Being a sex symbol is a heavy load to carry – especially when one is tired, hurt and bewildered.' (Marilyn Monroe)

'It's strange to become a sex symbol at 40. And even to be described as a kind of Warren Beatty. The truth is that, until I met my wife at 35, I only had two girlfriends.' (Colin Firth)

'I come from a strict Catholic upbringing and sex was a taboo subject. That makes you crave sex 10 times more for the rest of your life.' (Salma Hayek)

'It sounds strange for me to be saying this, but I've come around to the idea that sex really is for procreation.' (Eric Clapton)

'Sex is important, but by no means the only important thing in life.' (Mary Whitehouse)

'Sex is about as important as a cheese sandwich. But a cheese sandwich, if you ain't got one to put in your belly, is extremely important.' (Ian Dury)

'The only unnatural sexual behaviour is none at all.' (Sigmund Freud)

'I always thought coq au vin was love in a lorry.' (Victoria Wood)

'I honestly prefer chocolate to sex.' (Dale Winton)

'It's been so long since I made love, I can't remember who gets tied up.' (Joan Rivers)

'Sex appeal is 50 per cent what you've got and 50 per cent what people think you've got.' (Sophia Loren)

'If you were married to Marilyn Monroe – you'd cheat with some ugly girl.' (George Burns)

'Sex – the poor man's polo.' (Clifford Odets)

'My favourite sexual fantasy is smearing my naked body with chocolate and cream – then being left alone to lick it off.' (Jo Brand)

'It [sex] ruins friendships between men and women.' (Julia Roberts)

'It has to be admitted that we English have sex on the brain – which is a very unsatisfactory place to have it.' (Malcolm Muggeridge)

'I'm never through with a girl until I've had her three ways.' (John F. Kennedy)

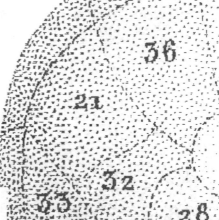

'I know it does make people happy but to me it is just like having a cup of tea.' (Cynthia Payne)

'I believe that sex is the most beautiful, natural and wholesome thing that money can buy.' (Steve Martin)

'If I took all my clothes off I wouldn't be sexy any more. I'd just be naked. Sex appeal is about keeping something back.' (Jennifer Lopez)

'The greatest pleasure that one person can offer another is carnal pleasure.' (Coco Chanel)

'The number of available orgasms is fixed at birth and can be expended. A young man should make love very seldom or he will have nothing left for middle age.' (Ernest Hemingway)

'I've never considered myself addicted to anything, but if I was, sex was it.' (Clint Eastwood)

'What comes first in a relationship is lust, then more lust.' (Jacqueline Bisset)

'Sex is a bad thing because it rumples the clothes.' (Jacqueline Kennedy Onassis)

**'A man with an erection is in no need of advice.'
(Samuel Pepys)**

'Sex has never interested me much.
I don't understand how people can waste so much time over sex.
Sex is for kids, for movies – it's a great bore.' (Sir Alfred Hitchcock)

'Sex is as important as food and drink.' (Britt Ekland)

'Some things are better than sex and some things are worse, but there's nothing exactly like it.' (W.C. Fields)

'The minute you start fiddling around outside the idea of monogamy, nothing satisfies any more.' (Richard Burton)

'Accursed from their birth they be/ Who seek to find monogamy./ Pursuing it from bed to bed/ I think they would be better dead.' (Dorothy Parker)

'You know, of course, that the Tasmanians, who never committed adultery, are now extinct.' (W. Somerset Maugham)

'All this fuss about sleeping together; for physical pleasure I'd sooner go to my dentist any day.' (Evelyn Waugh)

Pure trivia

Velcro was invented by a Swiss man who noticed the way burrs attached themselves to clothing.

Physicist Murray Gell-Mann picked the name quarks from a line in James Joyce's Ulysses, 'Three quarks for Muster Mark!'

When a film is in production, the last shot of the day is known as 'the Martini shot'.

Goldfish can suffer motion sickness.

The distress term 'Mayday' comes from the French term 'm'aidez' meaning 'help me'.

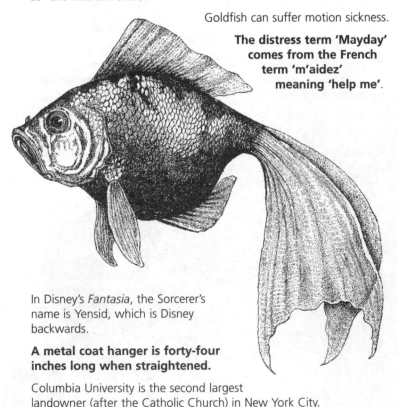

In Disney's *Fantasia*, the Sorcerer's name is Yensid, which is Disney backwards.

A metal coat hanger is forty-four inches long when straightened.

Columbia University is the second largest landowner (after the Catholic Church) in New York City.

The most common name in Italy is Mario Rossi.

Roosters can't crow if their necks aren't fully extended.

Shirley Temple always had 56 curls in her hair.

The three largest landowners in England are the Queen, the Church of England and Trinity College, Cambridge.

Most American car horns beep in the key of F.

Native speakers of Japanese learn Spanish much more easily than they learn English.

Dirty Harry's badge number was 2211.

The US has never lost a war in which mules were used.

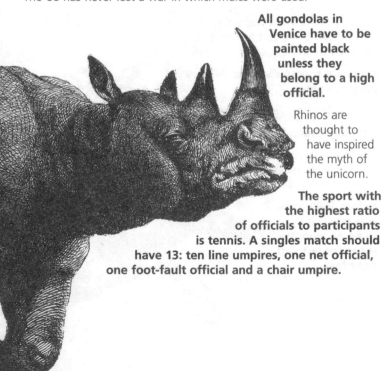

All gondolas in Venice have to be painted black unless they belong to a high official.

Rhinos are thought to have inspired the myth of the unicorn.

The sport with the highest ratio of officials to participants is tennis. A singles match should have 13: ten line umpires, one net official, one foot-fault official and a chair umpire.

The shortest intercontinental commercial flight is from Gibraltar (Europe) to Tangier (Africa). The distance is 34 miles and the flight takes 20 minutes.

The quartz crystal in a wristwatch vibrates 32,768 times a second.

The US has more bagpipe bands than Scotland.

There's no sand in sandpaper.

Mark Wahlberg has a third nipple (airbrushed out of the Calvin Klein underwear ad).

Elvis Presley never gave an encore.

Gone With the Wind was set in the US Civil War but didn't feature a single battle scene.

Flamingo tongues were a delicacy in ancient Rome.

Frosties' Tony the Tiger turns 50 in 2005.

The Jolly Green Giant turns 77 in 2005.

The YKK on a zip stands for Yoshida Kogyo Kabushibibaisha, the world's largest zip manufacturer.

Before 1800 there was no such thing as separate shoes for left and right feet.

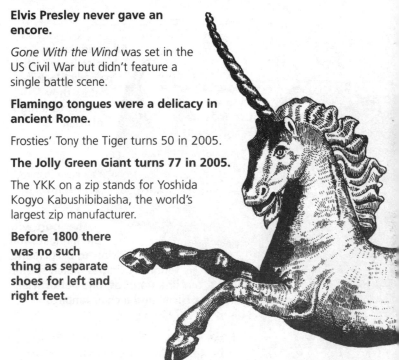

THINGS SAID ABOUT LAWYERS

'The first thing we do, let's kill all the lawyers.' (William Shakespeare, *King Henry VI, Part Two*)

'Ninety-nine per cent of lawyers give the rest a bad name.' (Steven Wright)

'A town that can't support one lawyer can always support two.' (Lyndon B. Johnson)

'Woodpeckers and lawyers have long bills.' (Dr K.C. Allen)

'There is never a deed so foul that something couldn't be said for the guy. That's why there are lawyers.' (Melvin Belli)

'I don't think you can make a lawyer honest by an act of legislature. You've got to work on his conscience. And his lack of conscience is what makes him a lawyer.' (Will Rogers)

'The trouble with law is lawyers.' (Clarence Darrow)

'Lawyers, I suppose, were children once.' (Charles Lamb)

'To some lawyers all facts are created equal.' (Felix Frankfurter)

'Between grand theft and a legal fee, there only stands a law degree.' (Anon)

'People whose profession it is to disguise matters.' (Sir Thomas More)

'If law school is so hard to get through, how come there are so many lawyers?' (Calvin Trillin)

'If you laid all of the lawyers in the world, end to end, on the equator – it would be a good idea to leave them there.' (Anon)

'God works wonders now and then. Behold! A lawyer, an honest man.' (Benjamin Franklin)

'Two farmer were arguing over the ownership of a cow. While one farmer pulled the head, the other pulled the tail. The lawyer sat in the middle milking the cow.' (Hebrew proverb)

'The legal trade is nothing but a high-class racket.' (Professor Fred Rodell)

'A lawyer is a learned gentleman who rescues your estate from your enemies and keeps it for himself.' (Lord Brougham)

'It is the trade of lawyers to question everything, yield nothing, and to talk by the hour.' (Thomas Jefferson)

'He saw a lawyer killing a viper on a dunghill hard by his own stable/ And the Devil smiled, for it put him in mind of Cain and his brother Abel.' (Samuel T. Coleridge)

'Lawyers are the only persons in whom ignorance of the law is not punished.' (Jeremy Bentham)

'Old lawyers never die, they just lose their appeal.' (Anon)

'What happens when a lawyer takes Viagra? He gets taller.' (Anon)

'An incompetent attorney can delay a trial for months or years. A competent attorney can delay one even longer.' (Evelle J. Younger)

'Lawyers are like rhinoceroses: thick-skinned, short-sighted but always ready to charge.' (Anon)

'Everyone ought to take every opportunity to blast lawyers.' (Marlin Fitzwater)

'As we watched Judge Clarence Thomas's Supreme Court confirmation hearings, all of the commentators said the same thing: "One of these people in the room is lying." Do you believe that? You've got two lawyers and fourteen senators in the room, and only *one* of them is lying?' (Jay Leno)

'Lawyers spend a great deal of their time shoveling smoke.' (Oliver Wendell Holmes)

'Win your lawsuit, lose your money.' (Spanish proverb)

'If all the lawyers were hanged tomorrow, and their bones sold to a mahjong factory, we'd be freer and safer, and our taxes would be reduced by almost half.' (H. L. Mencken)

'A man may as well open an oyster without a knife as a lawyer's mouth without a fee.' (Barten Holyday)

'A lawyer is a man who helps you get what's coming to him.' (Laurence J. Peter)

'No poet ever interpreted nature as freely as a lawyer interprets truth.' (Jean Giraudoux)

'Those who use the law as shoemakers use leather; rubbing it, pressing it, and stretching it with their teeth, all to the end of making it fit their purposes.' (King Louis XII)

'If it weren't for lawyers, we wouldn't need them.' (Anon)

'How do you get along at the office? Do you trust each other? Or does each have a separate safe for his money?' (Groucho Marx to his lawyer)

'I think we may class the lawyer in the natural history of monsters.' (John Keats)

'He is no lawyer who cannot take two sides.' (Charles Lamb)

A GUIDE TO CHIPS

The chip was first made in France – hence the name 'French fries'.

In Britain the first mention of chips is to be found in an 1854 recipe book, *Shilling Cookery*, in which chef Alexis Soyer referred to a recipe with 'thin cut potatoes cooked in oil'.

In 1857, Charles Dickens referred to plates of 'potato sticks cooked in oil'.

Gram for gram, chips contain a quarter of the fat of doughnuts.

In Britain we eat over two million tonnes of chips every year – that's 37 kg for each person every year.

Chips are the biggest-selling frozen vegetable in the world.

There are 8,500 fish and chip shops in the UK. In the 1950s there were more than 30,000. Nevertheless, fish and chip shops are still the most popular take-away restaurants in the UK.

69 per cent of us put salt on our chips; 57 per cent vinegar; 24 per cent tomato ketchup; 8 per cent brown sauce; 5 per cent mayonnaise and 2 per cent gravy.

Only the British sprinkle their chips with vinegar. The French usually have a pinch of salt, the Belgians use mayonnaise, while the Americans use tomato ketchup.

At the largest frozen chip factory in Britain, 3.5 tonnes of potatoes are processed every hour.

In 1996, the Irish introduced edible bags for chips to cut down on litter. According to someone who ate one, the bags 'taste a bit like mashed potato'.

When Arsene Wenger became manager of Arsenal, one of the first things he did was to ban chips from his players' diets.

American *Vogue* ran into trouble when it published a recipe that recommended using horse lard to cook tastier French fries.

80 per cent of the population visit fish and chip shops at least once a year. 22 per cent go at least once a week.

In the 19th century fish- and chip-fryers were social outcasts because of the strong odour of frying, which remained on their clothes.

Chippies officially remained an offensive trade until 1940. If the fat was not changed every day, the shops smelt awful and were usually confined to the poorer districts of town. As their popularity grew, however, the equipment and premises became more sophisticated.

Chips are a good source of vitamin C and complex carbohydrates in the form of starch. They also provide protein, fibre, iron, and other vitamins.

Every year British fish and chip shops chop up 500,000 tons of potatoes for chips – that's one twelfth of all the potatoes eaten in Britain.

The Germans have invented a revolutionary oven that produces a greaseless chip.

CELEBRITIES AND CHIPS

According to her mother, Carol Vorderman and her siblings were fed chips every day.

The actress Cameron Diaz says she has a 'love affair with French fries', which plays havoc with her skin. 'I've always been a salty, greasy kind of girl,' she declares.

Nick Faldo shocked the American golfing establishment when he ordered chips for the 1997 Masters dinner. As defending champion, it was up to him to choose the menu for the Past Champions dinner in the Augusta National clubhouse. After his two previous victories, he chose steak and kidney pie and shepherd's pie, but in 1997 he selected British fish, chips and, of course, mushy peas.

In *Pulp Fiction*, John Travolta, as Vincent Vega, the heroin-addled hit man, tells Samuel L. Jackson, 'Did you know McDonald's serves French fries with mayonnaise in Amsterdam?'

HEIGHT INDEX

4 foot 11: Charlene Tilton, Nancy Walker, Lynsey De Paul, Lil' Kim

5 foot: Dawn French, Geraldine Chaplin, Sir Norman Wisdom, Jada Pinkett Smith, Lucy Benjamin

5 foot 1: Kylie Minogue, Danny DeVito, Ronnie Corbett, Petula Clark, Sheena Easton, Carrie Fisher, Debbie Reynolds, Stevie Nicks, Lucy Liu, Lulu

5 foot 2: Holly Hunter, Sally Field, Joan Rivers, Linda Ronstadt, Sissy Spacek, Gloria Estefan, Rachel Stevens, Joan Collins, Jane Horrocks, Dame Judi Dench, Emma Bunton, Geri Halliwell, Suzanne Shaw, Jodie Marsh, Reese Witherspoon

5 foot 3: Julia Sawalha, Mickey Rooney, Sarah Michelle Gellar, Bernie Ecclestone, Prince Naseem Hamed, Christina Aguilera, Kerry McFadden, Helena Bonham Carter, Kathy Bates

5 foot 4: Madonna, Michael J. Fox, Roman Polanski, Drew Barrymore, Britney Spears, The Queen, Anne Robinson (and half an inch), Melinda Messenger, Tina Turner, Scarlett Johansson

5 foot 5: Belinda Carlisle, Sachin Tendulkar, Mel B, Jennifer Aniston, Natasha Hamilton, Joe Pesci, Sanjeev Bhaskar

5 foot 6: Pauline Quirke, Martin Amis, Princess Anne, Jayne Middlemiss, Calista Flockhart, Victoria Beckham, Carol Vorderman, Elijah Wood

5 foot 7: Laura Bailey, Sir Mick Jagger, Laetitia Casta, Tom Cruise, Kate Winslet, Catherine Zeta-Jones, Mark Wahlberg, Keira Knightley

5 foot 8: Phil Collins, Anne Bancroft, Rita Coolidge, Lauren Hutton, Billy Joel, Ringo Starr, Robin Williams, Robert Redford, Mel Gibson, Ali Landry, Elizabeth Hurley, Tobey Maguire, Mackenzie Crook

5 foot 9: Claire Rayner, Vic Reeves, Lauren Bacall, Liam Gallagher, Prince Charles, Shannon Elizabeth, Cameron Diaz, Richard Whiteley, Abs Breen, Liz McLarnon, Nell McAndrew

5 foot 10: Naomi Campbell, Harry Enfield, Lily Tomlin, Fiona Bruce, Nicole Kidman, Natasha Henstridge, Paul Nicholls, Gwyneth Paltrow, Minnie Driver

5 foot 11: George Michael, Bea Arthur, Vanessa Redgrave, Brooke Shields, Sigourney Weaver, Adam Rickitt, Claudia Schiffer, Jerry Hall, Lucy Lawless, Sophie Dahl

6 foot: Eva Herzigova, Terry Wogan, Brad Pitt, Macy Gray, Prince Edward, Prince Andrew, Tony Blair, Leonardo DiCaprio, Matthew Perry, Allison Janney

6 foot 1: Janet Street-Porter, Pete Sampras, Venus Williams, Pierce Brosnan, Freddie Prinze Jr, Janet McTeer, Chris Isaak, Enrique Iglesias, Jodie Kidd

6 foot 2: Julie T. Wallace, Russ Abbot, Chris Evans, Richard Madeley, Lindsay Davenport, Steve Penk, Tiger Woods, George W. Bush, Thierry Henry, Timothy Dalton

6 foot 3: Michael Barrymore, Clint Eastwood, Muhammad Ali, Jon Voight, Jamie Theakston, Al Gore, Brendan Fraser

6 foot 4: Frank Bruno, Chevy Chase, Louis Gossett Jr, Ralph Nader, Tom Selleck, John Wayne, Ben Affleck, Billy Campbell, Goran Visnijc, Benicio Del Toro, Heath Ledger, Rupert Everett, John Kerry

6 foot 5: Mick Fleetwood, John Leslie, Tim Robbins, Howard Stern

6 foot 6: Dolph Lundgren, Tommy Tune, Hulk Hogan

6 foot 7: Terry Waite, John Cleese

6 foot 9: Michael Crichton

7 foot 2: Richard Kiel

Brains

The brain is the second heaviest organ in the human body (after the liver and ahead of the lungs and the heart).

A brain weighs around 3 pounds. All but 10 ounces is water.

The brain uses more than 25 per cent of the oxygen required by the human body.

The brain uses less power than a 100-watt bulb.

Is eating fish good for the brain? Up to a point. The brain needs decosahexaenoic acid to develop and this is found in oily fish. P.G. Wodehouse's Jeeves attributed his brainpower to the eating of fish.

Albert Einstein's brain was preserved after his death. So was Lenin's.

Vincent van Gogh's brain was destroyed by the mercury he took to counteract syphilis.

Mensa people

Sir Clive Sinclair, Sir Jimmy Savile, Geena Davis, Carol Vorderman, Leslie Charteris, Jamie Theakston, Carol Smillie, Jeremy Hanley, Sally Farmiloe, Adrian Moorhouse.

John Thomson, Caroline Aherne, Bill Clinton and James Woods have all been measured at above Mensa entry level

THE BUFFALO THEORY

A herd of buffalo only moves as fast as the slowest buffalo. So when the herd is hunted, it is the weakest and slowest ones at the back that get killed first. This example of natural selection is beneficial for the herd because the regular culling of the weakest animals improves the overall and average health and speed of the whole group. Similarly, the human brain can only work at the speed of its slowest cells. Now, too much alcohol kills brain cells – but, importantly, the weakest and slowest cells first. Consequently, regular beer consumption, by eliminating them, is making your brain work faster and better.

So the moral of this theory is: drink more beer.

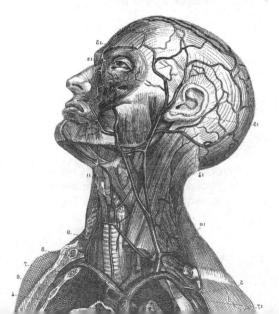

UNINTENTIONALLY FUNNY (GENUINE) NEWSPAPER HEADLINES

HIGH SCHOOL DROPOUTS CUT IN HALF

COMPLAINTS ABOUT REFEREES GROWING UGLY

ASBESTOS SUIT PRESSED

PHYSICIST RECOMMENDS BIGGER BALLS TO SLOW DOWN MALE TENNIS PLAYERS

NEW STUDY OF OBESITY LOOKS FOR LARGER TEST GROUP

PUPILS TRAIN AS COUNSELLORS TO HELP UPSET CLASSMATES

TWO CONVICTS EVADE NOOSE: JURY HUNG

PANDA MATING FAILS – VETERINARIAN TAKES OVER

ORGAN FESTIVAL ENDS IN A SMASHING CLIMAX

DEALERS WILL HEAR CAR TALK AT NOON

TWO SISTERS REUNITE AFTER EIGHTEEN YEARS AT CHECKOUT COUNTER

POLICE DISCOVER CRACK IN AUSTRALIA

WAR DIMS HOPE FOR PEACE

BOY WANTS TO MOUNT AUTOGRAPHED GUITAR

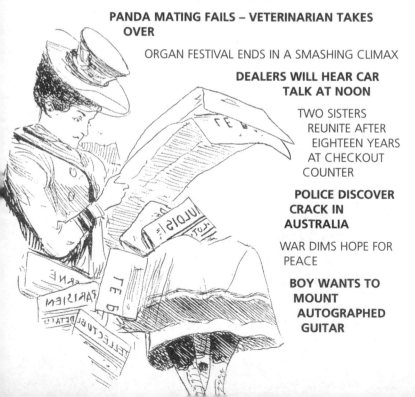

BODY FOUND ON BOAT SEIZED BY BAILIFFS AND DUE TO BE AUCTIONED

MILK DRINKERS ARE TURNING TO POWDER

TYPHOON RIPS THROUGH CEMETERY; HUNDREDS DEAD

BABIES USED TO SNEAK DRUGS INTO PRISON

ARAFAT SWEARS IN CABINET

BANGKOK LAUNCHES ANTI-BUTT CAMPAIGN

NEW AUTOS TO HIT 5 MILLION

MARCH PLANNED FOR NEXT AUGUST

NEW HOUSING FOR ELDERLY NOT YET DEAD

TUNA BITING OFF WASHINGTON COAST

JUDGE ACTS TO REOPEN THEATER

WOMAN ATTACKED BY TRAIN STATION

CHOPPER SEARCH FOR MAN IN UNDERPANTS

BRITON GORED BY BULL IN INTENSIVE CARE

BULGE IN TROUSERS WAS ECSTASY

CARIBBEAN ISLANDS DRIFT TO LEFT

SOMETHING WENT WRONG IN JET CRASH, EXPERT SAYS

GOLFERS WARNED NOT TO LICK BALLS

DRUGS FINE FOR BUSINESSMAN

COPS QUIZ VICTIM IN FATAL SHOOTING

SEX SCANDAL VICAR SEEKS NEW POSITION

CIRCUMCISION NOW SEEN AS POINTLESS

DOWN UNDER LOVE FOR PRINCESS ANNE'S DAUGHTER

BLIND BISHOP APPOINTED TO SEE

MAN WITH ONE ARM AND LEG CHEATS ON OTHER HALF

GIANT TEA BAGS PROTEST

POLICE CHIEF'S PLEDGE TO MURDER WITNESSES

MOST SURGEONS FACE CUTS

12 ON THEIR WAY TO CRUISE AMONG DEAD IN PLANE CRASH

STIFF OPPOSITION EXPECTED TO CASKETLESS FUNERAL PLAN

INCLUDE YOUR CHILDREN WHEN BAKING COOKIES

DAD WANTS BABY LEFT IN AEROPLANE

MALE NATURIST MEMBERS RISE

CUTS COULD HURT ANIMALS

CHEF THROWS HIS HEART INTO HELPING FEED NEEDY

PUBLIC SWINGS IN FAVOUR OF THE PRINCE

HALF MILLION ITALIAN WOMEN SEEN ON PILL

IDAHO GROUP ORGANIZES TO HELP SERVICE WIDOWS

L.A. VOTERS APPROVE URBAN RENEWAL BY LANDSLIDE

LESOTHO WOMEN MAKE GREAT CARPETS

EU MUST UNITE ON DRUGS

MEN RECOMMEND MORE CLUBS FOR WIVES

GUNMAN SHOT BY 999 COPS

PROSTITUTES TO HOLD OPEN DAY

SUBSTITUTE TEACHERS SEEKING RESPECT

NIGHT SCHOOL TO HEAR PEST TALK

HOME SECRETARY TO ACT ON VIDEO NASTIES

DIET OF PREMATURE BABIES 'AFFECTS IQ'

SEX UP AND DOWN AFTER SEPTEMBER 11

LARGEST AMOUNT OF CANNABIS EVER SEIZED IN JOINT OPERATION

STRAW'S PLEDGE TO RAPE VICTIMS

MAD COW TALKS

THE SENILITY PRAYER

God, grant me the senility to forget the people I never liked anyway, the good fortune to run into the ones that I do, and the eyesight to tell the difference.

DUMB THINGS PEOPLE HAVE SAID

'Everything that can be invented has been invented.' (Charles H. Duell, Commissioner, US Office of Patents, 1899)

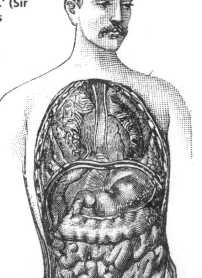

'This "telephone" has too many shortcomings to be seriously considered as a means of communication. The device is inherently of no value to us.' (Western Union internal memo, 1876)

'If we can just get young people to do as their fathers did, that is, wear condoms.' (Sir Richard Branson)

'My imagination refuses to see any sort of submarine doing anything but suffocating its crew.' (H.G. Wells)

'The abdomen, the chest, and the brain will forever be shut from the intrusion of the wise and humane surgeon.' (Sir John Ericksen, Queen Victoria's surgeon, 1873)

'Louis Pasteur's theory of germs is ridiculous fiction.' (Pierre Pachet, Professor of Physiology, 1872)

'No flying machine will ever fly from New York to Paris.' (Orville Wright)

'Drill for oil? You mean drill into the ground to try and find oil? You're crazy.' (Drillers responding to Edwin L. Drake in 1859)

'Airplanes are interesting toys but of no military value.' (Marshal Foch)

'Who the hell wants to hear actors talk?' (Harry Warner of Warner Brothers, 1927)

'The wireless music box has no imaginable commercial value. Who would pay for a message sent to nobody in particular?' (Anonymous businessman declining to invest in radio in the 1920s)

'So we went to Atari and said, "Hey, we've got this amazing thing, even built with some of your parts – what do you think about funding us? Or we'll give it to you. We just want to do it. Pay our salary, we'll come work for you." And they said, "No." So then we went to Hewlett-Packard, and they said, "Hey, we don't need you. You haven't got through college yet."' (Apple Computer co-founder Steve Jobs)

'I'm just glad it'll be Clark Gable who's falling on his face and not Gary Cooper.' (Gary Cooper turning down the role of Rhett Butler in *Gone With The Wind*)

'Heavier-than-air flying machines are impossible.' (Lord Kelvin, President of the Royal Society, talking in 1895)

'Stocks have reached what looks like a permanently high plateau.' (Irving Fisher, Professor of Economics at Yale just before the 1929 Wall Street Crash)

'The concept is interesting and well-formed, but in order to earn better than a C, the idea must be feasible.' (A Yale University professor's comment on Fred Smith's paper proposing an overnight delivery service. Smith later founded Federal Express.)

SUICIDE

Three times as many men commit suicide as women. But women attempt suicide two to three times more often than men.

The season for suicides is the spring; the winter months have the lowest number of suicides.

In 1926, a Budapest waiter committed suicide. He left his suicide note in the form of a crossword and the police had to get help from the public to solve it.

Vincent van Gogh committed suicide while painting *Wheat Field with Crows*.

COMMITTED SUICIDE

Bobby Bloom, Kurt Cobain, Michael Hutchence, Gig Young, Richard Manuel, Ian Curtis, Jerzy Kosinski, Pete Ham, Terry Kath, Ron 'Pigpen' McKernan, Donny Hathaway, Paul Williams, Cleopatra, Ronnie Scott, Ernest Hemingway, Margot Hemingway, Marc Antony, Screaming Lord Sutch, Del Shannon, Graham Bond, Brian Epstein, James Whale, John Kennedy Toole, Joseph Goebbels, Nick Drake, Brian Keith, Phil Ochs, Yukio Mishima, George Sanders, Tony Hancock, Hannibal, Freddie Prinze, Terence Donovan, Ted Moult, Primo Levi,

Adolf Hitler, David Bairstow, Stuart
Adamson, Robert Clive, Rory Storm, Nero,
Kid McCoy, Lord Castlereagh, Sylvia Plath,
Arthur Koestler, Pontius Pilate, Capucine,
Virginia Woolf, Carole Landis, Alan Turing,
Charles Boyer, Dorothy Dandridge, Herve
Villechaize, Faron Young, Pete Duel, The
Singing Nun, George Reeves, Margaret
Sullavan, Randy Turpin, Jean Seberg,
Thelma Todd, Lupe Velez, Spalding Gray

PEOPLE WHOSE FATHERS COMMITTED SUICIDE

Ernest Hemingway, Tara Fitzgerald, Hal Ashby, Phil Spector (on his
tombstone were the words 'To know him was to love him'), Ted
Turner, Betty Hutton, Rick Stein, Wendy Richard, Slobodan Milosevic,
Dawn French, Ben Hogan, Martina Navratilova, Steve Strange, Ruth
Prawer Jhabvala, Sarah Brightman, Jane Asher, Alger Hiss, Marsha
Hunt, Jean Cocteau

PEOPLE WHOSE MOTHERS COMMITTED SUICIDE

Dale Winton, Alan Ladd, Sid Vicious, Jane
Fonda, Sir Nikolaus Pevsner, Antonia de
Sancha, Christopher Hitchens, Mike
Oldfield, Slobodan Milosevic, Dame
Margaret Rutherford, Lena Zavaroni,
René Magritte, Truman Capote, Mikhail
Baryshnikov, Richard Todd, Spalding
Gray, Jean-Bedel Bokassa, Amos Oz,
Kurt Vonnegut, Peter Fonda

People whose sons committed suicide

Gregory Peck, Theodore Roosevelt, Paul Newman, Bing Crosby (two sons), Ian Fleming, Dan Dailey, Mary Tyler Moore, Bobby Womack, Hank Marvin, Thomas Mann, Charles Boyer, Richard Todd, Eugene O'Neill (two sons), Art Linkletter, Carroll O'Connor, Walter Winchell

People whose daughters committed suicide

Margaret Sullavan, Karl Marx, Robert Frost, James Arness, Marlon Brando, John Barrymore, Timothy Leary

Men whose wives committed suicide

Adolf Hitler (with him), Ted Hughes, Percy Bysshe Shelley, Timothy Leary, Jackson Browne, Henry Brooks Adams, Arthur Koestler (with him), Heinrich Mann, John Hiatt, Joseph Goebbels (with him), Joseph Stalin, Lord Melvyn Bragg, Henry Fonda

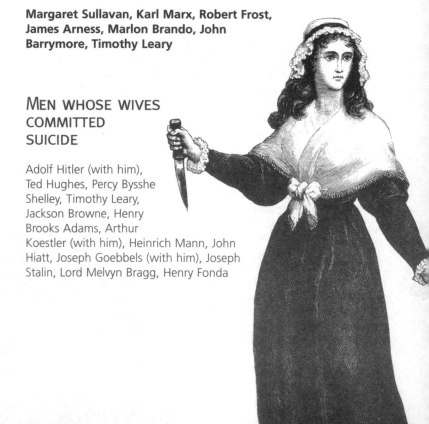

WOMEN WHOSE HUSBANDS COMMITTED SUICIDE

Courtney Love, Katharine Graham, Diana Dors (after her death), Joan Rivers, June Brown

SURVIVED SUICIDE ATTEMPTS

Drew Barrymore, Sir Elton John, Marianne Faithfull, Frank Sinatra, Tom Baker, Tuesday Weld, Danniella Westbrook, Billy Joel, Brenda Fricker, Sinéad O'Connor, Vanilla Ice, Gary Glitter, Mickey Rooney, Yannick Noah, Caroline Aherne, Jo O'Meara, Pamela Anderson, Mel B, Halle Berry, Jack Osbourne

ENOUGH TO END IT ALL?

In 1927, Edwin Wakeman of Manchester committed suicide leaving this note: 'I married a widow with a grown daughter. My father fell in love with my stepdaughter and married her – thus becoming my son-in-law. My stepdaughter became my stepmother because she was my father's wife. My wife gave birth to a son, who was, of course, my father's brother-in-law, and also my uncle, for he was the brother of my stepmother. My father's wife became the mother of a son, who was, of course, my brother, and also my grandchild, for he was the son of my stepdaughter. Accordingly, my wife was my grandmother, because she was my stepmother's mother. I was my wife's husband and grandchild at the same time. And, as the husband of a person's grandmother is his grandfather, I am my own grandfather.'

Died on Stage (literally)

Tommy Cooper

Sid James

Leonard Rossiter

Marie Lloyd

Simon Barere (pianist)

Les Harvey (Stone The Crows musician – electrocuted by touching a live microphone with wet feet in 1972)

Richard Versalle (opera singer – after singing the line 'Too bad you can only live so long' in 1996)

Linda Wright (nightclub singer)

Leonard Warren (opera singer)

DIED VIRGINS

Immanuel Kant, Sir J.M. Barrie, Nikolai Gogol, Queen Elizabeth I, Sir Isaac Newton, Anton Bruckner, Alma Cogan, Hans Christian Andersen, Edith Sitwell

DIED INTESTATE

Jayne Mansfield, George Gershwin, Karl Marx, Rita Hayworth, Howard Hughes, Abraham Lincoln, Pablo Picasso, Duke Ellington, Lenny Bruce, Paolo Gucci, Pat Phoenix, Phil Lynott, Sylvia Plath, Keith Moon

BELIEVE IN REINCARNATION

Jesper Parnevik, Glenn Hoddle, Eric Cantona, Joan Collins, Louise Jameson, k.d. lang, Keanu Reeves, Conchita Martinez, Tori Amos, Shirley MacLaine, Gillian Anderson, Sarah Jessica Parker

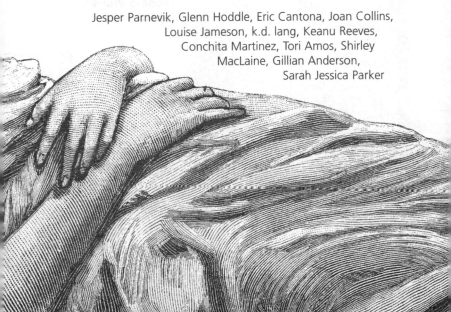

FAMOUS MEN'S LAST WORDS

'I'm still alive.' (Caligula, AD41)

'Tomorrow, I shall no longer be here.' (Nostradamus – possibly the only prophecy he got right, 1566)

'Friends, applaud, the comedy is over.' (Ludwig van Beethoven, 1827)

'Such is life.' (Ned Kelly, 1880)

'Who is it?' (Billy the Kid before being shot by Sheriff Pat Garrett, 1881)

'Go on, get out! Last words are for fools who haven't said enough.' (Karl Marx, 1883)

'I'm tired of fighting. I guess this is going to get me.' (Harry Houdini, 1926)

'Four o'clock. How strange. So that is the time. Strange. Enough.' (Sir Henry Morton Stanley, 1904)

'It is never too late for a glass of champagne.' (Anton Chekhov, 1904)

'Don't let it end like this. Tell them I said something.' (Pancho Villa, 1923)

'So little done, so much to do.' (Cecil Rhodes, 1902)

'If this is dying, I don't think much of it.' (Lytton Strachey, 1932)

'Never felt better.' (Douglas Fairbanks Sr, 1939)

'But, but, Mister Colonel ...' (Benito Mussolini, 1945)

'Go away. I'm all right.' (H.G. Wells, 1946)

'Born in a hotel room and – God damn it – died in a hotel room.' (Eugene O'Neill, 1953)

'Dying is easy. Comedy is difficult.' (Edmund Gwenn, 1959)

'Oh God, here I go.' (Max Baer, 1959)

'Dying is a very dull affair. My advice to you is to have nothing whatever to do with it.' (W. Somerset Maugham, 1965)

'It hurts.' (Charles de Gaulle, 1970)

'Drink to me.' (Picasso, 1973)

'OK, I won't.' (Elvis Presley, after his girlfriend told him not to fall asleep in the bathroom, 1977)

'That was a great game of golf, fellas.' (Bing Crosby, 1977)

'I would like two lightly poached eggs.' (Roy Jenkins, 2003)

'Channel 5 is all s*, isn't it? Christ, the c**p they put on there. It's a waste of space.' (Adam Faith, 2003)**

NB When Albert Einstein died in 1955, his final words died with him – the nurse at his side didn't understand German.

FAMOUS WOMEN'S LAST WORDS

'Hold the cross high so I may see it through the flames!' (Joan of Arc, 1431)

'All my possessions for a moment of time.'
(Queen Elizabeth I, 1603)

'Sir, I beg your pardon.' (Marie Antoinette, Queen of France, 1793, as she stepped on the executioner's foot)

'Nothing but death.' (Jane Austen, when asked if she wanted anything, 1817)

'Oh, I am not going to die, am I? He will not separate us, we have been so happy.' (Charlotte Brontë, 1855, to her husband of nine months)

'Beautiful.' (Elizabeth Barrett Browning, 1861, in answer to her husband's query as to how she was feeling)

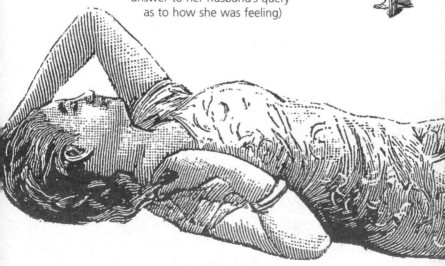

'I must go in, the fog is rising.' (Emily Dickinson, 1886)

'Is it not meningitis?' (Louisa M. Alcott, 1888)

'It is unbelievable.' (Mata Hari, 1917)

'Farewell, my friends. I go to glory.' (Isadora Duncan, 1927)

'Get my swan costume ready.' (Anna Pavlova, 1931)

'KHAQQ calling Itasca. We must be on you, but cannot see you. Gas is running low.' (Amelia Earhart, 1937)

'What is the question?' (Gertrude Stein, 1946 after her partner, Alice B. Toklas, asked her, 'What is the answer?')

'Is everybody happy? I want everybody to be happy. I know I'm happy.' (Ethel Barrymore, 1959)

'Am I dying or is this my birthday?' (Lady Nancy Astor, 1964)

'Codeine … bourbon.' (Tallulah Bankhead, 1968)

'Damn it! Don't you dare ask God to help me.' (Joan Crawford, 1977, to her housekeeper who was praying for her)

'My God. What's happened?' (Diana, Princess of Wales, 1997)

DIED BEFORE THE AGE OF 40

King Louis XVII of France 10

King Edward V 12

Saint Agnes 13

Saint Pancras 14

Anne Frank 15

King Edward VI 16

Lady Jane Grey 16

Ritchie Valens 17

Tutankhamun 18

Joan of Arc 19

Catherine Howard 20

Nancy Spungen 20

Dorothy Stratten 20

Duncan Edwards 21

Eddie Cochran 21

Stu Sutcliffe 21

Sid Vicious 21

Lillian Board 22

Aaliyah 22

Billy The Kid 22

Pocahontas 22

Buddy Holly 22

Freddie Prinze 22

Bonnie Parker 23

River Phoenix 23

Duane Allman 24

Tammi Terrell 24

Lee Harvey Oswald 24

James Dean 24

Frankie Lymon 25

Clyde Barrow 25

Françoise Dorleac 25

John Keats 25

Baron Manfred von Richtofen 25

Gram Parsons 26

Otis Redding 26

Sharon Tate 26

Nick Drake 26

Kurt Cobain 27

Jimi Hendrix 27

Robert Johnson 27

Brian Jones 27

Janis Joplin 27

Ron 'Pigpen' McKernan 27

Jim Morrison 27

Bix Beiderbecke 28

Caligula 28

Brandon Lee 28

Catherine Parr 28

Ruth Ellis 28

J. P. Richardson (aka 'The Big Bopper') 28

Karen Silkwood 28

Marc Bolan 29

Fletcher Christian 29

Ronnie Van Zant 29

Hank Williams 29

Anne Brontë 29

Percy Bysshe Shelley 29

Jean Vigo 29

Emily Brontë 30

Jim Croce 30

Sylvia Plath 30

Jeff Buckley 30

Andreas Baader 30

Steve Biko 30

Brandon DeWilde 30

Andy Gibb 30

Lisa 'Left Eye' Lopes 30

Nero 30

Keith Moon 31

John Bonham 31

Sandy Denny 31

Pete Duel 31

Karen Quinlan 31

Minnie Riperton 31

John Kennedy Toole 31

Rudolph Valentino 31

Patsy Cline 31

Florence Ballard 32

John Dillinger 32

Queen Mary II 32

King Richard III 32

Charles Rolls 32

Jane Seymour 32

Robert Walker 32

Bruce Lee 32

Keith Relf 32

Karen Carpenter 32

Bill Hicks 32

Carole Lombard 33

Dick Turpin 33

Alexander The Great 33

John Belushi 33

Eva Braun 33

Eva Cassidy 33

Charlotte Coleman 33

Sam Cooke 33

Mama Cass Elliot 33

Unity Mitford 33

Sanjay Gandhi 33

Donny Hathaway 33

Eva Perón 33

King Richard II 33

Yuri Gagarin 34

Gerald Hoffnung 34

Jesse James 34

Ayrton Senna 34

Joe Orton 34

Jayne Mansfield 35

Charlie Parker 35

Stevie Ray Vaughan 35

Wolfgang Mozart 35

Jesse James 35

Anne Boleyn 35

Guy Fawkes 35

Roger Tonge 35

King Henry V 35

Phil Ochs 35

Peter Revson 35

Marilyn Monroe 36

Robespierre 36

George Custer 36

Rainer Werner Fassbinder 36

Bob Marley 36

Mike Bloomfield 36

Princess Diana 36

Bob 'The Bear' Hite 36

Marie-Antoinette 37

Jill Dando 37

Bobby Darin 37

Rosalind Franklin 37

Lou Gehrig 37

Michael Hutchence 37

George Mallory 37

Sal Mineo 37

Christina Onassis 37

Irving Thalberg 37

Vincent van Gogh 37

Georges Bizet 37

Alexander Pushkin 37

Robert Burns 37

Charlotte Brontë 38

Felix Mendelssohn 38

Joanne Campbell 38

Harry Chapin 38

Stephen Foster 38

George Gershwin 38

Amelia Earhart 38

Florence Griffith Joyner 38

John Kennedy Jr 38

Mario Lanza 38

Federico Lorca 38

Van McCoy 38

David Rappaport 38

Che Guevara 39

Frederic Chopin 39

Dylan Thomas 39

Dr Martin Luther King 39

Blaise Pascal 39

Dennis Wilson 39

Pier Angeli 39

Neil Bogart 39

Tim Hardin 39

Wild Bill Hickock 39

Jim Reeves 39

Sabu 39

Fats Waller 39

Dinah Washington 39

Malcolm X 39

Emiliano Zapata 39

Lynne Frederick 39

Grace Metalious 39

John Garfield 39

Died in a plane crash

Roald Amundsen (1928)

Will Rogers (1935)

Carole Lombard (1942)

Leslie Howard (1943)

Charles Paddock (1943)

Antoine de Saint-Exupéry (1944)

Glenn Miller (1944)

Orde Wingate (1944)

Mike Todd (1958)

Duncan Edwards (1958)

Buddy Holly (1959)

J.P. Richardson ('The Big Bopper'; 1959)

Ritchie Valens (1959)

Dag Hammarskjöld (1961)

Patsy Cline (1963)

Jim Reeves (1964)

Herbert Marshall (1966)

Otis Redding (1967)

Yuri Gagarin (1968)

Rocky Marciano (1969)

Audie Murphy (1971)

Prince William of Gloucester (1972)

Jim Croce (1973)

Graham Hill (1975)

Ronnie Van Zant (1977)

Steve Gaines (1977)

Cassie Gaines (1977)

Sanjay Gandhi (1980)

Ricky Nelson (1985)

Larry Shue (1985)

General Muhammad Zia ul-Haq (1988)

Stevie Ray Vaughan (1990)

Senator John Tower (1991)

Bill Graham (1991)

Ron Brown (1996)

John Denver (1997)

Payne Stewart (1999)

John F. Kennedy Jr (1999)

DIED IN A ROAD ACCIDENT

T.E. Lawrence (1935)

Tom Mix (1940)

General George S. Patton (1945)

Margaret Mitchell (1949)

James Dean (1955)

Jackson Pollock (1956)

Prince Aly Khan (1960)

Eddie Cochran (1960)

Albert Camus (1960)

Ernie Kovacs (1962)

Jayne Mansfield (1967)

Françoise Dorleac (1967)

Duane Allman (1971)

Dickie Valentine (1971)

Brandon De Wilde (1972)

Marc Bolan (1977)

Harry Chapin (1981)

Grace Kelly (1982)

David Penhaligon (1986)

Cozy Powell (1988)

Falco (1988)

Pete DeFreitas (1989)

Diana, Princess of Wales (1997)

Dodi Fayed (1997)

Ian Bannen (1999)

Desmond Llewelyn (1999)

Aaliyah (2001)

Lisa 'Left Eye' Lopes (2002)

Helmut Newton (2004)

THE LAST LINE OF EVERY SHAKESPEARE PLAY

All's Well That Ends Well: 'Your gentle hands lend us, and take our hearts.' (King)

Antony And Cleopatra: 'Come, Dolabella, see/High order in this great solemnity.' (Octavius Caesar)

As You Like It: 'If I were a woman, I would kiss as many of you as had beards that pleased me, complexions that liked me and breaths that I defied not: and, I am sure, as many as have good beards, or good faces, or sweet breaths, will, for my kind offer, when I make curtsy, bid me farewell.' (Rosalind)

The Comedy of Errors: 'Nay, then, thus:/We came into the world like brother and brother;/And now let's go hand in hand, not one before another.' (Dromio of Ephesus)

Coriolanus: 'Though in this city he/Hath widow'd and unchilded many a one,/Which to this hour bewail the injury,/Yet he shall have a noble memory.—Assist.' (Aufidius)

Cymbeline: 'Never was a war did cease,/Ere bloody hands were wash'd, with such a peace.' (Cymbeline)

Hamlet: 'Take up the bodies: such a sight as this/Becomes the field, but here shows much amiss./Go, bid the soldiers shoot.' (Fortinbras)

Henry IV, Part One: 'Rebellion in this land shall lose his sway,/Meeting the check of such another day:/And since this business so fair is done,/Let us not leave till all our own be won.' (Henry IV)

Henry IV, Part Two: 'I will lay odds that, ere this year expire,/We bear our civil swords and native fire/As far as France: I heard a bird so sing,/Whose music, to my thinking, pleas'd the king./Come, will you hence?' (Lancaster – followed by an epilogue)

Henry V: 'Then shall I swear to Kate, and you to me;/And may

our oaths well kept and prosperous be!' (Henry V – followed by a chorus)

Henry VI, Part One: 'Margaret shall now be queen, and rule the king;/But I will rule both her, the king, and realm.' (Suffolk)

Henry VI, Part Two: 'Sound drums and trumpets, and to London all:/And more such days as these to us befall!' (Warwick)

Henry VI, Part Three: 'Sound drums and trumpets! farewell sour annoy!/For here, I hope, begins our lasting joy.' (Edward IV)

Henry VIII: 'This day, no man think/Has business at his house; for all shall stay:/This little one shall make it holiday.' (Henry VIII – followed by an epilogue)

Julius Caesar: 'So call the field to rest; and let's away,/To part the glories of this happy day.' (Octavius)

King John: 'Nought shall make us rue,/If England to itself do rest but true.' (Bastard)

King Lear: 'The weight of this sad time we must obey;/Speak what we feel, not what we ought to say./The oldest hath borne most: we that are young/Shall never see so much, nor live so long.' (Albany)

Love's Labours Lost: 'The words of Mercury are harsh after the songs of Apollo. You that way: we this way.' (Armado)

Macbeth: 'Of this dead butcher and his fiend-like queen,/Who, as 'tis thought, by self and violent hands/Took off her life; this, and what needful else/That calls upon us, by the grace of Grace,/We will perform in measure, time, and place:/So, thanks to all at once, and to each one,/Whom we invite to see us crown'd at Scone.' (Malcolm)

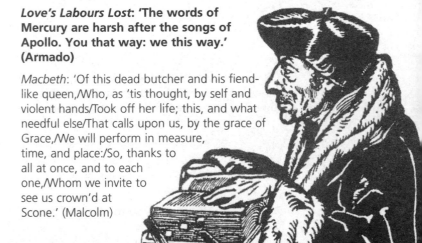

Measure For Measure: **'So, bring us to our palace; where we'll show/What's yet behind that's meet you all should know.' (Duke Vicentio)**

The Merry Wives of Windsor: 'Let it be so. Sir John,/To Master Brook you yet shall hold your word/For he, tonight, shall lie with Mistress Ford.' (Ford)

The Merchant of Venice: **'Well, while I live, I'll fear no other thing/So sore as keeping safe Nerissa's ring.' (Gratiano)**

A Midsummer Night's Dream: 'So, good night unto you all./Give me your hands, if we be friends,/And Robin shall restore amends.' (Puck)

Much Ado About Nothing: **'Think not on him till tomorrow:/I'll devise thee brave punishments for him./Strike up, pipers.' (Benedick)**

Othello: 'To you, lord governor,/Remains the censure of this hellish villain;/The time, the place, the torture: O, enforce it!/Myself will straight aboard; and to the state/This heavy act with heavy heart relate.' (Lodovico)

Pericles: **'So, on your patience evermore attending,/New joy wait on you! Here our play has ending.' (Gower)**

Richard II: 'Lords, I protest, my soul is full of woe,/That blood should sprinkle me to make me grow:/Come, mourn with me for that I do lament,/And put on sullen black incontinent:/I'll make a voyage to the Holy Land,/To wash this blood off from my guilty hand:/March sadly after; grace my mournings here;/In weeping after this untimely bier.' (Henry Bolingbroke)

***Richard III*: 'Now civil wounds are stopp'd, peace lives again:/That she may long live here, God say amen!' (Richmond)**

Romeo And Juliet: 'A glooming peace this morning with it brings;/The sun, for sorrow, will not show his head:/Go hence, to have more talk of these sad things;/Some shall be pardon'd, and some punished:/For never was a story of more woe/Than this of Juliet and her Romeo.' (Prince)

***The Taming of The Shrew*: ''Tis a wonder, by your leave, she will be tamed so.' (Lucentio)**

The Tempest: 'Now I want/Spirits to enforce, art to enchant,/And my ending is despair,/Unless I be relieved by prayer,/Which pierces so, that it assaults/Mercy itself, and frees all faults./As you from crimes would pardon'd be,/Let your indulgence set me free.' (Prospero)

***Timon of Athens*: 'Bring me into your city,/And I will use the olive with my sword,/Make war breed peace; make peace stint war; make each/Prescribe to other, as each other's leech./Let our drums strike.' (Alcibiades)**

Titus Andronicus: 'See justice done on Aaron, that damn'd Moor,/By whom our heavy haps had their beginning:/Then, afterwards, to order well the state,/That like events may ne'er it ruinate.' (Lucius)

***Troilus And Cressida*: 'Brethren and sisters of the old-door trade,/Some two months hence my will shall here be made:/It should be now, but that my fear is this,/Some galled goose of Winchester would hiss:/Till then I'll sweat, and seek about for eases;/And at that time, bequeath you my diseases.' (Pandarus)**

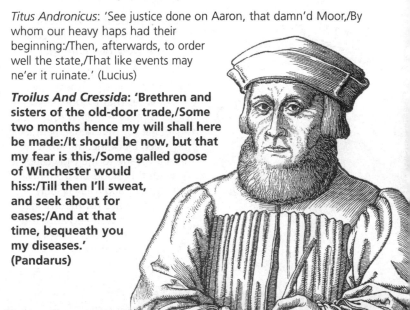

Twelfth Night: 'Cesario, come:/For so you shall be while you are a man;/But, when in other habits you are seen,/Orsino's mistress, and his fancy's queen.' (Duke – followed by Clown's song)

Two Gentlemen of Verona: 'Come, Proteus; 'tis your penance but to hear/The story of your loves discovered:/That done, our day of marriage shall be yours;/One feast, one house, one mutual happiness.' (Valentine)

The Winter's Tale: 'Good Paulina,/Lead us from hence, where we may leisurely/Each one demand, and answer to his part/Perform'd in this wide gap of time, since first/We were dissever'd: hastily lead away!' (Leontes)

FINALLY ...

'All I've ever wanted was an honest week's pay for an honest day's work.' (Steve Martin)

'Early to rise and early to bed, makes a male healthy, wealthy and dead.' (James Thurber)

'I like long walks, especially when they are taken by people who annoy me.' (Fred Allen)

'I think a man can have two, maybe three affairs, while he is married, but three is maximum. After that, you're cheating.' (Yves Montand)

'You can kill, you can maim people, but to be boring is truly a sin. And God will punish you for that.' (Burt Reynolds)

'Gluttony is not a secret vice.' (Orson Welles)

'Wickedness is a myth invented by good people to account for the curious attractiveness of others.' (Oscar Wilde)

'Tip big and tip quietly. Fold the bills three times into small squares and pass them in a handshake.' (Frank Sinatra)

'Remember that as a teenager you are in the last stage of your life when you will be happy to hear that the phone is for you.' (Fran Lebowitz)

'My best feature's my smile. And smiles – pray heaven – don't get fat.' (Jack Nicholson)

'Life is a tragedy when seen in close-up but a comedy in long-shot.' (Charlie Chaplin)

'Happiness in life is good health and a bad memory.' (Ingrid Bergman)

'I do not believe that friends are necessarily the people you like best; they are merely the people who got there first.' (Sir Peter Ustinov)

'I did not become a vegetarian for my health. I did it for the health of the chickens.' (Isaac Bashevis Singer)

'At fifty everyone has the face he deserves.' (George Orwell)

'To his dog, every man is Napoleon, hence the constant popularity of dogs.' (Aldous Huxley)

'There are only two things a child will share willingly – communicable diseases and his mother's age.' (Benjamin Spock)

'You never really know a man until you have divorced him.' (Zsa Zsa Gabor)

'The worst part of having success is to try finding someone who is happy for you.' (Bette Midler)

'Whenever a friend succeeds, a little something in me dies.' (Gore Vidal)

'Punctuality is the virtue of the bored.' (Evelyn Waugh)

'That is the essence of science: ask an impertinent question, and you are on the way to a pertinent answer.' (Jacob Bronowski)

'When you sit with a nice girl for two hours, you think it's only a minute. But when you sit on a hot stove for a minute, you think it's two hours. That's relativity.' (Albert Einstein)

'I can take any amount of criticism, so long as it is unqualified praise.' (Noel Coward)

ACKNOWLEDGEMENTS

I had so much fun compiling *That Book* – and the reaction to it was so gratifyingly (and surprisingly) generous – that I couldn't resist putting together this imaginatively entitled sequel.

As with the first book, most of it has been acquired 'organically' over the past 20 years (yup, that's the sort of man I am). However, I am obliged to acknowledge material culled from the internet – especially in the sections *insects etc., the human condition, fish etc., geography, birds etc., history, animals etc.* and *science*. Apart from the indispensable Google, I used LexisNexis, the best and the most user-friendly search tool I've ever come across. It was also on the net that I first saw the ultimate college application and was instantly dazzled by Hugh Gallagher's genius. I have made many attempts to contact him (for permission to use his essay) but to no avail. So I made the decision to include it – out of homage to its author and in the hope that, by so doing, I might bring his wonderful idea to a wider audience.

Meanwhile, I am still on the lookout for fascinating trivia and ideas that I might be able to use in a third book (inevitably entitled *The Other Book*). So if you have anything you think might be of interest – or even if you simply want to get in touch to point out all my mistakes, then please write to me at: thatbook@mail.com

This Book required ingenuity, cleverness and talent. Fortunately, I had the help of a group of people who possess such qualities by the bucket-load. Step forward and take a bow (in alphabetic order): Hugh Adams, Luigi Bonomi, Penny Chorlton, Patrick Janson-Smith, Mari Roberts (even if she did talk me out of including the fascinating fact that the average person has fewer than two arms …) and Doug Young.

In addition, I'd also like to thank the following people for their help, contributions and/or support (moral or otherwise): Russell Ash, Paul Ashford, Alison Barrow, Jeremy Beadle, Marcus Berkmann, Joel Cadbury, Jeremy Clarkson, Amelia Cummins, Paul Donnelly, Chris Ewins, Jonathan Fingerhut, Vanessa Forbes, Jenny Garrison, Rachel Jane, Robert Kilroy-Silk, John Koski, Richard Littlejohn, Tricia Martin, Keiran Mellikof, Emanuel Mond, William Mulcahy, Bee Musson, Rex Newman, Nicholas Ridge, Simon Rose, Charlie Symons, Jack Symons, Louise Symons, Chris Tarrant, David Thomas, Martin Townsend, Roy Wells, Katrina Whone, Rob Woolley and Stewart Wright.

If I've missed anyone out, then please know that – as with any mistakes in the book – it's entirely down to my own stupidity.